★★ THE 10 CENT WAR ★★

THE 10 CENT
WAR

Comic Books, Propaganda, and World War II

Edited by Trischa Goodnow and James J. Kimble

University Press of Mississippi / Jackson

www.upress.state.ms.us

The University Press of Mississippi is a member of
the Association of American University Presses.

First printing 2016

∞

Library of Congress Cataloging-in-Publication Data

Names: Goodnow, Trischa, editor. | Kimble, James J., 1966– editor.
Title: The 10 cent war : comic books, propaganda, and World War II / edited
by Trischa Goodnow and James J. Kimble.
Other titles: Ten cent war
Description: Jackson : University Press of Mississippi, 2017. | Includes
bibliographical references and index.
Identifiers: LCCN 2016032588 (print) | LCCN 2016033011 (ebook) | ISBN
9781496810304 (hardback) | ISBN 9781496810311 (epub single) | ISBN
9781496810328 (epub institutional) | ISBN 9781496810335 (pdf single) |
ISBN 9781496810342 (pdf institutional)
Subjects: LCSH: Comic books, strips, etc.—United States—History and
criticism. | World War, 1939–1945—Literature and the war. | National
characteristics, American, in literature. | Literature and society—United
States—History—20th century. | BISAC: LITERARY CRITICISM / Comics &
Graphic Novels. | SOCIAL SCIENCE / Popular Culture. | HISTORY / Military /
World War II.
Classification: LCC PN6725 .A13 2017 (print) | LCC PN6725 (ebook) | DDC
741.5/973—dc23
LC record available at https://lccn.loc.gov/2016032588

British Library Cataloging-in-Publication Data available

For Robert P. Newman and in Memory of James E. and Mathilda M. Goodnow

My heroes, from World War II and beyond

and for Michael and Rita Potuto

★★ CONTENTS ★★

★★ ACKNOWLEDGMENTS ★★

An edited book is an exercise in patience. We thank the contributing authors for being so gracious about the long process of getting this book to completion. The editors also thank Vijay Shah, who did an admirable job in continuing to believe in the project in spite of delays, as well as Pete Halverson, Lisa McMurtray, Randy Bytwerk, Harry Brod, Walter Biggins, countless helpful archivists and librarians, and the anonymous manuscript reviewers, whose advice was excellent. Trischa would like to thank Steve Johnson for providing ideas for the Superman chapter, and Forest Ledbetter for providing valuable information in general on the comic book industry. Jim thanks Stephanie Plunkett, Karen Gevirtz, Amy Hunter, and Susan A. Nolan for their wise counsel, and Tina Potuto Kimble for the constant inspiration and encouragement. Special thanks go to Dave Reynolds of Dave's American Comics for access to his copy of *Uncle Sam Quarterly* #5, adapted for the cover of the book.

★★ THE 10 CENT WAR ★★

★★ INTRODUCTION ★★

James J. Kimble and Trischa Goodnow

A most unusual event occurred in the U.S. House of Representatives on March 4, 1943: the reading of a comic book. *The Life of Franklin D. Roosevelt: 32nd President of the United States of America* was a colorful, 16-page production of the Office of War Information, or OWI (1942). New York representative John Taber, one of Roosevelt's Capitol Hill nemeses, had been alerted to the publication of the comic book by a constituent in military service abroad. The savvy congressman knew a political vulnerability when he saw one. After sarcastically reading selections from the booklet for the record, he pronounced it "purely political propaganda" that was "designed entirely to promote . . . the dictatorship"—code words for FDR's potential fourth term as president ("Taber Attacks," 1943, p. 5).

Although Taber's comment about a dictatorship was no more than partisan hyperbole, he was on the mark in asserting that the comic book was a clever propaganda message, albeit one aimed at foreign readers. OWI's employees kept a meticulous record of reactions to the booklet in the dozens of countries where translations were sent. They reported with evident pride that the reception was overwhelmingly positive. As staffer Armitage Watkins wrote, "we have received from our foreign missions unqualified praise for this publication and requests for additional similar publications. . . . There is an enormous demand," he concluded, "for facts in cartoon form" (1943, p. 1).

The word *facts* in this context referred to the practice of disseminating propaganda, once the task of the Office of Facts and Figures but by the summer of 1942 the primary responsibility of OWI. These agencies typically practiced their craft through press releases, leaflets, newsreels, pamphlets, and posters (Winkler, 1978). The general aim of such activities was to influence wartime audiences, both domestic and foreign, in ways consistent with the Roosevelt administration's viewpoints. The government's vast propaganda operations were, in other words, tools of war. At first glance, the humble comic book—with its cheap price, pulp paper, and Charles Atlas ads—would seem to have had little to offer that sort of propaganda operation. A closer examination, however, reveals that comic books were rich sources of wartime propaganda.

Accordingly, the purpose of *The 10 Cent War* is to examine the role of comic books as World War II propaganda, ultimately revealing the numerous ways in which these often-overlooked cultural artifacts helped forge a united home front by cultivating a patriotic sensibility that celebrated both American triumphalism and virtue. This introduction lays the groundwork for that examination by first establishing a theoretical and historical context for both propaganda and comic books. It then explores the part that comic books played in the so-called cartoon war. A third section details the various impacts of comic books on the home front. Finally, the introduction summarizes the essays that make up the bulk of the book. Each of these sections provides a foundation for understanding the circumstances from which war-era comic books emerged. That foundation, in turn, presents a detailed context for understanding the various chapters that follow.

Propaganda and Comic Books

The U.S. home front during World War II was home to some 130 million citizens, less than half of today's population figure. Theirs was a world of ration stamps, painted-on nylons, the national 35-mph speed limit, the jitterbug, victory gardens, Kate Smith's patriotic songs, blue- and gold-star mothers, massive munitions factories, air raid wardens, and bond rallies. Theirs, too, was a world without television, satellites, personal computers, or the internet. In fact, civilians on the 1940s home front had far fewer sources of information or entertainment available to them compared to Americans today. But the media to which they did have access—primarily radio, newspapers, newsreels, and magazines—were typically a vibrant aspect of both individual and family life.

In such a time and place it was possible for both propaganda campaigns and comic books to thrive. Given the cultural salience of both on the home front, it was probably inevitable that they would intersect at some point. Occasionally, this confluence was more akin to a collision, as when Representative Taber blustered about OWI's "so-called magazine" and its "cheap propaganda" on the House floor (Moore, 1943, p. 1). More often, however, it simply went unnoticed. After all, there was a war going on. Who had time to wonder whether 10-cent booklets were echoing the government's own propaganda line?

Yet in retrospect, the intersection of comic books and propaganda on the World War II home front presented a remarkable and largely unplanned symbiosis. Unlike the magazine, advertising, and radio industries, the comic book trade had little or no connection to the Roosevelt administration; there were few outright attempts to organize the comic industry in service of the war.[1] Nonetheless, comic books during the war years repeatedly offered subtle and not-so-subtle messages that betrayed a striking similarity across covers, characters, and story lines. Even before Pearl Harbor, this chorus of four-color messages had effectively constructed a de facto propaganda campaign that was aimed at millions of readers. The unofficial campaign was as vigilant and patriotic as any government-sponsored poster and thus invites careful scrutiny.

The Nature of Propaganda

Of course, any in-depth exploration of the intersection of propaganda and comic books from the war period requires a contextual understanding of both elements. For its part, the so-called art of propaganda has ancient roots. Garth S. Jowett and Victoria O'Donnell (2015) contend that the eighth-century BCE Greek culture was perhaps the first to systematically adopt propagandistic messages. These messages were often embedded in public monuments, sculptures, and temples as a means of glorifying one particular city-state over all others. Propaganda appeals later became mobile with the Roman adoption of coins that circulated throughout the empire bearing Caesar's image for all to see (Luce, 1968). By the seventeenth century, when the Catholic Church first coined the word *propaganda* to describe its strategic reaction to the Protestant Reformation, the Western practice of propaganda was already over two millennia old (Guilday, 1921).

With the advent of mass communication formats, propagandists were able to broaden their reach considerably. The printing press, advances in photography and moving pictures, the news media, and broadcast technology enabled vast propaganda campaigns unlike any seen in the ancient world. *The Saturday Evening Post*'s insistent anti-German editorial stance in World War I, for example, reached almost 10 million readers every week (Jowett & O'Donnell, 2015, p. 115). The U.S. government also found the new technologies useful in appealing to millions of citizens during that war. As George Creel's *How We Advertised America* (1920) revealed to a shocked postwar public, the federal Committee on Public Information had used "the motion picture, the telegraph, the cable, [and] the wireless" as part of "a vast enterprise in salesmanship" that had aimed to inspire the home front to "the supreme effort of service and sacrifice" (pp. 4, 5). Ironically, Creel's mass propaganda methods subsequently became useful after the conflict in advertising campaigns that attempted to sell insurance, toothpaste, medicine, and home goods to that very same public (Marchand, 1985).

As this brief historical sketch demonstrates, propaganda has materialized in myriad formats and contexts in human history. But how can one adequately define a practice that can range from architecture to coinage, from posters to advertisements, and from editorials to religious campaigns? Jacques Ellul (1965) offers one solution in his well-known formulation suggesting that propaganda and information are effectively indistinguishable in a given case. Yet this approach seems overly broad, as one could interpret it to mean that all communication is propaganda. A slightly narrower approach that can still account for a variety of historical instances of propaganda is in order. Although scores of definitions are plausible, then, this book will consider propaganda to be a branch of persuasion that involves institutional messages that are mediated, systematic, and aimed at influencing a specific audience.

This definition clearly identifies OWI's widespread communications during World War II as propaganda efforts. After all, OWI was an institution using mediated messages (such as posters, press releases, and newsreels) in a systematic fashion in order to influence a specific audience: the American public.[2] But the definition simultaneously offers insight into how seamlessly the new genre of comic books was able to enlist in home-front propaganda campaigns on the eve of the war. While the comic book publishers were not to be confused with the federal government, they were still institutional in nature. Moreover, their popular products emerged in active media markets even as they systematically stressed similar themes that aimed to influence many of the same recipients of OWI's messages (Wright, 2001, p. 22). When one considers that a great many of these comic books enthusiastically devoted their covers and story lines to service on behalf of the Allied cause, it is difficult to consider them anything but an organized propaganda effort. "Comic books," agrees William W. Savage (1990) "became an integral part of the Allied propaganda machine, emphasizing the need for a maximum war effort" (p. 10).

Understanding Comic Books as Propaganda

Yet identifying the propagandistic nature of most comic books during the war in some ways raises the question of the nature of the booklets themselves. In short, to study comic books it is important to define what they are in the first place. One way to do so is to return to the first comic book prototypes to examine some of the precedents that they established. Those prototypes emerged in 1934, in the midst of the Great Depression. That was when—after years of experimentation and false starts among several publishers—the Eastern Color Printing Company and the Dell Publishing Company collaborated to begin producing the first recognizably modern comic book series: *Famous Funnies, the Nation's Comic Monthly*. Like most of its thousands of successors throughout the rest of the decade and into the 1940s, this publication had several identifiable characteristics: it was a softbound magazine with a compelling cover, it was established not as a singular production but as a regular periodical, it featured 64 pages of cartoon stories, and it sold in drugstores and at newsstands for 10 cents. In addition to these important precedents, the collaborative product was not just a reprinting of comic strip material. Instead, it provided readers with original features unique to the series (Crawford, 1978, p. 362; Lopes, 2009, p. 18).

The recurring nature of comic book characteristics from 1934 on suggests that a distinctly new genre had emerged from its predecessors, the comic strip and the pulp novel (Gabilliet, 2005/2010, p. 13). In the most general sense, these features make it possible to describe the genre with the traditional observation that comic books are "cheap, softcover magazines of serialised cartoons" (Bongco, 2000, p. 54). As it turns out, however, comic books are more complex than this definition indicates. Thus, it is worthwhile to draw on a number of scholarly discussions (Bongco; Duncan & Smith, 2009; Eisner, 1994; McCloud, 1993) to identify comic books—at least those from the World War II era—as soft cover, inexpensive magazines of sequential cartoons that integrate prose and illustrations to relate interactive narratives.

This definition of comic books has several important elements that invite further clarification in order to set the stage for the analyses that follow in the chapters of this book. First, the reference to cartoons that appear in a particular sequence suggests that unlike most traditional forms of visual art, comic books rely on a sense of serial arrangement and progression. Any trip to a museum of classic artworks rewards the viewer with hundreds of images that are in effect depictions of a singular moment in time: a pose, a profile, a still life, a portrait. In such images, the viewer can only imagine what events might or might not have occurred before or after a given artwork's singular moment.[3] Comic books, in contrast, provide readers with scores of images that follow an orderly trajectory. One need not wonder, for the most part, what happens after a particular scene, as the booklet generally portrays a subsequent event in the very next frame. This formal structure not only places story elements in juxtaposition but also enables the artist to construct and give forward motion to a story line.

The shape of that story line emerges in another part of the definition, which describes comic books' constant interplay of prose and illustrations. The interdependence between these two channels is one of comic art's most distinctive characteristics (Harvey, 1979, p. 641), a connection that Scott McCloud likens to the relationship between "partners in a dance" (1993, p. 156). As Will Eisner suggests (1994, p. 8), this potent combination allows comic book writers and artists to relate their tales with both "the regimens of art (e.g., perspective, symmetry, brush stroke) and the regimens of literature (e.g., grammar, plot, syntax)." The result is a profoundly yet deceptively complex communication form. In uniting the trappings of art and literature, comic books relate their tales using visual and verbal symbols even as they require readers to develop a hybrid style of comic book literacy if they want to enjoy the exploits of their favorite characters.

A final part of the definition that might require some explanation is its reference to interactive narratives. The combination of prose and illustrations mentioned above provides comic books with a more inherently narrativistic orientation than classical forms of display art (it is not that such artworks cannot relate narratives, but rather that their space to do so is quite limited in comparison to comic books). Yet even with dozens of pages and hundreds of frames, a given booklet itself has a finite amount of space to relate its stories. It would, of course, be impossible to display every consecutive second of a narrative within the frames available to the artist. Here is where McCloud's phrase "the invisible art" (1993, p. 74) plays a crucial role. In his terms, a comic book's so-called gutters (i.e., the spaces between the frames) are, paradoxically, where much of the story takes place. To illustrate, two juxtaposed frames might show, say, a character jumping from a rooftop and then landing safely on the ground below. The character's rapid descent in between the two depicted moments occurs not in a frame but in the gutter, forcing the reader to envision the missing moments. The process is called "closure," and it allows readers to "mentally construct a continuous, unified reality" (p. 67) from the limited number of scenes that are actually illustrated. "Readers fill in the gaps," adds Mila Bongco, to "make the leap ... from one panel to another" (2000, p. 65). In this sense, comic books are a thoroughly interactive medium, operating in such a way that artists and readers essentially meet at an intermediate point to co-create the details of the narrative. It is little wonder, then, that a captivated fan base followed the new medium from its very first days back in the Great Depression, thoroughly "ensnared ... in a magical world" (Robinson, 2004, p. 19).

As this discussion indicates, comic books have numerous unique qualities. These qualities in turn suggest an important reason why comic books were so suitable for propaganda messages on the home front: the new genre and its potent features made possible the depiction of almost anything imaginable, from dauntless American heroes to crafty spies to inhuman enemies. Among the other media sources of the day, radio was limited to what producers could depict audibly, while motion pictures were generally constrained by budgets that limited what they could portray in an affordable manner. Comic books, however, had no such restrictions. As Savage points out, the booklets "could show whatever the artist could draw, their lines and color directing imagination, their balloon-held texts defining time and space. Comic-book artists and writers," he concludes, "could produce that which could be conceived" (1990, p. 7). Such a quality was of great utility to any publisher that wanted to use its comic book line in service of the upcoming war effort.

But comic books were also a fertile propaganda environment for reasons apart from their form. Most obviously, they quickly grew into a major national medium that attracted a widespread reading audience. Consider that in 1935 there were only three organizations publishing comic books; by 1939 there were 18. The number of comic book releases saw a corresponding growth spurt, going from 19 in 1935 to an astonishing 322 four years later (Gabilliet, 2005/2010, p. 17). By 1940 the industry had clearly begun to mature, with some 10 million comic books sold every month. While this phenomenal growth was cause for alarm in the eyes of a number of social critics (e.g., North, 1940; "Feeding Your Children Horror?, 1941), it was good news for the comic industry and, simultaneously, for its ability to use the increasingly popular publications as a source of subtle and not-so-subtle propaganda messages.

Yet perhaps the most important reason that the new genre of comic books was a natural vehicle for propaganda was that it emerged and matured just as local conflicts and regional tensions were growing into a second worldwide war that would require an intense propaganda effort from all sides. Comic books swiftly became an essential aspect of that propaganda effort. In the late 1930s, as it turned out, the comic book industry soon found itself functioning as one of the nation's most powerful voices in support of U.S. involvement in the brewing world war.

Comic Books and the Roots of the Cartoon War

Long before Pearl Harbor, the unmistakable signs of violent international conflict were increasingly evident. As early as 1936, Germany had occupied the Rhineland. It subsequently forged alliances with both Italy and Japan, setting off alarm bells in Europe and prompting the *New York Times* to suggest that if France and Britain responded with their own pact, "war would result . . . probably sooner than later" (Cortesi, 1937, p. 62). The comic book industry at this point was still quite young, of course. However, there were signs that it was willing to voice its concerns about the international situation, even if those concerns were allegorical in form. For instance, Chesler Publications' *Star Comics* #3, published in May 1937, featured a story involving a conflict on the planet

Venus between the Sun Country, whose citizens were "friendly" and whose "lands . . . were theirs by right of inheritance," and the enemy Dark Country, "where the sun never shone and the natives were hardy, vicious, grasping, ever watching for a chance to swoop down" upon their neighbor (Fitch, 1937, p. 31).[4] Although the Dark Country's military helmets used a death's head insignia that was not unlike the design already in use by Adolf Hitler's SS, the comic book did not overtly indicate that its story referred to the growing unrest in Europe. Still, the tale's light–dark metaphor was a telling trope, one that would gradually become prevalent in a great deal of home-front propaganda.

The simultaneous rise of Nazi militarism and the continuing growth of the comic book industry presented myriad opportunities for ever-more specific propaganda allegories. Many of the trade's writers and artists were Jewish, and they could not help but be aware of Germany's increasingly ominous restrictions on and violent actions toward Jews (Scott, 2007). Not surprisingly, then, more and more comic book stories began to offer thinly disguised warnings about Hitler's intentions. Not long before Germany's September 1939 invasion of Poland, for example, *Smash Comics* featured the hero Black Ace fighting against a ruthless dictator who has taken over South America and is now planning to attack the United States. With his brownshirt uniform and favored female spy (conveniently named Mara Hani), there is little doubt that the villain was a stand-in for Hitler—even though the comic specified, tongue-in-cheek, that "any similarity to persons living or dead is purely coincidental" (Erwin, 1939, p. 1).[5] Such allegories became increasingly overt in the late 1930s as alarmed comic book artists felt more and more justified in using the considerable tools at their disposal to attempt to influence the American public's perspective on the Axis powers in general, and on Nazi Germany specifically (Wright, 2001, p. 39). It might have been propaganda for sale at only 10 cents per issue, but there was by now no doubt that it was indeed propaganda.

The anti-Axis parables lurking in all of this comic book propaganda began to adopt a more actively interventionist tone after a watershed event in 1938. Even as Japanese troops carried out the infamous rape of Nanking, and even as Germany forcibly annexed Austria, the growing comic book industry was approaching a colorful explosion of red and blue. It was time for Superman's June 1938 debut in *Action Comics* number 1. Here was the sudden emergence of a tremendously powerful icon, a visual embodiment of U.S. power, righteousness, and willingness to take action in a time of world crisis. The comic book universe—and its growing propaganda efforts—would never be the same.

The sensational, near-instantaneous success of National Comics' Superman character prompted numerous costumed superheroes to join him in taking the comic world by storm. National's Batman was one of the immediate followers, but he was soon joined by countless others, including (to name a few) Human Torch, Shock Gibson, and the Sub-Mariner in 1939; Green Lantern, the Shield, and Uncle Sam in 1940; and Miss America, Spirit of '76, and Wonder Woman in 1941. These characters, and many more, openly fought against Axis soldiers and spies even before the Pearl Harbor attack brought the United States into the fight—with the most famous encounter, perhaps, being Captain America's punch to Hitler's jaw on the March 1941 cover of the Captain's self-titled debut issue. The United States itself was still officially neutral in the conflict, but the comic book industry was no longer being subtle in using its growing clout to identify the Axis powers as enemies worth fighting.

Compelling propaganda images and story lines like these were already reaching millions of home-front readers as the nation reacted to the shock of the Pearl Harbor attack and as Congress formally declared war in December 1941. By this point comic books were inching closer to becoming "the most popular form of entertainment in America," now attracting a vast audience that rivaled those reached by older media such as radio, magazines, and motion pictures (Hajdu, 2008, p. 5). As many as 15 million new comic book issues were flying off drugstore shelves and newsstand racks every month (Littledale, 1941). Each copy was avidly read not just by its purchaser, but by another four or five siblings or friends (Frakes, 1942), multiplying the power of the industry's messages exponentially. It was, to use Steve M. Barkin's phrase, a sign that the nation's "cartoon war" (1984, p. 117) was already an indispensable aspect of the war effort itself.

To be sure, comic books were not the only front in this unprecedented cartoon war. Daily newspaper comic strips, for instance, were all but saturated with war themes after Pearl Harbor. By late 1942 an OWI study found that nearly all of the protagonists in the funnies had already enlisted for war service—although the government did express concern that many such comic strip characters defeated their cartoon enemies much too easily (Blum, 1976, pp. 36–37). Editorial cartoons, of course, also featured prominently in newspapers, with the Axis leaders and their sympathizers becoming regular subjects of caricature, ridicule, or condemnation (Somers, 1996). Dr. Seuss's hundreds of editorial cartoons, published by the New York daily PM, presented a particularly incisive viewpoint early in the war, allowing the famous artist to use his allegorical wit against enemies both foreign and domestic (Minear, 1999). Animated cartoons were an indelible part of the home-front experience as well. Several of them resulted from close cooperation between the government and movie studios, such as The Spirit of '43, a U.S. Treasury–sponsored short that reminded citizens to pay their quarterly income taxes on time (Goodnow, 2009). Others were produced with little or no government supervision. Most prominent of this group, perhaps, was Disney's popular *Victory Through Air Power*, which made the case for disabling Fortress Europe through relentless air bombing (Van Riper, 2011). Whatever their origin, hundreds of war-themed animations emerged during the conflict, with most of them reaching weekly audiences numbering in the millions (Shull & Wilt, 1987, p. 3).

Although it is difficult to make comparisons across genres, the comic book industry was arguably the most significant of these cartoon fronts. Animated productions, of course, reached massive audiences in the theaters. Unlike comic books, however, animations were not portable and could not be carried from place to place and transferred from friend to friend. They were also ephemeral; once a given movie's run was finished, there was no going back to see it again, since theaters would already have moved on to new titles. For their part, comic strips and editorial cartoons also tended to be ephemeral, since they appeared in an "intrinsically disposable medium" (Hajdu, 2008, p. 21); indeed, most wartime newspapers were discarded or recycled in scrap-paper drives when individuals or families were finished reading them. Moreover, the funnies and editorial cartoons faced the additional disadvantage of a cluttered canvas, due to their role as constituent elements within the context of dozens of other daily newspaper features.[6]

Comic books, in contrast to these other facets of the cartoon war, were self-contained, portable units that were eagerly anticipated, continually savored, and even jealously hoarded by countless readers during the war (Lupoff, 1973). At only 10 cents per issue, they were also quite affordable for all but the very poorest civilians. By the summer of 1942, these qualities had made the maturing genre a formidable force on the home front. At that point, to the delight of industry insiders, comic book circulation had risen to between 150 million and 180 million per year, with about 50 million citizens—nearly 40% of the country—reading comic books every month (Frakes, 1942, p. 1349; Waugh, 1947, p. 344). There could no longer be any doubt that the colorful booklets were not only a vital part of the cartoon war but also an indelible aspect of the home-front experience itself.

The Impact of Comic Books on the Home Front

The propaganda appeals that emerged in wartime comic books were particularly remarkable in that they emerged not from a government-sponsored source but from a thoroughly private industry. Although the government itself did dabble in the production of comic books early in the war, there was ultimately no federally appointed comic book czar, and no official propaganda handbook for superhero depictions. Despite this rather independent status, however, the comic book industry almost universally supported the government's perspective on everything from war strategy to rationing to civilian engagement in the conflict. If anything, comic book propaganda was frequently ahead of the government's appeals, calling for outright intervention long before Pearl Harbor, and for opening more battlefronts long before the military was prepared to do so. The situation was so striking, notes Bradford W. Wright, because it "marked a rare convergence of interests between publishers, creators, readers, and government policy" (2001, p. 54).

Significantly, when OWI's domestic budget was slashed after the summer of 1943, comic books became almost overnight one of the largest remaining sources of propaganda on the home front. This shift of the government's traditional propaganda responsibility into private hands was a risky choice in some respects. Yet the comic book industry demonstrated that its propaganda efforts—despite their corporate, private origin—were up to the challenge. To examine this claim in further detail, it is worthwhile to consider the war-era comic books' story lines, ideological outlook, multiple audiences, and long-term impact.

Comic Book Story Lines

What kinds of tales did these ever-present booklets present to their avid home-front fans? The ubiquitous superhero comic books, for their part, tended toward a simplistic, triumphalist, and often bluntly racist perspective on the conflict. While some costumed characters—among them Superman and Batman—kept their war contributions indirect, most were actively involved in the struggle, either in ferreting out spies on the home front or in direct combat with Axis forces. Their adventures, however, were often rather formulaic. A typical story line featured a nefarious new Axis strategy or weapon, demonized Germans or dehumanized Japanese figures, a costumed crusader with a secret identity and a flippant, can-do attitude, a generous measure of cartoon violence, and, just in time for the ending, a convincing Allied victory. "Even an illiterate," comments Savage, would be able to deduce from these sorts of stories "the virtue of the American cause" (1990, p. 11). Mike Conroy adds that although such adventures tended to be "gung-ho, jingoistic . . . [and] blatantly racist," they ultimately "gave the public what they wanted" (2009, p. 12).

To be sure, not every wartime comic book featured caped beings with super powers of one sort or another. Titles such as *War Stories*, *War Heroes*, and *True Comics* often described the exploits of both fictional and nonfictional GIs and Marines in battle, occasionally with a dash of spying adventures thrown in for good measure. Some of the comic world's story lines about such flesh-and-blood heroes even had an international flavor, as in the exploits of Will Eisner's *Blackhawks*, a ragtag guerilla group with members from several Allied nations. While traditionally valiant U.S. characters still tended to receive top billing in most of these stories, readers did find themselves exposed to positive views of other cultures therein. The resulting adventures did not rely on extraordinary powers or on super-beings but rather on American (or Allied) virtues such as toughness, tenacity, and bravery under fire. As a result, their protagonists also usually ended up beating their foe-of-the-month, ultimately providing more propagandistic support for the idea that an Axis defeat was inevitable.

Intriguingly, a significant number of home-front comic books featured tales involving regular, everyday civilians and their role in the war. The characters in these stories were not soldiers, nor did they possess superhuman powers. Rather, they were responsible citizens who did their patriotic duty with enthusiasm and determination. Often, of course, their adventures brought them into contact with Axis spies and saboteurs, with predictable results. *Banner Comics*'s Paul Revere Jr., for instance, was a young patriot who teamed up with his friends (the aptly named Betsy Ross and Patrick Henry) and his reporter father to defeat Nazi agents before they could complete their evil missions. The Standard Comics company provided a similar character in the preteen Jimmy Cole, Boy Sleuth. While most Americans would never come across an Axis spy in their own lives, such highly patriotic characters undoubtedly provided important role models for many readers.

For those comic book fans who craved more exotically themed stories, there was even a subgenre of sequential cartoons that emerged from the nation's small Japanese American culture. Jun Atsushi Iwamatsu, a Japanese refugee who served as an artist in the government's wartime Office of Strategic Services, published *The New Sun* in 1943 (under the pen name Tarō Yashima) to critical acclaim. As Frederik L. Schodt notes, Iwamatsu's visceral sketches of life under the emperor served as a "devastating critique of Japan's militarist government" (2014, p. 311). Miné Okubo's haunting depictions of life in a detainee camp, meanwhile, provided a devastating critique of their own, offering American readers a poignant glimpse into a reality that many had previously ignored. *Fortune*, which published many of her serial cartoons before they emerged as a complete book, was moved to conclude that "the Constitution and the Bill of Rights were severely stretched if not breached when U.S. citizens," like Okubo and her family, "were put in prison" ("Issei, Nisei, Kibei," 1944, p. 8). Although such comic publications, due in part to their unusual subject matter, could not have achieved the same levels of circulation and saturation as their more mainstream siblings in the American comic book industry, the variant viewpoints on the war that they provided were surely enlightening to those who came across them on the home front.

Still, while comic book superheroes, soldiers, civilians, and even artists in the marginalized Japanese American subculture typically dealt with the ongoing war directly, it is worth mentioning that amidst the many fantastic, realistic, and heart-wrenching war tales, some comic book story lines on the home front seemed to avoid references to the conflict altogether. At first glance, the propaganda value of such comics would seem to be rather limited. After all, how could a comic book story line support the war effort without any reference to war itself? Here it is important to recognize that even if a specific narrative was not overtly propagandistic, it could still act in propagandistic ways through its juxtaposition with nearby narratives. The Archie Andrews series, for instance, in many respects occurred in a narrative world without war—even though the character first appeared just as the country declared war and thrived as the conflict progressed. Yet the series' very evocation of life in the United States as desirable and worthwhile likely intimated to wartime readers that the nation itself embodied the better side in a struggle of good vs. evil.

This notion was particularly true for Archie, given the placement of his series throughout most of the war as an interior feature within *Pep Comics*. Since the narratives surrounding his story line generally featured heroic figures such as the Shield and the Hangman fighting Axis spies and saboteurs, the war was in fact just a few pages away from serene Riverdale. A reader, in other words, could easily have come to see the casual life of Archie and Jughead and Betty and Veronica as the exact American ideal that superpatriots like the Shield were fighting for within the same issue. No doubt this type of propaganda message was less direct than that of its superheroic relatives. But while the strength of superhero propaganda appeals emerged in their boldness and audacity, the strength of the less belligerent comic story lines, such as that exemplified by Archie and his friends, emerged in a more ideologically subtle use of propaganda (see Parry-Giles, 1994).

Ideological Outlook

The lighthearted ideological underpinnings of the Archie narratives were actually just a small subset of the heavy-handed ideological messages that frequently emerged in the story lines that were produced by the comic book industry. For the most part, regardless of genre, the booklets overtly supported American geo-political aims and, even more specifically, the policies of the Roosevelt administration. This practice started well in advance of Pearl Harbor. As Christopher Murray contends, Superman creators Jerry Siegel and Joe

Shuster modeled their mythology on "the Rooseveltian ideal of a benevolent yet capitalist society, with their hero fighting on behalf of the average American, opposing corruption in the legal system and in big business" (2011, p. 12). Wonder Woman, too, was a New Deal convert, occasionally taking time from her focus on villains to tackle domestic social issues such as children's nutrition and workers' rights (Wandtke, 2007, p. 157). Other superheroes followed in this idealistic and activist mold, meaning that comic books were effectively enthusiastic New Deal supporters from their earliest days.

The approach of war indirectly tied the comic book publishers to the Roosevelt administration's ideology in other ways. FDR, hemmed in by a strong isolationist movement, could not proactively bring the United States into what a great many Americans viewed as a European struggle. As early as 1937, however, the president's speeches began to betray an increasingly militant undertone, suggesting that he was determined to confront Germany and Japan one way or another (Edwards, 2009, pp. 30–31; Kaiser, 2014, pp. 15–17). The comic book industry, of course, had much more freedom to express such a belligerent agenda openly. When its superheroes pointedly (and repeatedly) grappled with the Axis powers in the years before Pearl Harbor, then, the industry was essentially expressing the administration's tacit ideology.

Once the United States actually became an active participant in the war, the ideological affinity between the White House and the comic book industry became more and more obvious. Whether they were encouraging readers to recycle paper, gather scrap, purchase war stamps, or simply cheer on the Allies, comic protagonists were outwardly avid in both encouraging and modeling the very same domestic behaviors and beliefs touted in official propaganda appeals. Not surprisingly, the nation's war aims also received admiring commentary from such characters. Fawcett Publication's Radar, the International Policeman, even began his career as a superhero after a secret 1944 meeting with FDR, Winston Churchill, Chiang Kai-shek, and Josef Stalin, who charged him to help "the Allies win the peace as well as the war" ("Captain Marvel," 1944, p. 13). Radar thus joined numerous other comic book protagonists as they explicitly endorsed—and fought on behalf of—the Atlantic Charter, the Four Freedoms, and the international stability represented by the United Nations.

Of course, the interconnections between the ideologies expressed by the Roosevelt administration and the comic book industry were not always so admirable. The relationships depicted between male and female characters, for instance, tended to emerge in patriarchal and even misogynistic tones. Even superheroines, despite their powers, were often the subjects of demeaning behavior (and not just from villains)—providing an unflattering view of the nation's ideological beliefs involving gender relations. Enemy figures, especially the Japanese, frequently appeared as little more than beasts or vermin, likewise exposing an ideological belief system that allowed and encouraged the dangerous practice of dehumanization. Elsewhere, the recurring genre of "'jungle' comic books" (Wright, 2001, p. 36) visibly supported a colonialist and overtly racist attitude on the part of Westerners toward the developing world. Indeed, regular readers of *Jumbo Comics*, *Jungle Comics*, and similar titles would have become quite familiar with relentless depictions of savage native groups whose seemingly inferior intelligence and capabilities made them suitable for mastery by white overseers. If the United States and its allies were truly fighting to spread the Four Freedoms across the globe, such story lines seemed to suggest, then they would do so whether or not the inferior natives were in favor of such a grand idea. Clearly, while comic books conveyed ideological messages of all sorts, at least some of those underlying messages verged on the odious.

The Wartime Audience for Comic Books

The ideological attitudes residing within comic books' propagandistic messages during the war were powerful enough on their own but likely ended up being all the more potent given the surprising variety of readers that they reached across the country. There was no doubt that many adults perceived the booklets "as another nutrient-free but essentially harmless confection for kids" (Conroy, 2009, p. 35). Nonetheless, adult readers were not at all uncommon. In 1943, according to figures gathered by the Market Research Company of America, around 35% of adults between the ages of 18 and 30 regularly read at least six comic books per month. The industry even had fans in the age group over 30, with some 15% reading comic books regularly and another 10% admitting to being occasional readers (as cited in Waugh, 1947, p. 334).[7] It was no accident, then, that when one *Captain Marvel* write-in contest received over 46,000 entries, the average age of the prize winners turned out to be 30—with one winning reader already past the age of 70 (Zorbaugh, 1944, p. 201). Although these adult readers were certainly not the primary target of the industry's products, the very presence of this unlikely reading audience indicated how quickly comic books and their ideological outlooks had infiltrated the national consciousness during the national emergency.

Millions of those in the armed forces were also tremendous fans of comic book publications. More than half of servicemen in training for deployment overseas were occasional or regular readers (Muhlen, 1949, p. 81), while in stores on military bases, comic books outsold the combined totals of *Life*, the *Saturday Evening Post*, and *Reader's Digest* at an astounding rate of 10 to 1 (Waugh, 1947, p. 334). By one estimate, in fact, comic books made up 80%

of the reading material on U.S. Army posts (Robinson, 2004, p. 21). The army itself, well aware of the reading desires of its enlistees, became the comic book industry's largest institutional customer during the war (Gabilliet, 2005/2010, p. 22); by 1943 copies of the latest Superman comic book were being rushed to troops in battle zones ("Escapist Paydirt," 1943). "A lot of GIs," confirmed Ethan Roberts, "went to war with a comic book rolled up in their back pants pocket" (cited in Rhoades, 2008, p. 40). The nation's GIs—many of them still quite young themselves—evidently found the dramatic booklets to be an entertaining escape from the stresses of wartime duty.

Despite the significant numbers of adult and military readers, however, the comic book industry's primary audience during the war consisted of the nation's youth. In less than 10 years, comic books had established an impressive beachhead among the youngest Americans. Surveys indicated that over 90% of those aged 11 or younger were regular readers, while more than 80% of their older siblings—up to age 17—read comic books just as avidly (Zorbaugh, 1944, p. 197).[8] A 1942 study in Indiana offered even more data by monitoring the reading habits of 696 grade school students for seven days. The researchers reported that, altogether, the students had read 2,370 comic books that week, for an individual average of nearly five titles per day (Frakes, 1942). At the same time, the booming war economy left many youngsters with ample pocket change, enabling their comic passion. The inevitable result was a comic book generation, one raised on harrowing, four-color adventures that insistently touted the virtues of America, condemned the dastardly nature of the Axis powers, and implored every reader, young and old, to find ways to help bring the final victory closer.

The Long-Term Impact of Comic Books

There is, of course, no way to quantitatively measure the success of these kinds of propaganda appeals, particularly some 75 years after the fact. However, there were some on the home front who were willing to attest to the powerful impact of comic books on readers' beliefs and behaviors. Child psychologists Lauretta Bender and Reginald S. Lourie, for instance, admitted that "anyone in contact with children of school age . . . becomes conscious of the extent to which the constant reading of comic books has invaded their thinking, daily activities, and play" (1941, p. 541). Sidonie M. Gruenberg of the Child Study Association of America specifically focused on the ideological impact of the ubiquitous booklets, suggesting that, "for better or worse, they are more potent than many of our other instruments for influencing people's understanding and attitudes" (1944, p. 208). And, somewhat more pragmatically, sociologist Harvey Zorbaugh noted that Captain Marvel's appeal was so magnetic that his fan club had garnered 573,119 members, and that the character himself was receiving nearly 600 fan letters per week. The "impact on our culture" of such cartoon figures, he concluded, "is seen at every hand" (1944, p. 200, 201).

In later years, some readers themselves have attested to the profound influence of the ever-present comic propaganda on the home front. Michael Rockland remembered in an oral history that as a 10-year-old during the war, "all my comic books were nothing but … Superman was killing Nazis, Batman was killing Nazis, and so, that was a very important part of my formation, that I wanted to kill Nazis, too" (2009, p. 10). Similarly, Dick Lupoff recalled that dramatic comic book stories prompted him and his friends to imagine themselves, "faces and hands darkened with lampblack, dogtags taped together to avoid sound, parachuting silently into occupied France" to help prepare "for the great day of liberation that lay ahead" (1973, p. 64). For many youngsters on the home front, apparently, the industry's consistent propaganda appeals were quite involving.

Still, while it is likely that comic book characters' frequent appeals to recycle paper, purchase war stamps, and collect scrap metal found a reading audience that was at least sympathetic during the war, the ultimate impact of comic propaganda was not always predictable. Captain America, for instance, constantly encouraged his wartime fans to enlist as members of the Sentinels of Liberty. For only 10 cents, enlistees would receive a badge and would then be expected to sign an oath pledging to "assist Captain America in his war against spies in the U.S.A" (quoted in Jewett & Lawrence, 2003, p. 33). Unfortunately, youthful members occasionally took this pledge a bit too literally. As comic book artist Derek Skinn recalled, the publisher began to receive "quantities of mail, with the young patriots reporting such un-Americanisms as Teutonic-sounding names and strange noises from parents' bedrooms" (1994, p. 12). These eager but misguided Sentinels surely had their hearts in the right place. Yet in their zealous desire to follow Captain America's instructions, they had ended up demonstrating that even comic book propaganda in the midst of the largest war in history had its limits.

By the war's end, however, the comic industry had to be extremely pleased with the overall impact of its endeavors. Comic book sales had continued to soar during the conflict and would eventually reach a peak of 60 million issues per month by 1947 (Abrams, 2003, p. 436). The direct result of this success was not only more and more readers, but ever-increasing profits. Unfortunately, the artists and writers within the industry typically saw little of those massive profits. Their interest was thus less financial and more ideological. They were, in a sense, soldiers with sketch books, using their positions and talents to help the

nation win the war as quickly as possible. By providing millions of avid readers with compelling story lines involving Allied bravery and Axis perfidy, their
propaganda appeals arguably helped to shape the home front as surely as the
government's own opinion makers. And while many in the comic book industry saw combat in the literal war—and some lost their lives in battle (Robinson,
2004, p. 22)—it was their role in the cartoon war that touched the greatest number of people.

Looking back some 75 years later, the tidal wave of World War II comic book
propaganda has not been forgotten. Indeed, in many ways it remains a distinctive aspect of our cultural heritage. Official reprints of the wartime story lines
are increasingly popular, even as scarce copies of the original issues remain
in high demand on auction sites. In 2000, Michael Chabon's Pulitzer Prize–
winning novel *The Amazing Adventures of Kavalier & Clay* brought the vibrant
world of the war-era comic book artists back to life, reviving for another generation the complex motivations that lay behind the industry's propaganda
campaign. And, of course, many classic propaganda heroes from the war years
have made big-screen comebacks in recent years, with Batman and the Green
Hornet among the most recent.[9] The most telling revival, though, has been Captain America's 2011 blockbuster (Feige & Johnston, 2011). The movie was a tremendous hit for a number of reasons. But the most intriguing aspect for many
World War II buffs was the ending title sequence, which overlaid the usual production credits upon numerous war posters from the home-front years. Here
was a tacit but powerful acknowledgment of the intimate connection between
the wartime comic book universe and propaganda appeals. It was a connection
that, decades ago, reached millions of home-front readers, soldiers abroad, and
even members of Congress—but it is also a connection that remains relevant in
our cultural memories today.

Overview of Chapters

Clearly, after all these years there is still a great deal of interest in wartime comic
books and the captivating nature of their potent, inspiring, and (at times) con-
troversial form of domestic propaganda. The contributors to this volume enthusiastically share that interest. Accordingly, the original analyses that follow
investigate a number of specific instances of comic book propaganda from
the Golden Age. The subject matters vary from chapter to chapter, as do the
analytical and methodological choices of the authors. Each chapter, however, is
an important contribution to what has become a vibrant scholarly discussion
about the role of comic books in American cultural history (see, e.g., Hajdu,
2008; Nyberg, 1999; Savage, 1990; Wright, 2001).

In the first chapter, Christina M. Knopf scrutinizes portrayals of militarized women and their part in the war, with an emphasis on depictions of the famous WACs and WAVES in comic books. Chapter 2, by Zou Yizheng, then examines how U.S. comic books portrayed China and its citizens, effectively educating readers about the Eastern ally even as they simultaneously contrasted the industrious and stalwart Chinese people with Japanese perfidy.

Jon Judy and Brad Palmer turn in chapter 3 to the trope of heroic sidekicks. By examining the characters of Bucky Barnes (who was paired with Captain America) and the Boy Commandos (who supported the military directly), they show how comic books appealed to young male readers, encouraging them to develop a wartime mentality. And in chapter 4, John R. Katsion focuses on the common portrayal of kid gangs in war-era comic books. This trope, he argues, provided younger fans with a number of coping mechanisms during the stress of the home front. These two chapters approach the identification that young readers could have with comic book characters. In both chapters, Judy and Palmer, and Katsion, using differing methodologies, consider how the comic adventures of adolescent heroes could have encouraged countless young readers to imagine themselves aiding in the war effort.

The book then turns to the better-known comic book characters made popular during World War II, the larger-than-life figures who helped to save the day with their extraordinary powers. Travis L. Cox's essay in chapter 5 explores the exploits of the superhero Uncle Sam, whose prewar struggle against the Nazis continued with renewed enthusiasm as the United States entered the conflict in late 1941. Chapter 6 also explores the propaganda evident in prewar comic books. Trischa Goodnow's analysis of the allegorical dimensions of Superman illustrates how his Jewish creators furthered the position of interventionism espoused by many comic book creators. In chapter 7, Deborah Clark Vance examines the rise of Captain America in early 1941, showing how his story line drew on cultural myths to construct a wartime atmosphere while it also supported the virtue of the Allied cause and condemned the evil nature of the Axis powers. Chapter 8 sees Elliott Sawyer and Derek T. Buescher examine Wonder Woman—particularly her magic lasso and its astounding lie-detection capabilities—as an exemplar of the desire for control of the Axis enemy.

The concluding chapters of the book examine the lesser-known comics and presses that also aided the war effort. As Steven E. Martin reveals in chapter 9, the *True Comics* series actively debunked Hitler's master-race philosophy, mocking the Nazi leader and encouraging readers to avoid racial stereotypes. David E. Wilt explores, in chapter 10, the myriad ways that wartime comic books adopted story lines to which readers young and old could personally relate in order to actuate civilian participation in the war effort. Such narratives,

Wilt shows, were a vital part of the comic industry's propaganda function on the home front. James J. Kimble's chapter 11 examines *War Victory Adventures*. This Family Comics series, he contends, provided national character roles for the United States, its allies, and the enemy—ultimately constructing an epic struggle between good and evil that gave readers no choice but to sympathize with the Allied war effort. The last chapter, Wilt's study of characteristics of the strategies of comic book propaganda, provides a summary of the strategies examined in depth in previous chapters.

Taken together, these 12 chapters provide new insights into the intertwined roles of comic books and propaganda on the home front in World War II. In hindsight, there can be no question that the genre had its failings: it was often violent, overly polarized, frequently repetitive, invariably sexist, occasionally distorted, and routinely racist. Yet at the same time, the comic book propaganda of the Golden Age can serve as an intriguing window into a vibrant time in U.S. history, one that continues to reverberate in popular culture and in public memory. *The 10 Cent War*, even as it acknowledges the negative aspects of its subject, thus hopefully serves as a reminder of the indelible quality of this period in our history, and of the long-term potency of its comic depictions.

Notes

1. Eventually, the national Writers' War Board—an unofficial group of writers and publishers working to support the government's war effort—did establish some connections with the comic book industry. However, the group's *Cartoonists' Bulletin*, apparently meant to be disseminated to those involved in the creation of comic books, did not begin publication until May 1944, with the war's climax already on the horizon. See Writers' War Board (1945, p. 5).

2. OWI also had authority over most of the nation's international propaganda as well. After significant budget cuts in mid-1943, OWI's domestic responsibilities waned and foreign appeals became its primary focus (Winkler, 1978).

3. There are, of course, exceptions, with the most obvious being William Hogarth's 18th-century artworks *A Harlot's Progress* and *The Rake's Progress*, which portray two lives in a series of sequential scenes (Kidson, 1999).

4. Throughout this book, references to page numbers in comic books adopt a uniform system that views the first page after the cover and inside cover as page 1, then proceeding throughout the booklet until reaching the inside back cover and the back cover—regardless of any internal page numbers used by individual story lines within a given comic book.

5. Will Erwin was one of Will Eisner's pseudonyms.

6. To be sure, the funnies were often one of the top attractions in a newspaper (Duncan & Smith, 2009, p. 27). Editorial cartoons were also popular, though as Vultee (2007) has noted, their impact on readers' opinion is unclear. They are thus "perhaps better seen as a reflection of converged sentiment than as a signal for action" (p. 160). Regarding paper scrap drives, while Captain America suggested that readers look for newspapers, magazines, cardboard, and envelopes to recycle for the war effort, he did not mention recycling comic books (see

Conroy, 2009, p. 65). Lupoff (1973) recalled that children gave up their comics for scrap drives quite reluctantly.

7. When divided by sex, the numbers for regular adult readers were 41% (men) and 28% (women) in the 18–30 bracket, while 16% (men) and 12% (women) aged 31 and older were regular readers. The research also reported that, for the oldest group, 13% (men) and 10% (women) were occasional readers (Waugh, 1947, p. 334).

8. As before, the numbers varied somewhat by sex. In the 6–11 age bracket, 95% of boys were regular readers, compared to 91% of girls. For the adolescents, the numbers were 87% and 81%, respectively (Zorbaugh, 1944, p. 197).

9. While the Green Hornet did have a lively comic book career during the war, he actually had an earlier career in radio serial dramas.

References

Abrams, N. (2003). From madness to dysentery: "Mad's" other New York intellectuals. *Journal of American Studies, 37*, 435–451.

Barkin, S. M. (1984). Fighting the cartoon war: Information strategies in World War II. *Journal of American Culture, 1-2(7)*, 113–117.

Bender, L., & Lourie, R. S. (1941). The effect of comic books on the ideology of children. *American Journal of Orthopsychiatry, 11*, 540–550.

Blum, J. M. (1976). *V was for victory: Politics and American culture during World War II.* New York, NY: Harcourt Brace Jovanovich.

Bongco, M. (2000). *Reading comics: Language, culture, and the concept of the superhero in comic books.* New York, NY: Garland.

Captain Marvel presents "Radar" the international policeman. (1944, May). In *Captain Marvel Adventures* (pp. 2–13). (No. 35). Louisville, KY: Fawcett.

Chabon, M. (2000). *The amazing adventures of Kavalier & Clay: A novel.* New York, NY: Random House.

Conroy, M. (2009). *War stories: A graphic history.* New York, NY: Collins Design.

Cortesi, A. (1937, January 24). Italo-Reich unity a force in Europe. *New York Times*, p. 62.

Crawford, H. H. (1978). *Crawford's encyclopedia of comic books.* Middle Village, NY: Jonathan David.

Creel, G. (1920). *How we advertised America: The first telling of the amazing story of the Committee on Public Information that carried the gospel of Americanism to every corner of the globe.* New York, NY: Harper & Brothers.

Duncan, R., & Smith, M. J. (2009). *The power of comics: History, form, and culture.* New York, NY: Continuum.

Edwards, G. C. III. (2009). *The strategic president: Persuasion and opportunity in presidential leadership.* Princeton, NJ: Princeton University Press.

Eisner, W. (1994). *Comics and sequential art.* Tamarac, FL: Poorhouse.

Ellul, J. (1965). *Propaganda: The formation of men's attitudes.* New York: Knopf.

Erwin, W. (1939, August). Espionage! In *Smash Comics* (pp. 1–9). (No. 1). Cleveland, OH: Everett M. Arnold.

Escapist paydirt. (1943, December 27). *Newsweek*, pp. 55, 58.

Feeding your children horror? (1941, February 21). *Delta Democrat-Times* [Greenville, MS], p. 2.

Feige, K. (Producer), & Johnston, J. (Director). (2011). Captain America: The first avenger [Motion picture]. United States: Paramount Pictures.

Fitch, K. (1937, May). True colors. In *Star Comics* (pp. 31–35). (Vol. 1, no. 3). St. Louis, MO: Chesler Comics.

Frakes, M. (1942, November 4). Comics are no longer comic. *Christian Century*, 1349–1351.

Gabilliet, J. (2010). *Of comics and men: A cultural history of American comic books*. Jackson: University Press of Mississippi. (Original work published 2005)

Goodnow, T. (2009). Ultimate images in Disney's *The Spirit of '43*. *Journal of the Northwest Communication Association, 38*, 17–27.

Gruenberg, S. M. (1944). The comics as a social force. *Journal of Educational Sociology, 18*, 204–213.

Guilday, P. (1921). The sacred Congregation de Propaganda Fide (1622–1922). *Catholic Historical Review, 6*, 478–494.

Hajdu, D. (2008). *The ten-cent plague: The great comic-book scare and how it changed America*. New York, NY: Farrar, Straus and Giroux.

Harvey, R. C. (1979). The aesthetics of the comic strip. *Journal of Popular Culture, 12*, 640–652.

Issei, Nisei, Kibei. (1944, April). *Fortune, 8*, 22, 32, 74, 78, 84, 94, 106, 118.

Jewett, R., & Lawrence, J. S. (2003). *Captain America and the crusade against evil: The dilemma of zealous nationalism*. Grand Rapids, MI: Eerdmans.

Jowett, G. S., & O'Donnell, V. (2015). *Propaganda & persuasion* (6th ed.). Thousand Oaks, CA: Sage.

Kaiser, D. (2014). *No end save victory: How FDR led the nation into war*. New York, NY: Basic Books.

Kidson, M. (1999). William Hogarth: Printing techniques and comics. *International Journal of Comic Art, 1*(1), 76–89.

Littledale, C. S. (1941, March). What to do about the "comics." *Parents' Magazine*, 26–27, 93.

Lopes, P. D. (2009). *Demanding respect: The evolution of the American comic book*. Philadelphia, PA: Temple University Press.

Luce, T. J. (1968). Political propaganda on Roman Republican coins: Circa 92–82 B.C. *American Journal of Archaeology, 72*, 25–39.

Lupoff, D. (1973). The propwash patrol. In D. Thompson & D. Lupoff (Eds.), *The comic-book book* (pp. 63–86). New Rochelle, NY: Arlington House.

Marchand, R. (1985). *Advertising the American dream: Making way for modernity, 1920–1940*. Berkeley: University of California Press.

McCloud, S. (1993). *Understanding comics: The invisible art*. New York, NY: HarperCollins.

Minear, R. H. (1999). *Dr. Seuss goes to war: The World War II editorial cartoons of Theodor Seuss Geisel*. New York, NY: New Press.

Moore, W. (1943, March 5). House laughs at OWI's new F.D.R. "comic." *Chicago Daily Tribune*, p. 1.

Muhlen, N. (1949, January). Comic books and other horrors: Prep school for totalitarian society? *Commentary*, 80–87.

Murray, C. (2011). *Champions of the oppressed? Superhero comics, popular culture, and propaganda in America during World War II*. Cresskill, NJ: Hampton.

North, S. (1940, May 8). A national disgrace. *Chicago Daily News*, p. 21.

Nyberg, A. K. (1999). Comic book censorship in the United States. In J. A. Lent (Ed.), *Pulp demons: International dimensions of the postwar anti-comics campaign* (pp. 42–68). Cranbury, NJ: Associated University Presses.

Office of War Information. (1942). *The life of Franklin D. Roosevelt: 32nd president of the United States*. Washington, DC: OWI. RG 208, Records of the Office of War Information, New York Office, Publications for Overseas Distribution, Box 8, folder "'Roosevelt Cartoon Book,' English." National Archives, College Park, MD.

Parry-Giles, S. J. (1994). Rhetorical experimentation and the Cold War, 1947–1953: The development of an internationalist approach to propaganda. *Quarterly Journal of Speech, 80*, 448–467.

Rhoades, S. (2008). *A complete history of American comic books*. New York, NY: Peter Lang.

Robinson, J. (2004). The ultimate fantasy. In William Breman Jewish Heritage Museum, *ZAP! POW! BAM! The superhero: The golden age of comic books, 1938–1950* (pp. 11–23). Atlanta, GA: William Breman Jewish Heritage Museum.

Rockland, M. A. (2009). An interview with Michael Aaron Rockland. Interviewers: S. Illingworth, D. Ruggiero, & K. Thomas. Rutgers Oral History Archives. New Brunswick, NJ. Retrieved from oralhistory.rutgers.edu/Interviews/pdfs/rockland_michael_part1.pdf

Savage, W. W. (1990). *Comic books and America, 1945–1954*. Norman: University of Oklahoma Press.

Schodt, F. L. (2014). *Dreamland Japan: Writings on modern manga*. Berkeley, CA: Stone Bridge Press.

Scott, C. (2007). Written in red, white, and blue: A comparison of comic book propaganda from World War II and September 11. *Journal of Popular Culture, 40*, 325–343.

Shull, M. S., & Wilt, D. E. (1987). *Doing their bit: American animated short films, 1939–1945*. Jefferson, NC: McFarland.

Skinn, D. (1994, February 14). The man who framed America's superheroes. *Guardian* [London], p. 12.

Somers, P. P. Jr. (1996). "Right in the Führer's face": American editorial cartoons of the World War II period. *American Journalism, 13*, 333–353.

Taber attacks OWI pamphlet on Roosevelt. (1943, March 5). *Washington Post*, p. 5.

Van Riper, A. B. (2011). *Learning from Mickey, Donald, and Walt: Essays on Disney's edutainment films*. Jefferson, NC: McFarland.

Vultee, F. (2007). Dr. FDR & Baby War: The world through Chicago political cartoons before and after Pearl Harbor. *Visual Communication Quarterly, 14*, 158–175.

Wandtke, T. R. (2007). *The amazing transforming superhero! Essays on the revision of characters in comic book, film and television*. Jefferson, NC: McFarland.

Watkins, A. (1943, March 19). Letter to George T. Balch. RG 208, Records of the Office of War Information, General Records of Ruth Ames, 1943–1946, NC-148, Box 1720, folder "Requests for-Correspondence on THE LIFE OF FDR." National Archives, College Park, MD.

Waugh, C. (1947). *The comics*. New York, NY: Macmillan.

Winkler, A. M. (1978). *The politics of propaganda: The Office of War Information, 1942–1945*. New Haven, CT: Yale University Press.

Wright, B. W. (2001). *Comic book nation: The transformation of youth culture in America*. Baltimore, MD: Johns Hopkins University Press.

Writers' War Board: Third annual report. (1945, January). National Association of Manufacturers Records, Series III, Box 846, folder "'quick answer' activities." Hagley Museum and Library, Greenville, DE.

Yashima, T. (1943). *The new sun*. New York, NY: Henry Holt.

Zorbaugh, H. (1944). The comics—there they stand! *Journal of Educational Sociology, 18*, 196–203.

"Hey Soldier!—Your Slip Is Showing!"

Militarism vs. Femininity in World War II Comic Pages and Books

Christina M. Knopf

When the war started, the girls and women of comics met the challenge—both the artists and the heroines. As in other industries, many women filled in for deployed men in comic creation. These women illustrators often excelled at creating and drawing female characters and produced a number of wartime heroines, both costumed and quasi-military, including Yankee Girl, Blond Bomber, Girl Commandos, Black Cat—an actress with an alter-ego who un-covered Nazi plots, Flyin' Jenny—an aviatrix who battled Nazis—Jane Martin—a nurse turned aviatrix, and Mopsy—a working girl who wore the uniforms of the WAAC, the WAVES, the Army Nurses, and the Motor Corps (Hajdu, 2008; Robbins, 1993; Wright, 2001). Tessie the Typist, the first career-girl comic book, debuted with its namesake holding down three war-related jobs: a lion tamer in a circus whose animal trainers were in the service, a showgirl entertaining the troops, and a factory worker who uses a hairpin to fix a machine capable of producing hundreds of armored tanks (Robbins, 1999). Wonder Woman came to the United States to help save democracy. So-called Victory Girls like Miss America, Miss Victory, Pat Patriot, and Liberty Belle came from all walks of American life to don masks and secret identities to carry on wartime activities (Madrid, 2009).

Most of these heroines were designed to appeal to men and women alike during the war years, offering new civic ideals for the women, and shapely young pinups for the male military readership (Hajdu, 2008). Although such portrayals in many respects stereotypically emphasized appearance and sexuality over ability (McGrath, 2007; Wolk, 2007), Will Eisner points out that the stereotype is an essential part of the language of comics and sequential art: "In the creation of a character, physical differences help make the character recognizable to the viewer, visually unique from the other characters, and 'readable'" quickly and without interpretation (Eisner, 2008, p. 145).

Other heroines in syndicated serials or single-issue publications were strictly military women, such as the mysterious War Nurse and the cheeky Winnie the WAC. At least two scholars have pointed to such depictions of female military personnel as reinforcing, if not propagating, prejudices against women in the armed forces. Historian Leisa D. Meyer (1996) frequently cites cartoon depictions of WACs emasculating or sexually entertaining/provoking men in her book *Creating GI Jane*, while English professor Laura Browder (2006) also criticizes the frequently sex-starved comic heroines of the WWII era as reinforcing women's unreliability with firearms.

Comics, however, historically have provided a safe outlet for dissent or questioning of the status quo, precisely through this kind of reinforcement, rather than destruction, of social norms (see Black, 2009). From the perspective of social judgment theory (Sherif, Sherif & Nebergall, 1965), comics can change attitudes by challenging social norms within the audience's latitude of acceptance—the range of ideas that individuals perceive as reasonable. Subversive content in comics, however, tends toward the fringe of that latitude, which can then create attitude change in the audience by expanding the latitude of acceptance itself. This chapter considers the ways in which comic depiction of female military personnel during WWII might have helped to foster tolerance for the newly created women's corps by using recognized gender stereotypes as contrary evidence to dominant social complaints about women's military service. In other words, the chapter explores how the comics reframed gender norms to depict feminine stereotypes as strengths, rather than weaknesses, in military service. In this way they illustrated compatibility between society's expectations of women and the needs of the military and the war.

Women at War

WWII required and received total mobilization of men, women, and children, but there were concerns about what kinds of service were appropriate for women and what effect women's involvement in the war would have on the war effort and on society. Women's direct participation in the military was particularly troublesome, and female service members generated widespread skepticism, civilian scorn, resentment in the male armed forces, and even consternation in the female forces (see, for example, Yellin, 2004).

Between May 1942 and July 1943, the Women's Army Auxiliary Corps (WAAC, later shortened to WAC), the Women Accepted for Volunteer Emergency Service (the Navy WAVES), the Semper Paratus—Always Ready (SPARS) division of the Coast Guard, the women's Marines, and the Women's Airforce Service Pilots (WASPs) were established. As early as September 1942, polls indicated tremendous support for drafting single women (rather than those who were married) into military service, but the reality of recruitment told a different story (Weatherford, 2008; Yellin, 2004). Nurses were already serving military duty when Pearl Harbor was attacked. Nursing, however, was not considered a proper job for young ladies because of the menial cleaning tasks, the necessity of seeing men naked, and the knowledge of inappropriate topics such as venereal disease—and military nursing was even more distressing to families of such young women (Neidel-Greenlee & Monahan, 2003; Stern, 1942). Women who were interested in nursing, or in flying, could not always afford the training required as a prerequisite for service. Others found better pay and more satisfaction working in defense plants; not only could they help the war effort, but they could meet their new financial responsibilities and enjoy more personal freedom than their enlisted sisters. Some were generally uninterested in the physical demands of military training and service, only to end up doing clerical or domestic work; many knew their skills were likely to be underutilized as babysitters, personal servants, or "mop commandos" (Weatherford, 2008).

The most pervasive challenge to female military recruitment, however, was public opinion. Women's families and sweethearts often disapproved of the independence and risk involved with military service (Weatherford, 2008; Yellin, 2004). Churches denounced women's military service as antithetical and disruptive to Christian teachings (Meyer, 1996; Weatherford, 2008). Rumors of sexual promiscuity and homosexuality were, at times, rampant; claims of military service turning women into lesbians or prostitutes were common, and false reports of high overseas pregnancy rates made their way into the news (Meyer; Weatherford, 2008; Yellin, 2004). Many, males and females alike, did not believe that women were capable of military duty and would be a potentially dangerous detriment to the armed forces (Meyer, 1996; Weatherford, 2008). Because the primary function of the women's corps was to undertake a support role and desk duties, allowing more men to fight, some families of servicemen were angry that the women's corps put more of their sons and husbands on the frontlines (Yellin, 2004). Some feared for the safety of women, because the recruits were stepping outside the protection of men (Meyer, 1996). Others were worried that military training for women would disrupt the entire gendered structure of home and family and of politics and economy; men would surely be emasculated by the women's newfound abilities and authority (Meyer, 1996; Weatherford, 2008). As a result, those women who did enlist often encountered open hostility from their male counterparts, gawks and jeers from civilians, and confusion or embarrassment from their families (Meyer, 1996; Weatherford, 2008; Yellin, 2004).

Public relations efforts were thus crucial to the mission of recruiting women into military service. The government sought to meet employment needs in both military and civilian sectors and to manage public response to the sacrifices required of them through propaganda efforts. From 1942 to 1943, magazines flooded the public with stories of how women could help the war effort—though the stories often focused on morale-boosting trivialities, such as the design of women's uniforms, than on issues or areas of substance (Weatherford, 2008; Yellin, 2004).

Cooperation among the Office of War Information, the War Advertising Council, and the Joint Army–Navy Personnel Board fostered intense recruitment campaigns in 1943 and 1944 aimed at bringing women into war work and at changing public attitudes about female enlistment. Traditional prejudices against working women had to be dispelled in the name of patriotism. Men were advised to accept women into their ranks, while women were encouraged to expand their self-expectations and dreams—but only for the duration (Honey, 1984; Meyer, 1996).

Propaganda campaigns therefore idealized the image of women war workers, portraying them as strong and competent, yet feminine and temporary. Mediated portrayals of women's war experiences were premised on the assumption that women's war labor was a short-term, if necessary, inconvenience. As such, they were depicted not only as secondary to the experiences of men but also as motivated by the desire for male approval. In order to overcome public opposition to women in the workforce and the military, women's patriotic commitment was emphasized alongside representations of their commitment to beauty and domesticity (Yesil, 2004; also, Friedman, 2005; Honey, 1984; Kimble & Olson, 2006; Marcellus, 2005). For example, recruitment slogans like "Be a Marine, Free a Marine to Fight" demonstrated women's ancillary function in the military. A Woman Ordnance Worker poster that declared, "'The girl he left behind' is still behind him; she's a WOW," emphasized feminine desire for male approval and reaffirmed commitment to the domestic ideal of marriage. Elizabeth Arden cosmetics advertisements endorsed women's commitment to both duty and beauty by promoting lipstick shades like Victory Red that complemented uniforms of khaki and blue and made men "aware of the woman" (see Dallal, 2010, graphic).

Methodology

Recognizing that in the 1940s comic strips and comic books were frequently indistinct, the comics discussed in the following pages were found in newspapers, serial comic books, and hardcover tomes.[1] The comics were selected based on historical prominence and cultural significance, on representation of the women's branches, and on representation of male and female creators. They cover a range of the war years and offer insight into comics aimed at American youth and those aimed at adults. The principle comics include "Pat Parker, War Nurse," from *Speed Comics* (debuting 1941), "Girl Commandos" from *Speed Comics* (1941), *They're All Yours, Uncle Sam!* by Barsis (1943), *Winnie the WAC* by Cpl. Vic Herman (1945), *Up Came a Ripple* by Y3C Dorothea Byerly (1945), *Meet Molly Marine* by Pfc. Barbara Bristol (1945), and "Pvt. Joe Dope" by Will Eisner (1945).[2]

War Nurse is part of the superhero genre, defined as discrete comic heroes with selfless mission, secret or alternate identities, special costume, and superior powers or abilities (Coogan, 2009). She is also one of the first female comic characters to actually be in the war theater. Pat Parker is a British nurse who becomes a critical link between the RAF and the Army Air Corps. She is compelled to do more to stop the Nazis than just treat wounded allies and so develops the War Nurse alter-ego to fight the enemies undercover. She appears next to, and is sometimes assisted by, the Girl Commandos—an international Nazi-fighting force of five women in paramilitary uniforms representing the United Nations.

Baris's (1943) somewhat historical account follows twin "babes in arms who became women at arms" (p. 12) when Maribelle joins the Army and Claribelle joins the Navy. The book was promoted as "a revelation to the women" to see "how much fun there is along with the work" (inside back cover). Herman was an advertising illustrator who was commissioned to create a morale-boosting cartoon for the army base newspaper when he was a corporal during the war; Winnie's appearance was modeled after real-life WAC Althea Semanchik, but her experiences were based on every WAC. Winnie was a hero to the Women's Army Corps, to civilian children, and even to the male army who voted her Ordnance Joe—an honor that had always gone to a living man. Winnie's trials and tribulations began around 1943 and were syndicated in 1,200 of the army's camp newspapers; she was introduced to the American public through features in *Life and Look* magazines, and in 1945 through a bound collection, with a foreword by actress Carole Landis, that sold 85,000 copies (Maw, 1971; "Speaking of," 1945).

Byerly (1945) was a servicewoman who wrote of her experience as a WAVE in a comic book described by the Women in Military Service for America Foundation as one woman's story, still typical for women serving today (Byerly, 1946, inside cover). Bristol's work was also semi-autobiographical, and her comic book, and other comic art, served promotional purposes for the "Lady Leathernecks" (N. Wilt, personal communication, August 31, 2011). "Joe Dope" was a serial featured in *Army Motors* magazine commissioned expressly for the purpose of teaching new recruits safety and warning them of the dangers of not following procedure. In at least one of Joe Dope's adventures, the character of Pvt. Ona Ball, WAC, was also a titled player. The sections that follow analyze and discuss these characters through the lens of cultural criticism. Qualitative analyses of comics often look to a text's culturally symbolic meanings in relation to myths (Duncan & Smith, 2009). Myths are enduring stories of how society works, or should work; they involve characters on quests who serve as moral guides for proper action. They may also be abbreviated fantasy themes that serve as concrete expressions of current values. Mythic criticism involves identifying familiar motifs in the comics and understanding how they relate to the larger culture in which they were produced (for more, see Foss, 1996; Hart, 1997; Rushing & Frentz, 2005). This chapter is also concerned with ideology—how those mythic themes reveal certain cultural assumptions and interpretations of society. The analysis proceeds in two steps. The first step draws on historical accounts of women's military experiences to pinpoint the social and political expectations of women in American life and military service that were represented in the vignettes and stories. The second step is premised on social judgment theory (Sherif, Sherif & Nebergall, 1965) and examines how the comics used cultural assumptions and popular stereotypes, thereby working within the public's latitude of acceptance in order to broaden it, regarding women's roles, abilities, and military service.

Analysis and Discussion

Ironically, the main arguments often made against women in the military and the dominant cultural assumptions of their military service during WWII also appeared as the primary themes in female military comics: Women who served in the military were, or would become, sexually promiscuous; women's military service would emasculate men and disrupt the social order of home and family; women were too incompetent for military service; and women's military involvement was designed to please or support men. Table 1.1 provides an overview of these ideological assumptions and their related cultural myths, along with representative examples of each in the comics.

The overriding supposition that ties these four main themes together is that, at face value, femininity and soldiering were incompatible. This point of view emerged most succinctly in one Herman (1945) vignette when an MP shouts to Winnie, "Hey soldier!—Your slip is showing!" (p. 47). The humor in the scene is based entirely on the juxtaposition of the masculine image of the soldier against the feminine article of the slip. Jenny Dare of the "Flyin' Jenny" serial was not a servicewoman, but then again neither were many of the real female pilots who flew planes for the war effort—such as members of the Women's Auxiliary Ferrying Squadron (WAFS), who were civilian employees on three-month contracts, not affiliated with any military branch, who wanted to use their skills in service to their country (Weatherford, 2008). The story line (and its title character) were inspired by the JN-40 training plane, known as the fly-ing jenny, and was eventually written by a former navy pilot. Early in the series, it was made clear that men expected little ability from a pretty face. "She's too beautiful to have brains even if she could fly!" one character remarks, and when reporters see her in grease-covered coveralls, they remark that "she's a regular guy!" (Keaton, 1987, pp. 2, 5).

Another postulation at the heart of each theme is that women did not know what they were getting themselves into when they enlisted. Baris's Claribelle and her bunkmate in the WAVES quickly discover a lack of closet space for the multiple suitcases worth of dresses, hats, stockings, and shoes they have brought to basic training. Real-life servicewomen actually did bring unneces-sary and excessive clothing with them to their posts, primarily because they lacked realistic expectations for military life. When army nurses, for example, arrived in Manila harbor in 1940, they did so carrying chiffon dresses, coordi-nating hats and high heels, white gloves, and evening gowns, having been given no instruction regarding their duties or living conditions (Neidel-Greenlee & Monahan, 2003). This circumstance, however, suggests that even if women were not quite ready for the military, the military was not ready for them, either. In one of Herman's (1945) scenes, Winnie stands in baggy coveralls rolled at the ankles and explains: "I asked the supply sergeant for my correct size and all I got was hysterical-wild laughter!" (p. 10). Byerly's Ripple is also outfitted in sleeves too long and shoes too large in several scenes. Such vignettes ac-curately captured the experience of at least some women—such as the WACs who received all-size-18 winter bathrobes and the WACs in the South Pacific who suffered jungle rot on their feet because the army had no overshoes in women's sizes (Weatherford, 2008). The lack of military readiness for females in the ranks was humorously and succinctly captured in one *Winnie the WAC*

Table 1.1		
Ideological Assumption	**Cultural Myth**	**Examples**
Servicewomen are sexually promiscuous	Women's morality and purity are rooted in domesticity	-Winnie asks a WAVE if she has a man in every port -War Nurse's costume is compared to a chorus girl's -Pat Parker's nurses get lovestruck over pilots -Winnie tries to attract a rescue plane by stripping -Molly falls for a smooth-talking gyrene
Women in the military would disrupt the social order and emasculate men	Women are the center of the home and family	-Winnie shows off a sweater her boyfriend knitted for her -War Nurse uses a gun on male allies to get them to allow her to join them on a mission against Nazis -While in formation at orientation, a Barsis recruit rejects her scrawny suitor -A mother admonishes Winnie to not keep her son out too late -Molly has no interest in her hometown beau when she joins the Marines
Women are too incompetent for military service	Women's greatest asset is beauty, being physically and mentally inferior to men	-Winnie puts the 12th Armored Division on the wrong continent -Barsis recruits show up for drills in decorative high-heeled shoes -Winnie calls for the Cpl. of the Guard because of a mouse in the barracks
Women's military service designed to please men	Men are dominant and women's activity is secondary to men's	-Wonder Woman joins the Navy as "Diana Prince" to be closer to her love interest -Cpt. Pat Parker and her nurses use hospital space to have a party for pilots -Molly frees Elmer, a sign painter at Parris Island, to fight in Japan, much to Elmer's joy

comic where a male officer cannot seem to figure out where to pin a medal on Winnie's shapely chest.

By reinforcing the status quo in order to challenge it, such comics depended on stereotypes. Quite often, the stereotypes of womanhood were translated into the requirements for soldiering—two concepts that were culturally at odds with each other. These ladies would prove otherwise; as Ellen, one of the Girl Commandos, says, "Only girls, punk! Well I ain't no wallflower" ("The Greeks Say: Fight!" 1991, p. 4). The next section examines how the comics coped with these female-vs.-soldier tensions.

Connecting Femininity and Soldiering

The fact that so many of the Victory Girls were average American citizens (not aliens like Superman, wealthy like Batman, or even goddess royalty like Wonder Woman) who took on alter egos in order to do war work reveals that women's opportunities were frequently limited. According to Mike Madrid, "putting on a cape and mask liberated these women to live the kind of life that they dreamed of—one where they could help make their world a better place" (2009, p. 5). For Winnie, Maribelle, Claribelle, and the Ripple, that liberating costume was the uniform of the country's military. Real-life WAC Jane Pollocj wrote that when she was a civilian she had been afraid to go out after dark, but she felt perfectly safe on evening strolls when she wore her army uniform (Weatherford, 2008). Even in these comics, then, the women's preoccupation with clothing was not female vanity, but an awareness of what the clothing represented and the empowerment that it could provide.

> Though it is doubtful that many women chose a military branch on the basis of the clothing offered, the uniform was truly an important part of the military experience. For men and women alike, it was essential to the definition of who they were and what role they played in the war. To be without one was indeed to be without identity (Weatherford, 2008, p. 49).

Such significance was not lost on Herman's Winnie, who, in one scene, is discovered by her sergeant off base wearing long underwear with her army cap, proudly explaining, "But it's my first pair of longies!" (Herman, 1945, p. 16). Pride in her uniform and what it represents appeared again when she sewed her Private First Class chevron onto all of her clothes, including her brassiere. Byerly's Ripple also enthusiastically stitched an eagle and crossed quills onto her jacket when promoted to Yeoman 3rd Class; the insignia was so prominent in the scene that Byerly drew it as a live bird perched on Ripple's shoulder (see Figure 1.1).

Doris Weatherford points out that "the ability of a uniform to bring welcome attention was thoroughly recognized; millions of women who did not join the military nonetheless found a way to get themselves into uniform" (2008, p. 50). This circumstance was particularly telling in Barsis's (1943) work when Maribelle and Claribelle's mother—the "only female civilian" in the family— went shopping for her own uniform at the AWVS War Shop (p. 92). War Nurse's masked-hero costuming, designed "for action" (Harvey, 1941, p. 61), however, also acknowledged that even the military uniform did not provide women with a full opportunity to serve (see Figure 1.2). Not only were the skirted uniforms restrictive in a practical sense, but they also reflected the civilian distinctions of gendered activities. Additionally, though some women appreciated the interest they generated when seen in the uniforms, others faced reproach or even violence from those who did not approve of women doing men's work or those who blamed the women for freeing more military men for combat duty.

Figure 1.1: The Ripple shows the significance of the female serviceperson uniform (Byerly, 1945, p. 80).

Responding to Gender Norms and Sexuality

In emphasizing the fragile femininity and sexy capabilities of women recruits, these comic artists and their heroines rejected the image of the ersatz man. For example, observers in the Barsis (1943) story remarked, "Whad'ya know, the Rockettes" (p. 45), while witnessing a sharp line of in-step WAVES in a comparison of military maneuvering to sexy dancing that simultaneously linked femininity with successful soldiering. One of Herman's (1945) scenes bolsters this same idea when Winnie gives instruction to a line of showgirls to "dress it up" (p. 111). For her part, Molly Marine is "not a Hedy Lamarr or a Shirley Temple—oh no! But she did ALL RIGHT" (Bristol, 1945, p. 5), and during her two weeks of mess duty she is specifically ordered to "wipe the lipstick off those cups" (p. 29), offering further evidence of femininity even in the marines. The opening scene of an episode of "Girl Commandos" depicted the women gazing admiringly at their new plane, while nearby they "are themselves gazed at, but with eyes not admiring" (1991, p. 22), as Nazis planned the Commandos' demise. Such narration reminded the audience that the Girl Commandos were women who were attractive and capable of earning a male gaze even as they were a dangerous threat to be taken seriously by the enemy. Wonder Woman, too, blended distinctly feminine qualities with fighting skill and masculine strength. William Moulton Marston created Wonder Woman and her alter ego, WAVE Diana Prince, as "psychological propaganda for the new type of woman who should, I believe, rule the world. . . . I have given Wonder Woman this dominant force but have kept her loving, tender, maternal and feminine in every other way" (as

Figure 1.2: War Nurse, in her revealing costume, shows
that even servicewomen can be alluring (Wanted,
1993, p. 6).

cited in Daniels, 2004, pp. 26–27). Her physical abilities were softened through
her depiction in a low-cut bustier; her fighting prowess was made feminine
through her fashion-related signature weapons: bullet-deflecting bracelets and
a lasso formed from the golden girdle of Greek mythology.

Barsis (1943) went so far in rejecting the masculinized female soldier as to
show a naval officer telling a receiving officer, "I don't want her" (p. 41), when
presented with a recruit in a pantsuit. The scene not only emphasized the
femininity of these new soldiers but also discouraged notions of lesbianism
in the ranks by indicating that women with masculine characteristics were not
welcome. Similarly, suggestions of sexual promiscuity, such as scenes where
Winnie is sitting on the laps of soldiers to cheer them up or because of inad-
equate seating, or giving kisses to all the men before leaving on furlough, ran
counter to society's fear that the women's ranks were comprised of lesbians.
Nonetheless, higher-ranking women, usually sergeants, were depicted with less

femininity. For example, two young shoe-shiners ask a stout female officer in the Barsis (1943) text, "Shine Sir?" (p. 56). This scene, however, was likely more a result of cartooning style than social commentary about women in positions of authority. In fact, comic men in authority positions also tend to be large, stern, imposing figures, whereas men without authority are often small and skinny. The tall, broad, or rotund commanding officer in comparison to the short, petit, or spindly private was common in military-themed comics. The 1950s Owen Fitzgerald comic *Here's Howie*, which featured its own *Winnie the WAC* serial, used these stereotypes in both the male and female divisions of the army. The "Pvt. Joe Dope" serial that Will Eisner (1945) wrote during his WWII service used similar characterization. Joe Dope was short, soft-looking, and baby-faced, whereas his commanding officers were muscle-bound, sporting five-o'clock shadows and bearing angry expressions.

Suggestions of old-fashioned romantic integrity and naiveté destabilized the promiscuous image of female servicepersons. For example, scenes such as Winnie commenting during KP duty, under the watchful eye of her commanding officer, "When I get married I'm going to be the sergeant!" (Herman, 1945, p. 8), or when she tried to order a lower-class male private into the marriage bureau, or built a snowman because, "Well—it's a man!" (Herman, 1945, p. 68), indicated both a desire for marriage and a lack of male companionship. Bristol's (1945) work also undermined notions of female promiscuity in the ranks while suggesting *male*-soldier philandering. Molly was quite heartbroken by a marine named Mack who wooed her with a "snow job" (p. 43) and then never wrote after shipping out for war. She shied away from the attentions of the other servicemen after that and gained new appreciation for the "drip" of a boy she knew at home (p. 6)—the heroic GI Joe she would ultimately decide to marry after the war. Mack, on the other hand, went on to snow a very topless overseas native.

Responding to Women's Competence

It was not only femininity that was compatible with soldiering, but womanhood and so-called women's work more broadly. Bristol cast women's military service into the broader social and historical context of women in war; before joining the Marines, Molly bought bonds, gave blood, and rolled bandages. Her decision to join was a logical extension of these gender-appropriate activities and was in line with historical precedent and the American spirit. "My greatgreat grandmammy didn't sit home weeping under her old gray bonnet," Molly said. "She just latched onto a covered wagon and fought side-by-side with the men" (Bristol, 1945, p. 10). Barsis (1943) devoted six pages of Maribelle's time in the WACs to training and duties, captioned with "Woman's Work is Never Done" (p. 52). These pages show the WACs making beds, sweeping, washing windows, scrubbing floors, doing the dishes, and cooking. The considerable space devoted to these tasks suggests their importance to the military experience. The caption reminds the reader that these were the same tasks the civilian women were doing. This idea is reaffirmed near the end of the story when the audience is told, "Maribelle, too, became a soldier" (Barsis, 1943, p. 100). Above this caption is what appears to be a "before" image of the woman in civilian dress, hunched over a typewriter, while a male boss in a business suit stands over her. The same two people appear below the caption, now in military uniforms, doing the exact same actions. "Up Came a Ripple" has several similar passages where the reader witnesses the title character doing the dishes and the laundry, ironically captioned, "Home was never like this!" (Byerly, 1945, p. 26). Even Molly "learned to iron a shirt" in the Marines (Bristol, 1945, p. 26). Pat Parker's adventures as War Nurse also began through gender-appropriate interests; while treating a patient, Pat was tipped to the possibility of germ warfare by the Nazis—which she set out to uncover and stop. Not only was this mission fitting for a nurse, but at the end of her first adventure readers are told that "the dashing, glamorous new Pat Parker . . . as War Nurse for her beloved Britain . . . continues her heroic battle against the hidden foes that she encounters in the line of duty!" [ellipses original] (Harvey, 1941, p. 61)—further linking femininity with military action. Moreover, for War Nurse, the link between her activities and feminine duty gave nursing a more respectable and even heroic reputation than it had enjoyed during World War I.

One can also glimpse how the women's non-military mentality and their alleged feminine illogic did not necessarily mean incompetence or incompatibility, but creative—if unintentional—military success. Pat Parker and the Girl Commandos, for example, are heralded for their use of "feminine intuition" ("Murder and Masquerade," 1991, p. 4) and "Girl Commando ingenuity" ("Devil's Sister," 1991, p. 4). Other examples of nonconformist approaches used by these comics' heroines included Winnie shopping for a talking parrot to answer roll call for her, hanging her laundry in front of the company bugler to dry it before inspection, suggesting that they convert to coal to avoid cutting down a large tree, and riding around in a jeep to make the sergeant's malted milk.

In reality, women's unorthodox style of problem solving was often admired by military men. In naval offices, for example, efficiency increased when WAVES replaced the men in noncombat duties, and reporters were awed by WACs who set water-filled helmets in the sun to warm for bathing (Weatherford, 2008)—an activity that Herman captured in one comic where Winnie is seen bathing nude behind modestly placed bubbles in her helmet. Such a high estimation of the women's abilities clearly emerges in Eisner's work through his use of aptronyms—character names that are appropriate to, or reflective of, character attributes. His blundering male private, for instance, is named Joe Dope, clearly labeling the GI's inadequacies, whereas Eisner's female private is named Ona Ball, a type of mondegreen or malapropism, deliberately using homophony with the phrase on the ball, a reference to the character's sharp capabilities (Eisner, 1945, p. 302).

Responding to Gender Roles and Social Order

Recognition of women's military success raised additional concerns about gender roles and the effect that female soldiers would have on male–female relationships and men's sense of identity. Part of the traditional cultural structure placed men as the protectors and women as the protected. Many soldiers fought, in part, for their wives and sweethearts at home. As a result, some opponents to women's military involvement were concerned about both the morale of male troops and the safety of females in battle (Meyer, 1996). In real life, therefore, women were not permitted to engage in combat. In the comics, most women were similarly kept far away from weaponry. In Woman Ordnance Worker posters, women were touted as "Soldiers without Guns," and the same could be said of the female soldiers in comics. Wonder Woman's weaponry of bullet-deflecting bracelets and a lasso that compels the captured to tell the truth are both peaceful in nature; Moulton's conception was one in which submission was Wonder Woman's (and all women's) greatest strength (Daniels, 2004). No weapons appeared in *Up Came a Ripple*, nor did they in *Meet Molly Marine*. The same was true of *They're All Yours, Uncle Sam!*— though the women in this comic were shown training in hand-to-hand combat.

When comic servicewomen were shown with firearms, it typically demonstrated that women and guns were not a desirable mix. For example, Winnie was shown with a tank only thrice. In one instance, she used the tank to coerce a date from a male soldier. In another, she and another WAC peeped down the gun barrel to catch a glimpse of the "cute" soldier inside (Herman, 1945, p. 65). War Nurse, when in her own comics, relied on athletic prowess and cunning. When she joined forces with the Girl Commandos, weapons were occasionally used. The Girl Commandos, however, were as likely to make advantageous use of available enemy armory as their own weapons, because they had no real need to be armed. As War Nurse said in one adventure, "We still have our fists, haven't we" ("Girl Commandos," 1991, p. 26). Molly and her fellow Marines were depicted in one scene, in marching formation, wielding brooms over their shoulders the way most troops would present their arms—fully embodying the mop commando moniker (see Figure 1.3). By limiting female military personnel's use of weapons, these comics reinforced gender norms that women were still mostly defenseless, while still showing them as capable of service.

In one Girl Commandos story line, Commando Mei-Ling eagerly undertakes a covert operation against Japanese spies to avenge the death of her fiancé—directly linking women's service with support for men while simultaneously undergirding the women's roles as wives and sweethearts, and, by extension, mothers. Such traditional family roles helped to reinforce the temporary status of women in the military. It was assumed that when the war was over, women would be not only willing but even eager to leave their emergency wartime posts in the male sector and return to home and hearth. Byerly's (1945) Ripple was portrayed as one of these women, showing joy at seeing news of victory in Japan and happily anticipating her move to "civilian, first-class" (p. 86). At the end of her story, Molly Marine is contentedly engaged to a hometown boy, indicating a return to the home after the war (Bristol, 1943). Herman's (1945) Winnie also reflected the ideal of temporary status, asking, "Do you mean to tell me I'm not fired?" (p. 19) when she breaks a stack of dishes while on KP duty. This scene demonstrated that women anticipated, even hoped for, their eventual departure from service—while it also poked fun at their lack of preparation for the military lifestyle. Later in the run, Winnie would gleefully walk off the base, suitcase and hatbox in hand, wearing a floral civilian dress (which still brandished her stripe on the sleeve) and cheerfully waving goodbye to the MP at the gate.

Conclusion

Despite modern criticisms of the portrayal of female military personnel in WWII comics, it is clear that the artists/authors and their characters did much to demonstrate women's aptitude and acceptability in the armed forces. They did so while working within the confines of dominant ideologies, or the public's latitudes of acceptance, that were both incredulous and antagonistic toward women entering traditional masculine fields. The messages of these comics fully echoed the jingoistic slogans of wartime propaganda, demonstrating their function within the country's persuasive campaigns: for girls with star-spangled hearts, this was their war, too, and they enlisted in a proud profession. Even though they were soldiers without guns, women's work was never done, because they were helping to win by doing man-sized jobs to free real men to fight.

Figure 1.3: The Lady Leathernecks are depicted as "Mop Commandos" doing evening details (Bristol, 1945, p. 23).

The success they had can be seen, in part, by their reception and popularity. Winnie the WAC was described by Carole Landis, who played Winnie in a film adaptation that never made it to theaters, as the "baby" of the WACs, because "she kidded them kindly instead of unkindly" (Landis, 1945, p. 3). Winnie and her creator—who himself was known as a hero to the WACs—went on recruiting and morale-boosting tours, received hundreds of fan letters, and served as inspiration for males and females to serve their country (Herman, 1945, Maw, 1971; "Speaking of," 1945). In 2002 Winnie returned to duty, prompted by the events of September 11, 2001; Virginia Herman, Vic Herman's widow and a former WAVE herself, republished Winnie, believing it was a time to "share her with today's military . . . and anyone else who welcomes the benefits of laughter" (Herman, 2002, p. 1). The Girl Commandos appeared in special collected reprints of war comics during Operation Desert Shield/Storm, some of which were dedicated to the United States Armed Forces (see Lorne-Harvey, 1991, inside front cover).

Up Came a Ripple was republished in the mid-to-late 1990s as part of fundraising efforts for a women's military service memorial in Arlington National Cemetery. *Meet Molly Marine* was very popular with the Pacific-based corps, as few had ever seen a female marine in person (N. Wilt, personal communication, August 31, 2011). *Flyin' Jenny* lasted from 1939 until 1946.

One of the longest-running comics, *Wonder Woman* was started anew in September 2011 by DC Comics. The day-in-the-life stories of male and female military personnel were a comic genre popular enough to continue after the war. The 1950s brought about *Here's Howie* by Owen Fitzgerald, a comic book series that followed the title character into the army and provided antic-filled adventures on the base—including those of an all-new Winnie the WAC, another lovely, well-intentioned, but somewhat ditzy character who meets with incredible military success thanks to unintentional outcomes of harebrained schemes.

Beyond the immediate public relations boost these comics offered the war effort, the enduring significance of characters like Winnie and the Ripple point to more lasting effects. Though many have argued that women's progress during the war years was limited at best (see, for example, Yesil, 2004), inroads for women were made by demonstrating possibilities: people got to see what women were capable of doing and accomplishing, without society crumbling as a result; that even if women had a different work approach or style, it was not necessarily inferior; and that femininity and hard work were not incompatible. As illustrated—literally and figuratively—by these comics, femininity and soldiering had a lot in common: Military marching formations were not unlike showgirl dance routines; KP, latrine, or mess duty was parallel to housework; and creative problem solving could occur through women's allegedly irrational thinking.

Moreover, characters like Winnie, the Ripple, Maribelle, Claribelle, and Molly helped to validate and publicize the unique experience of servicewomen in (and since) WWII. When *Up Came a Ripple* was released to raise funds to build the Women In Military Service For America Memorial, it was because the book represented not only one woman's experience in the WAVES during World War II, but also the experiences of women serving in the Armed Forces today; and, as such, it reinforced the Memorial's goal of making visible "the largely untold story of women's service to the nation" (Byerly, 1945). As John Ward Bayly (1943) wrote in the foreword to Barsis's book:

> Men, as a part of the race, and again as individuals, are progressively learning about women. They have needed no new education, however, to become aware that in time of trial woman can be relied upon with complete faith to offer herself, freely and gladly, for whatever sacrifice is needed. "They're All Yours" is woman's immemorial statement of her case. It cannot be improved. (p. 3)

In the end, the female military personnel in World War II comics may have been cast as capricious and comely coquettes, but they were courageous and competent. As such, they taught their generation, and those of their descendants, about women's service in times of trial and that acting like a girl can be an asset to any task.

Notes

1. More precisely, this chapter accepts the broad definition of comics put forth by Heer and Worcester (2009), wherein "the term most often refers to comic strips, comic books, manga, and graphic novels, but also encompasses gag cartoons, editorial cartoons, and New Yorker–style cartoons" (p. xiii; also see Wolk, 2007).

2. Samples of comics that appeared serially—"Pat Parker," "Girl Commandos," and "Pvt. Joe Dope"—were acquired based on availability. The characters of Wonder Woman by Charles Moulton (debuting 1941/42) and Flyin' Jenny from Bell Syndicate (1941) are also mentioned in the discussion, but due to limited obtainability were not central to the analysis. All quotations from the comics that are included in the discussion have been carefully reproduced to preserve the original spellings, punctuation, and capitalization.

References

Barsis, (1943). *They're all yours, Uncle Sam!* New York: Stephen Daye.

Bayly, J. W.(1943). Foreword. In Barsis, *They're all yours, Uncle Sam!* (pp. 1–3). New York: Stephen Daye.

Black, J. E. (2009). Amoozin' but confoozin': Comic strips as a voice of dissent in the 1950s. *ETC: A Review of General Semantics, 66,* 460–477.

Bristol, B. (1945). Meet Molly Marine. n.p.: Robert J. Weaver. Archives of the Women of the Corps Collection, Castle Rock, CO.

Browder, L. (2006). *Her best shot: Women and guns in America.* Chapel Hill: University of North Carolina Press.

Byerly, D. (1945). *Up came a ripple.* East Orange, NJ: Greenwood Press.

Coogan, P. (2009). The definition of the superhero. In J. Heer & K. Worcester (Eds.), *A comics studies reader* (pp. 77–93). Jackson: University Press of Mississippi.

Dallal, F. (2010, November 8). 100 years behind the iconic red door. *Vanity Fair.* Retrieved from http://www.vanityfair.com/online/beauty/2010/11/100-years-behind-the-iconic-red-door

Daniels, L. (2004). *Wonder Woman: The complete history.* San Francisco: Chronicle Books.

The devil's sister (1991). In *War sirens and liberty belles* (Vol. 1). Larchmont, NY: Lorne-Harvey.

Duncan, R., & Smith, M. J. (2009). *The power of comics: History, form & culture.* New York: Continuum.

Eisner, W. (1945). Joe Dope and Pvt. Ona Ball, WAC. In *Army Motors,* 5(10), 302–303.

Eisner, W. (2008). *Expressive anatomy for comics and narrative.* New York: W. W. Norton.

Foss, S. J. (1996). Rhetorical criticism: Exploration & practice (2nd ed.). Prospect Heights, IL: Waveland.

Friedman, B. (2005). "The soldier speaks": Yank coverage of women and wartime work. *American Journalism,* 22(2), 63–82.

Girl Commandos (1991). In *War heroes classics* (pp. 22–27). (No. 1). Larchmont, NY: Lorne-Harvey.

The Greeks say: Fight! (1991). In *War sirens and liberty belles.* (Vol. 1). Larchmont, NY: Lorne-Harvey.

Hajdu, D. (2008). *The ten-cent plague: The great comic-book scare and how it changed America.* New York: Farrar, Straus and Giroux.

Hart, R. P. (1997). *Modern rhetorical criticism* (2nd ed.). Boston, MA: Allyn and Bacon.

Harvey, A. (1941). Pat Parker, War Nurse. *Speed Comics* #15. Retrieved from private collection at http://www.jhalpe.com/items/view/00625

Heer, J., & Worcester, K. (2009). Introduction. In J. Heer & K. Worcester (Eds.), *A comics studies reader* (pp. xi–xv). Jackson: University Press of Mississippi.

Herman, V. (1945). *Winnie the WAC*. Philadelphia, PA: David McKay.

Herman, V. (2002). Winnie is back. In V. Herman, *Winnie the WAC: The return of a World War II favorite* (p. 1). Carlsbad, CA: T. G. Graphics.

Honey, M. (1984). *Creating Rosie the Riveter: Class, gender, and propaganda during World War II*. Amherst: University of Massachusetts Press.

Keaton, R. (1987). *Flyin' Jenny*. Greenfield, WI: Arcadia. (Original work published 1941)

Kimble, J. J., & Olson, L. S. (2006). Visual rhetoric representing Rosie the Riveter: Myth and misconception in J. Howard Miller's "We can do it!" poster. *Rhetoric & Public Affairs, 9*, 533–570.

Landis, C. (1945). Foreword. In V. Herman, *Winnie the WAC* (pp. 1–4). Philadelphia, PA: David McKay.

Madrid, M. (2009). *Supergirls: Fashion, feminism, and fantasy, and the history of comic book heroines*. Minneapolis, MN: Exterminating Angel.

Marcellus, J. (2005). Bo's'n's whistle: Representing "Rosie the Riveter" on the job. *American Journalism, 22*(2), 83–108.

Maw, D. (1971, July). Herman's hacienda. *San Diego Magazine*, 68–9, 91, 94.

McCloud, S. (1994). *Understanding comics: The invisible art*. New York, NY: Harper Paperbacks.

McGrath, K. (2007). Gender, race, and Latina identity: An examination of Marvel Comics' *Amazing Fantasy* and *Araña*. *Atlantic Journal of Communication, 15*, 268–283.

Meyer, L. D. (1996). *Creating GI Jane: Sexuality and power in the Women's Army Corps during World War II*. New York, NY: Columbia University Press.

Murder and masquerade of Mei-Ling! (1991). In War sirens and liberty belles (Vol. 1). Larchmont, NY: Lorne-Harvey.

Neidel-Greenlee, R., & Monahan, E. (2003). *And if I perish: Frontline U.S. Army nurses in World War II*. New York, NY: Knopf.

Robbins, T. (1993). *A century of women cartoonists*. Northampton, MA: Kitchen Sink.

Robbins, T. (1999). *From girls to grrrlz: A history of ♀ comics from teens to zines*. San Francisco, CA: Chronicle Books.

Rushing, J., & Frentz, T. (2005). The mythic perspective. In J. A. Kuypers (Ed.), *The art of rhetorical criticism* (pp. 241–269). Boston, MA: Pearson.

Sherif, C., Sherif, M., & Nebergall, R. (1965). *Attitude and attitude change: The social judgment-involvement approach*. Philadelphia, PA: W. B. Saunders.

Speaking of pictures . . . (1945, March 19). A soldier cartoonist makes a WAC his heroine. *Life*, 12–14.

Stern, E. M. (1942, February). Nurses wanted: A career boom. *Survey Graphic, 79*, 179.

Wanzo, R. (2009). The superhero: Meditations on surveillance, salvation, and desire. *Communication and Critical/Cultural Studies, 6*, 93–97.

War heroes classics. (1991). (June, No. 1). Larchmont, NY: Lorne-Harvey.

Weatherford, D. (2008). *American women and World War II*. Edison, NJ: Castle Books.

Wolk, D. (2007). *Reading comics: How graphic novels work and what they mean*. Cambridge, MA: Da Capo Press.

Wright, B. W. (2001). *Comic book nation: The transformation of youth culture in America*. Baltimore, MD: Johns Hopkins University Press.

Yang, M. (2005). Creating the kitchen patriot: Media promotion of food rationing and nutrition campaigns on the American home front during World War II. *American Journalism, 22*(3), 55–75.

Yellin, E. (2004). *Our mothers' war: American women at home and at the front during World War II.* New York, NY: Free Press.

Yesil, B. (2004). "Who said this is a man's war?" Propaganda, advertising discourse and the representation of war worker women during the Second World War. *Media History, 10,* 103–117.

★★ 2 ★★

Flying Tigers and Chinese Sidekicks in World War II American Comic Books

Zou Yizheng

The rise of comic books in the United States before WWII was based primarily on commercial interests. As the war approached, however, publishers recognized that the new medium could also serve as a means of war-related propaganda. In time, both commercial and propaganda interests would become particularly evident in the publication of a vibrant subgenre of comic book stories in U.S. culture—those that focused on China, one of America's critical wartime allies in the fight against the Axis powers.

While Chinese-themed story lines in WWII-era comic books typically appeared as backup features—serving as support for more prominent lead stories and established characters—they were a surprisingly common phenomenon on the U.S. home front. Such themes emerged in at least two different ways. Some story lines focused on American combatants as protagonists (especially the so-called Flying Tigers), with Chinese characters acting in an enthusiastically supportive manner. Others looked specifically at Chinese characters (including the Nationalist army and guerrillas), with Americans generally taking up secondary roles. In both kinds of stories, the comic book industry was effectively educating its readers about the most important American ally in the Pacific theater of the war, even as it used the theme to help sell comic books.

Yet the industry seemingly could not avoid depicting a vast and mysterious culture to readers, one filled with alien wonders and strange, though frequently heroic, people. Bradford W. Wright (2003) has noted many of the biased inaccuracies exhibited by wartime comic book story lines involving China. Before Pearl Harbor, he points out, many stories had depicted Chinese characters "as mysterious and sinister villains who schemed to promote racial domination from the opium dens, torture chambers, and laundries of fog-bound American Chinatowns" (Wright, 2003, p. 49). When the United States went to war that image adjusted, but even so the Chinese "never quite measured up to Western standards" (Wright, 2003, p. 49). In some wartime cases, for example, comic books implied that Chinese people were so hapless that they all but required the assistance of American superheroes, such as Captain Battle (Wright, 2003, p. 42), to make any progress in the fight against the Japanese. In one especially memorable story line, that assistance came from a Pat Patriot, a superheroine sent by the United States on a rather "humiliating" mission to "whip the Chinese into shape as an effective fighting force" (Wright, 2003, p. 49). No doubt, these sorts of depictions were unlikely to send a reassuring message about the Chinese ally to American readers.

On the other hand, many aspects of the Chinese-themed comic book plots were reflections of actual people and events. The Flying Tigers, for example, began as a real group of American pilots and support personnel who volunteered to defend Chinese interests against Japanese forces. They were training for combat in China even before Pearl Harbor, and while many stories exaggerated their exploits, the comic book portrayal of the cooperation between the Tigers and local Chinese partisans was frequently accurate. Although there were some neglected historical facts in many of the stories, as I will demonstrate, much of the image of the Flying Tigers and their adventures in China was based in reality.

The mixing of accuracies and inaccuracies should not be surprising, of course. American comic book artists did not observe the Chinese struggle against the Japanese in isolation. Consciously or unconsciously, the artists seem to have depicted events and people in China as a means of strengthening the bonds among the Allies. Americans—whether they were civilians reading comic books at home or soldiers reading them in a war zone—probably appreciated the positive messages of unity in them. Nevertheless, as a propaganda tool ultimately supporting American interests, such comic books tended to relay stories that echoed the official American diplomatic position toward China. The Flying Tigers were obviously a positive reflection on Allied cooperation, and so the U.S. State Department could only be pleased with the media attention directed toward them. But comic books seldom reported what some postwar scholars have described as the corruption of Generalissimo Chiang Kai-shek's Nationalist government and its conflicts with another anti-Japanese party, the Communist Party of China (Cohen, 2009). To put it differently, comic books depicted a pro-American Chinese Nationalist government and cooperative Chinese images—a construction that was only a part of the actual story.

In many respects, then, American comic books during the war largely disguised some of the baser motives of the United States regarding China at the time. The American military strategy essentially aimed to use Chinese forces as a tool to disrupt and distract the Japanese military while American war planners focused on their Germany-first policy (Cohen, 2009). By more or less sacrificing numerous Chinese lives, the United States shored up its territorial security in the Pacific, diverted some elements of the Japanese army, and relieved much of the pressure it was facing in that theater of the war. Not surprisingly, many Chinese observers did not appreciate this approach, coming to view the conflict as little more than a struggle among imperialist countries. For some, in fact, the American image in early stages of the war was as an accomplice that was actually helping imperial Japan to carve up China; others saw the United States as a backstage manipulator that supported the corruptions of Chiang Kai-shek and the Nationalist Party (Lary, 2007; Tanner, 2009).

Comic books naturally painted a very different picture of America's role in China for their readers. The booklets generally created an attractive illusion of that theater, making its strategic military approach seem more rational and less risky than it really was. Indeed, because many comic books simultaneously condemned the Japanese enemy, they effectively reinforced the perceived righteousness of the Allied struggle in the Pacific even as they overlooked the meager support that Chinese forces actually received from Americans. While this comic book reality helped promote understanding and sympathy between the American people and the Chinese people, it was biased in many respects. Worst of all, the constructed view of the conflict in this region might well have helped plant the seeds for ideological conflict in what would become the Cold War once this earlier war was won.

Such are the themes that serve as the backdrop for the analysis I undertake in this chapter. My primary goal herein is to examine how American comic books created and described the characteristics and mutual engagements of the Flying Tigers, enemy Japanese figures, and cooperating Chinese characters during the war—keeping in mind that these story lines often deviated from the actual events they purported to present. The analysis begins with the historical context that gave rise to these stories, then focuses on the series of cultural images that emerged in the China-centric comic book accounts. I conclude by considering how the images produced in these comic books might have been harbingers of the increasingly troubled Sino-American relationship that was to emerge after the war.

Historical Background of the Flying Tigers and Their Chinese Allies

Following World War I, the relationship between the United States and China became increasingly fraught with tension. The May Fourth Movement, which was the product of a widespread protest at Chinese mistreatment in the post-war settlement, the related New Culture Movement, and the growth of what amounted to a culture war between East and West led many Chinese to feel that America's fabled qualities of democracy and freedom were but thin disguises for colonialism and imperialism. Although there were still many Nationalists who supported the United States, for others America gradually lost its exalted status in China (Elleman, 2002).

The rise of imperial Japan and its military ambitions in the 1930s helped thaw the Sino-American relationship somewhat. President Franklin D. Roosevelt developed a diplomatic antipathy toward Japan, effectively meaning that he required an ally in the region. China and its Nationalist government under Generalissimo Chiang was a logical choice, since it had already become involved in a full-scale war against invading Japanese troops. By the late 1930s, the relationship between the two leaders had warmed to the point that Chiang risked asking Roosevelt for financial and military support in the struggle against Japanese expansion (Cohen, 2009). While FDR was receptive to these requests, the forthcoming support never met Chinese expectations (Frillman & Peck, 1968).

One of the highlights of America's assistance was the program that would come to be known as the Flying Tigers. Since 1937 Claire Lee Chennault, a retired Army Air Corps colonel, had been advising the Chinese in the fight against Japan. At Chiang's urging, Chennault returned to the United States in 1940 in order to approach the White House with a request for more direct assistance. In particular, he sought any surplus planes that could be used in China, along with volunteer pilots and support personnel who could put the planes into the fight (Perret, 1993). The United States was not at war at that point (and the Lend-Lease operation was still in the distant future), so no actual military support was officially possible. However, Roosevelt tacitly encouraged the founding of what would soon become the American Volunteer Group (AVG). With scores of volunteer recruits in tow, Chennault eventually returned to China to begin training with his new unit. The Flying Tigers became involved in combat operations against the Japanese only a few weeks after Pearl Harbor. By that point, its pilots had already begun to paint what would become their internationally famous symbol: ferocious, grinning tiger shark faces located on the noses of their P-40s (Frillman & Peck, 1968).

The new fighting group, at first officially known as the 1st AVG, was welcomed with open arms by Chiang's government. The force's pilots received

$600 per month from China, with a bonus of $500 for every Japanese plane they destroyed ("Flying Tigers in Burma," 1942). Eventually, the U.S. military made them into an official army unit, designated as the 14th Air Force, and broadened their mission to include not only combat against Japanese forces but also "flying over the Hump," as the pilots termed the dangerous process of supplying the region over the Himalayas (Haulman, 1993, p. 4). Chennault remained in command, however, and the larger unit retained the Flying Tigers moniker as well as the intimidating tiger shark markings.[1]

Although the Flying Tigers' prowess in combat against the Japanese soon became fodder for legend, numerous casualties still occurred (Janda, 2005). Among the most famous was Bert Christman, who ironically had created DC Comics' Sandman hero before becoming involved in the growing war. The former comic book artist was shot down over Burma in January 1942 in action against the Japanese (Klinkowitz, 1999). The later supply missions over the Hump also took their toll, with nearly 1,500 deaths attributable to the dangers of that particular route (Correll, 2009). Despite the casualties, however, the Flying Tigers were generally acknowledged to be very successful in their missions, leading to numerous admiring profiles in the American press.[2]

Part of the Flying Tigers' story involved the direct cooperation of Chinese soldiers and civilians. Although no authoritative statistics exist, numerous pilots from the unit, at one time or another, found themselves fleeing on foot in unfamiliar territory after landing a damaged aircraft or, in some cases, parachuting to relative safety. Often, they were assisted in their return by local Chinese civilians. To help assure this kind of emergency help, the Flying Tigers carried so-called blood chits into combat. These were messages in the local vernacular affirming a flyer's role as an American combatant and requesting rescue from any pursuing enemies (Eisel, 2009, p. 30; Samson, 2012, p. 279). Surprisingly, the bitter partisan rivalries between Nationalists and Communists going on in China at the time appear to have had little effect on such rescues. In the southern Guangdong region, for example, the Communist-led army of the East River Column rescued eight Flying Tiger pilots during combat operations (Zhao, 2011).

There were, to be sure, occasional misunderstandings due to language and cultural barriers. For instance, American pilots carried identification documents approved by Chiang's Nationalist government. If the pilots were rescued by soldiers or peasants with Communist sympathies, such documents were bound to create tension. On at least one occasion, in fact, members of a rescued Flying Tiger crew found themselves accused of spying against the Communists ("Minutes of Meeting," 1945). For the most part, however, the Communists were friendly toward American pilots (Samson, 2012). In one memorable occurrence, several Communist soldiers disguised themselves in order to rescue a number of downed flyers from an area occupied and patrolled by the Japanese (Xia, 2005). Later, Chennault presented the Communists with munitions as a way of acknowledging such support of the Flying Tigers and their missions in China (Yu, 2009).

All too often, however, Chinese rescuers paid a heavy price for their actions. The Japanese army was not unaware of the rescue operations and occasionally engaged in revenge killings of nearby peasants. Officials occasionally suffered too, as in the case of the magistrate of Xingzi County, Zhang Guoyou, who suffered from brutal retaliation after he rescued seven American pilots who had survived an accident on August 17, 1944 (Zhang, 2003). In brief, without the intervention of such courageous Chinese allies, the Flying Tigers could not have succeeded; despite the existing language and cultural barriers, good relations generally persisted between the Flying Tigers and the militaries and local citizens of China.

Cultural Images in "Flying Tigers" Comics

Not long after the Flying Tigers began combat operations, in late 1941, their unexpected initial triumphs over Japanese forces gained widespread media attention in America. Japan's surprise attack against the unprepared U.S. Navy at Pearl Harbor in December had dispirited many journalists, who became desperate for inspiring news stories. As if on cue, writes Lance Janda (2005), tales from China suddenly began to emerge about "a group of ragtag American heroes battling against impossible odds and scoring victory after victory over the seemingly invincible Japanese war machine" (p. 82). Reporters flocked to the story of the apparently dauntless fighters. *Life* ("General Chennault," 1942), *Newsweek* ("General Chennault," 1943), and *Time* ("Chennault," 1943) devoted their covers to the unit's grizzled leader, while book publishers began to tell the unit's story as well (e.g., Hotz, Paxton, Neale, & Dupouy, 1943; Mims & Shenton, 1943; Whelan, 1942). Hollywood even began filming a Flying Tigers movie, starring a young John Wayne (Grainger & Miller, 1942). The legend of the Flying Tigers had emerged.

As one might expect, these media accounts about the dashing new unit tended to deify Chennault and his men and simultaneously to exaggerate their accomplishments. In such accounts it seemed that the Americans could do no wrong and that they were, almost single-handedly, defeating Japanese ambitions in the East. Imperial publications in Japanese-occupied areas of China, on the other hand, provided overwhelmingly unflattering views of the Flying Tigers. According to the Japanese authors, Chennault's men were little more than flying brutes who assaulted Chinese women, bullied and oppressed Chinese men, were undisciplined in their living and fighting habits, and tended to flee when faced with the better-equipped Japanese pilots (Ge, 2001). The truth about the Flying Tigers, no doubt, tended to lie in between the two extremes.

The American comic book industry had been among those to take notice of the Flying Tigers' legend, leading many publishers to set about incorporating it into their publications using prominent backup features. Comic book story lines thus regularly began to feature Flying Tigers adventures that capitalized on their growing popularity. Given the nature of the industry, those stories tended to dramatize the most positive aspects of the legend for their younger reading audience. Indeed, as this section demonstrates, they focused primarily on providing a series of easy-to-grasp cultural images of the major players in that theater of conflict. Not surprisingly, the images tended to echo the traditional comic book narrative lineup, pitting heroes against villains—with sidekicks providing important (though occasionally unpredictable) support for the cause.

Americans as Swaggering Heroes

The comic book industry's primary audience during the war consisted of younger readers, most of them in the United States—with members of the American military making up a sizeable secondary audience (Gabilliet, 2005/2010). Considering this readership, it is no surprise to find that American characters in China-based story lines tended to serve as the primary narrative protagonists. More to the point, in story line after story line, they almost invariably played heroic daredevils with deadly fighting skills and a jaunty, carefree attitude.

Perhaps the most immediately obvious characteristics of these Americans were their tough temperament and talk. Narration in the comic books typically introduced them by emphasizing their inherently aggressive nature. These were the "hard-hitting, devil-may-care pilots of the American volunteer group," begins one admiring narrator (Carnahan, 1942, p. 3). The "independent squadron of devilcats," intones another, is hurling "thundering defiance" at the Japanese invaders (Barry & Ulmer, 1943, p. 34). A third narrator presents the Flying Tigers as "daredevils, brilliant fighting men clearing the skies" over China ("In the Name," 1943, p. 2). If even half of these sorts of introductory comments were truthful, Chennault's men were indeed a tough breed.

The comic pilots' preferred mode of talking within the stories was remarkably tough as well. Consider the confident remark of one new volunteer, who is leaving the United States for his Chinese adventure: "So long for a while,

America—we're gonna help set the rising sun!" (Carnahan, 1942, p. 4. Another cartoon flyer is thoroughly unfazed by the prospect of death in battle against a tough foe, matter-of-factly telling his commanding officer that it is "all in a day's work for a flying tiger" ("The Flying Tigers," 1943a, p. 9). Even the unit's songs signal determined defiance to avid readers. "We're the Flyin' Tiger squadron and we're off to blast Japan," shrills one jaunty tune. "An' we take no guff or propwash stuff from any flyin' man" (Barry & Ulmer, 1943, p. 32). Such aggressive messages, no doubt, represented fighting words and then some, suggesting that the American protagonists were more than ready for battle in the Chinese theater.

Yet these cartoon Flying Tigers did much more than think and talk like tough guys; they were clearly tough fighters, too. In the space of only six pages, for instance, pilot Art Shaw single-handedly outduels and destroys several attacking fighter planes, turns away two knife-wielding assailants with his bare hands, knocks out an enemy with one punch, and disables another with the stock of his service weapon—all so that he can save the entire Flying Tigers unit from ingesting a deadly poison that has been planted in their communal meal by a spy (West, 1942). Captain Spin Shaw, for his part, successfully strafes an entire Japanese infantry division while simultaneously downing three attacking Zeros (Smith, 1943). As Captain Shaw and his fellow Flying Tigers could profess, their adventures somehow find them constantly outnumbered, fighting with limited resources, or facing seemingly hopeless odds. Despite these obstacles, they almost always defeat the enemy in a resounding fashion. Even their allegorical representations are fierce. *Air Ace Comics'* regular feature on the unit, for example, always opens with an oversized frame showing variations on a literal tiger in the act of graphically mauling, crushing, or otherwise savaging Japanese soldiers (e.g., "The Flying Tigers," 1943a, 1943b, 1943c, 1943d, 1944). Whether it was combat skill or sheer animalistic power, these sorts of representations made it clear that the cartoon American pilots were menacing fighters to be feared in combat.

In combination, the bravado and the fighting prowess of the Flying Tigers characters made for a constant display of swaggering, fearless action. In episode after episode, the pilots express their thrill at encountering enemies, then proceed to engage and destroy them by any means possible. "YAHOO! JAP ZEROS! Let's give 'em the business, boys!" exclaims one squadron leader (Barry & Ulmer, 1943, p. 36). He and his unit quickly and efficiently carry out "the old flippo" (Barry & Ulmer, 1943, p. 37), a daring maneuver that traps and destroys the enemy fighters in only four frames. Meanwhile, a Flying Tiger known as Woody suddenly finds his craft under fire from numerous directions. He gamely yells to his comrades that they have "a reception!" After battle debris disables his fuel tank, however, he steers the burning plane directly toward an enemy supply train below—then escapes the resulting explosion in a daring, last-second parachute jump. Although he subsequently gripes to a colleague that he "feels like an overtoasted wienie," he is still hearty enough to beat up several armed Japanese soldiers who converge on him after the crash ("The Flying Tigers," 1943a, pp. 11, 13, 14). Much like his many comic book comrades, this American character backs up his tough talk with action, bravery, and skill. Indeed, one incredible scene elsewhere showcases all of these traits by depicting the daring rescue that results when Confusion, a befuddled Chinese character, falls out of a plane. Working quickly, an American pilot flies directly underneath him, timing his path so accurately that the falling character lands safely on the nose of the fighter (Barry & Ulmer, pp. 41–42). Such a rescue would, of course, have been impossible in the real world. But in the comic book world inhabited by the American protagonists, it was yet another instance of both swagger and dramatic action.

Importantly, however, these brave and daring Flying Tigers represented much more than tough-talking, tough-acting characters. Rather, at the most basic level, the comic book artists consistently endowed them with a kind of nobility in the face of war's death and destruction. "From the Western world," comments one narrator, "came the Flying Tigers" in order "to help defend . . . freedom" ("The Flying Tigers," 1944, p. 35). Another narrator says that the unit is nothing less than "the intrepid vanguard of American heroism of World War II," concluding that this "gallant organization" will ultimately "live in the hearts of the Chinese forever!" ("The Flying Tigers," 1943d, p. 51). Even negative events in the stories ultimately transform into noble sentiments. When one pilot avidly expresses his enjoyment of the money he has earned in combat, for example, another character quickly corrects him, exclaiming that the Flying Tigers' mission is nothing less than "*the chance to fight for a free world!*" ("The Flying Tigers," 1943a, p. 5; italics original). Meanwhile, when a pilot named Red dies after being ambushed by Zeros, the narrator rushes in to reassure readers that here is "a man who finds a place of eternal rest in the skies he loved and lived in," adding that "fate pays tribute to a great fighter with a grave up in the clouds" (Barry & Ulmer, 1943, p. 43). Far from being sketched only as brute warriors, in other words, the pilots in these stories emerged with an overarching quality of worthiness and honor. They are not just fighting Americans, but noble Americans at war.

As comic book characters, then, the Flying Tigers were more or less militarized equivalents of superheroes. Christopher Murray notes that characters such as Superman, Batman, Captain America, and their numerous peers from the war era tended on the one hand to be "rugged, strong, straightforward, and invested with wisdom borne of hardship." On the other hand, he continues, they also "symbolized the supposed moral and military strength of the nation" (2011, p. 93). Readers who followed the Flying Tigers through their many comic book adventures during the war could surely see how similar the pilot protagonists were to their superhero associates. Indeed, because stories about Chennault's adventurous men in China appeared as backup features in the very same issues in which traditional superheroes thrived, those parallels would have been hard to miss. Ultimately, here were swaggering, heroic protagonists whose very cultural qualities all but required them to use their powers for good—even as they battled cartoon versions of one of the nation's deadliest foes.

Japanese Forces as Contrived Villains

Protagonists and antagonists, as their names imply, tend to coexist, rather like opposite sides of the same coin. As Mike Alsford has observed, "the hero and the villain have fought their eternal battle across all of human history and imagination" (2006, p. 8). The two sides require and define each other; narratively, to feature one is to create a need for the other. Hence, as the protagonists of their story lines, the Flying Tigers required by their very presence an antagonist against whom they could wage their noble struggle. Not surprisingly, Japanese forces capably took on this narrative role for comic book readers in the war period. Again and again, the Japanese characters in China-centric comic book stories emerged as inhuman cowards whose nefarious plans were as threatening as they were deceitful.

As with many cartoon villains, the most central characteristic of the Japanese enemy facing the Flying Tigers was his fundamentally evil nature.[4] Consistent with popular American perceptions of the real-world attack on Pearl Harbor, the Japanese characters were obsessed with perfidy and betrayal. Over and over again, observers described them as "treacherous Japs" (Carnahan, 1942, p. 6) and "treacherous invaders" ("In the Name," 1943, p. 2) who represented "a cowardly, treacherous nation" ("The Flying Tigers," 1943a, p. 3) and who were conducting a "treacherous attack" on China (Carnahan, p. 3). One story even helpfully uses an initial line-up of characters to introduce readers to a predatory-looking "Jap officer" as "the villain" ("Wing Lee," 1943b, p. 34). From the moment these players appear in their respective stories, their evil nature is a prominent part of the comic books' underlying message.

Predictably, the cartoon Japanese figures go on to embrace their inner evil through their deplorable actions. One enemy pilot allows himself to be captured, reassuring the Flying Tigers that he is "American educated" and has been "forced to fight with Japs" ("The Flying Tigers," 1944, p. 37). However, he soon proves to be treacherous in his own right, carrying out a devious plan to dupe the Americans by stealing their strategic intelligence. In another story a Japanese pilot comes across a Flying Tiger who is parachuting to safety; the enemy pilot gleefully attacks the "helpless drifting figure—guns spurting death!" ("The Flying Tigers," 1943a, p. 7). A nearby American witnesses this act, exclaiming, "*You #@%**# filthy Jap! . . . Killin' a guy who can't fight back! . . . I'll show you!*"; the "perfidious Jap," of course, quickly pays the price for his actions ("The Flying Tigers," 1943a, p. 8; ellipses and italics original). Other story lines offer depictions of similarly evil behavior: a Japanese soldier who brutalizes a vulnerable Chinese girl ("Wing Lee," 1943c); a Japanese unit intent on killing the children in a Chinese school ("The Flying Tigers," 1943c); and a Japanese spy who attacks an American nurse, yelling "white pig woman learn respect *superior* Jap man!" ("The Flying Tigers," 1943d, p. 58). In each case, the actions of the villains affirm the initial descriptions of their inherently evil nature. No wonder, then, that one narrator summarizes the Japanese enemy as being little more than the "savage Jap rapers of China" (Barry & Ulmer, 1943, p. 34).

To compound the evil status of the Japanese figures, the comic book artists undertake a complementary tactic by portraying the enemy as cowards at heart. To wit, not only do these villains attack those who appear to be defenseless (such as the schoolchildren, nurse, and parachuting flyer noted above), but they also are fearful of—or helpless against—those who can fight back. Numerous Japanese pilots, for example, find themselves outwitted by the Flying Tigers in combat and soon end up yelling in terror as they plummet to their deaths. Here the comic book artists seem to take special pleasure in showing the panicked facial expressions of the doomed enemy figures as well as recording their guttural final words (such as the "gaaawwrrk!" uttered by one dying figure in "The Flying Tigers," 1943c, p. 26). As much as the Americans insist that the Japanese characters "*come down here an' fight like men!* ("The Flying Tigers," 1943d, p. 54), the cartoon antagonists generally prefer to use sneak attacks, to focus on weaker targets, and to keep their distance from the brave Flying Tigers. They are, in a word, cowardly, a theme that pervades the comic book story lines.

Above and beyond their apparently evil and cowardly nature, however, the most damning trait of all for these comic book enemies is that their very humanity is in doubt. Frequently, for instance, the Japanese characters become protohuman figures who resemble real people but seem to lack essential human characteristics. They are "those little men with big teeth," in the words of one American ("The Flying Tigers," 1943b, p. 7), and one particularly dastardly figure is a "dirty, buck-toothed, so and so" (p. 8). Other characters describe the antagonists as being little more than "rising sons of Satan" ("The Flying Tigers," 1943d, p. 55) or "superiorly equipped Jap savages" ("The Flying Tigers, 1943c, p.

25). The American nurse, desperately defending herself from the Japanese spy, even finds the energy to cry "Owwww! Dirty—rotten—savage!" ("The Flying Tigers," 1943d, p. 58). If the enemy has any humanity in these sorts of references, it is marginal at best.

Just as frequently, the Japanese figures in these story lines become beasts, infestations, and worse. Simian metaphors are common, as when one Flying Tiger calls the enemy "educated baboons" ("The Flying Tigers," 1943c, p. 34), while another curses the "Jap monkey-men" and still another orders his comrades to "take on those winged monkeys" ("The Flying Tigers," 1944, pp. 36, 40). At other times, the antagonists become "little yellow rats" (Carnahan, 1942, p. 5), "low-down half-breed rattlesnakes" ("The Flying Tigers," 1943d, p. 54), or, simply, "the bestial Japanese" (Moreira, 1943, p. 33). Even worse, one narrator graphically describes "China's fight to exterminate the Jap disease invading her country" ("The Flying Tigers," 1944, p. 35). Tellingly, *Blazing Comics* felt comfortable detailing "the venomous octopus that is Japan," which was slithering its way "over China bent on ruthless conquest!" The accompanying drawing shows a bird's-eye view of the Pacific theater, with Japan having come to life as a tentacled, leering monster as it slowly strangles its neighbors ("The Green Turtle," 1944, p. 1). In each of these cases, the enemy's humanity was not only in doubt but was absent altogether.

Clearly, as with their Flying Tigers counterparts, such Japanese villains echoed figures from the traditional comic book canon. Of course, the analogs this time were the supervillains of the Golden Age, those figures who squared off against superheroes and menaced their very world. Evil, cowardly at heart, and often dehumanized in various ways, characters such as Doctor Psycho, Eviless, Ibac, and Ultra-Humanite embraced their duplicitous roles even as they tried to carry out their missions of mayhem. To be sure, the comic book Japanese villains did have authentic counterparts in the very real skies and battlefields of China itself. But the thoroughly corrupt nature of the cartoon Japanese was suitably contrived and exaggerated for readers, a trope not unlike that found in the personalities and actions of the supervillains found in the lead stories of many of those very same issues. It was in this sense, then, that the nefarious, cowardly, and inhuman Japanese characters were fitting narrative antagonists for the cartoon Flying Tigers and all that those noble American figures represented to the reading audience.

Chinese Characters as Erratic Sidekicks

It is perhaps ironic that this chapter has thus far focused primarily on American and Japanese characters. After all, the story lines in these comic books take place in China, a sovereign Allied nation with its own military forces and a population by this point well over 500 million people. For better or worse, however, China-themed comic books from the war period tended to treat Chinese characters as tertiary subjects. Even when those characters transcended the rather passive part of victims of Japanese aggression, their participation in what amounted to an American-themed war effort was often portrayed as unreliable at best and futile at worst. Still, it was important, at least for the American reading audience that was learning about its primary ally in the region, that those characters also appear to embody highly positive traits. In a narrative world populated with American protagonists and Japanese antagonists, these ambivalent vantage points thus inevitably relegated the cartoon Chinese figures to the supporting role of sidekicks—and erratic ones at that.

First, in setting up the context for their story lines, the comic book authors frequently expressed admiration for China and its people. In their view, it was apparent that—unlike the Japanese villains—many of their Chinese characters seemed to possess great courage and resolve. They were the "heroic[,] gun-hungry Chinese," according to one account (West, 1942, p. 16), and a "gallant people," in the view of another ("The Flying Tigers," 1943d, p. 51). "Under the able leadership of Generalissimo Chiang Kai-Shek," proclaimed a third, "China is determined, in time, to drive the Japanese out of China!" ("Chinese Hero No. 1," 1941, p. 52). In fact, as one narrator contended, the battle for China was actually "the fight of a peace-loving people aroused to hate-fervor, determined to sacrifice ALL rather than give up the freedom they cherish" ("The Flying Tigers," 1944, p. 35). With such admiring sentiments in place, there was clearly ample room in the narratives for notable Chinese characters and their actions.

As it turns out, a few Chinese characters did indeed emerge to play an exceptional role in their story lines. The most prominent, perhaps, was the teenager Wing Lee, touted by *New Blue Beetle* as the "boy patriot of China" ("Wing Lee," 1943c, p. 34). In one episode Wing and his gang of young misfits walk for 10 days as they seek to join Chiang's army (("Wing Lee," 1943c, p. 40). In another, they nearly defeat an armed squad of Japanese soldiers with their bare hands ("Wing Lee," 1943a, p. 50). Finding themselves imprisoned by the Japanese in another story, Wing exclaims that "worthy sons of China never surrender!" ("Wing Lee," 1943c, p. 37). Remarkably, there is even a scene where a downed Flying Tiger—who has linked up with Wing's ragtag commandos—discovers that his own father is being held by Japanese troops in a nearby compound. "Don't worry, Bill!" says Wing with conviction. "We'll help you rescue your father despite all the obstacles and dangers!" ("Wing Lee," 1943b, p. 36). The daring rescue proceeds as planned (albeit with some unexpected assistance from a Flying Tigers raid). Afterward, Wing and his group celebrate by vowing to "continue to fight behind the lines and keep on till victory is ours" ("Wing Lee," 1943b, p. 43). Although he is young and inexperienced, Wing is indeed a brave and determined character.

An even more impressive show of courage and resolve is evident in a story line that begins with an urgent, hand-delivered request to the Flying Tigers from a Chinese general. As the American commander reads the note, he is shocked to find that his unit is being asked to bomb several Yangtze River dikes. "But why?" asks a nearby pilot in disbelief. With countless local civilians living in the valley, he adds, "they're ordering their own suicide!" Grimly, the commander replies that the bombing will also drown a threatening "army of 35,000 Japs." The young Chinese messenger interjects, with great pride, that "every Chinese living in valley is willing to dlown with them to achieve such a *great victoly!*" Impressed, the pilot then shakes the messenger's hand. "Whata people you Chinese are . . . a people with guts!," he proclaims. The messenger concludes the exchange by reemphasizing his statement, in case anyone missed it the first time: "We not aflaid to die!" ("The Flying Tigers," 1943b, p. 6, ellipsis original).

At length, and after overcoming numerous obstacles, the Flying Tigers successfully arrive at the river dikes. On the ground, intones the narrator, "Chinese peasants who know the bombs carried in the planes flying overhead mean their extermination, happily wave them on!" The accompanying drawing shows a close-knit family of five placidly waving to the pilots overhead. Their impending sacrifice is made all the more poignant for readers by the shadows of the Flying Tigers' two planes, which cast two great crosses on the ground beyond the family ("The Flying Tigers," 1943b, p. 10). Soon thereafter, the great river's water is unleashed, and viewers see a meaningful contrast. In one frame, a half dozen Japanese soldiers, brute panic on their faces, run for their lives as "the deadly army of 35,000 Japs is wiped out in a single stroke!" The facing frame, meanwhile, depicts several Chinese peasants facing "this honorable death with brave smiles" ("The Flying Tigers," 1943b, p. 11). Their action, according to the narrator, amounts to "the greatest national sacrifice in history" ("The Flying Tigers," 1943b, p. 5). More to the point, it is a vivid and dramatic illustration of the bravery and determination possessed by many of the cartoon Chinese characters.

As it turns out, though, the comic books' occasional emphasis on the stalwart nature of their Chinese figures consistently runs up against an equally strong theme of contempt and, at times, outright suspicion. Consider, for instance, the basic assumption of many of the stories that the Chinese people have been little more than hapless targets of wartime Japanese aggression. This viewpoint appears to influence the development of many of the Chinese figures, who consistently act in passive and even ridiculous ways. Confusion, the character who falls out of his plane only to land safely on the nose of a well-positioned P-40, is a prime example. His name is a mocking nod to Confucius, of course, yet he is far from wise. As the narrator states, he has "a heart of gold and a head of lead" (Barry & Ulmer, 1943, p. 33). Indeed, his unpredictable, slapstick behavior leads the American pilots in the story to treat him as they might a pet or a mascot. Even his English skills seem designed for ridicule, as when he asks a pilot if he can ride along on a mission: "Mist Tliger! When is you tlake Confusion up in fishplanes to kill 'um tellible Japanese?" (Barry & Ulmer, 1943, p. 38). Like many of his cartoon peers, this character is more suitable for laughs than for admiration.

Wing Lee, the lead Boy Patriot, is undoubtedly a much stronger character than Confusion. His English skills in particular are excellent. Still, the comic book story lines find ways to marginalize him as well. Despite his moments of bravado, for example, all three of Wing's adventures would go nowhere without the timely intervention of one or more fortuitous (and unexplained) Flying Tigers attacks from above ("Wing Lee," 1943a, 1943b, 1943c). Moreover, in the character's second story line, the downed Flying Tiger Bill Anderson joins the group, and his presence diminishes Wing's leadership role significantly. At nearly every turn, in other words, Wing's strength as a character actually depends on American intercession of one sort or another.

However, the most unflattering depiction of Chinese characters remains the one in *Feature Comics*'s "Capt. Spin Shaw" story line (Smith, 1943). Here, a group of Chinese guerillas encounters the titular Flying Tiger after an emergency landing. Without identification papers, the pilot quickly falls under suspicion. Using a style of English not unlike that used by Confusion ("You!! Come this side quick! Go chop chop! Look see number one man! Hully up!"), the guerillas take Shaw before their leader, whose word bubbles contain no English at all, only kanji symbols (Smith, 1943, p. 36). The chief concludes that the pilot is a German spy and sends him away for immediate execution. On the way, Shaw complains that he "can't imagine Chinese shooting anyone without a fair trial!" (Smith, 1943, p. 37). The situation looks pretty dire for the American hero.

Fortunately, proof of Shaw's status as an authentic Flying Tiger arrives just in time, and the situation changes immediately as the Chinese bow before him in humility. "Now what's this??" he says. "First, you're going to shoot me and now you go kowtowing all over the place!! What gives?!!" (Smith, 1943, p. 37). One of the guerillas replies "We are lose face! Our humiliation knows no side bounds for grievous error—you forgive?" (Smith, 1943, p. 37). The turnabout is stunning; in only two pages, the pilot has gone from a death sentence to a reprieve, while the Chinese have gone from cruel and merciless executioners to hapless buffoons.

The Chinese guerillas ultimately end up cooperating with Shaw to destroy a Japanese division (Smith, 1943). Yet their apparently capricious behavior immediately after the pilot's capture seems to linger. By the end of the story, readers can hardly question the characters' determination, nor can they question their zeal. The Chinese figures' trustworthiness and judgment, in contrast, remain in serious doubt. The final victory scene ultimately makes it clear that the Chinese characters are important strategic allies in the context of the larger war effort. At the same time, though, the story line has obviously positioned them as erratic at best and unreliable at worst. As allies go, the story seems to conclude, these figures are far less than desirable.

A similar conclusion—albeit one that is subtler in tone—lurks in the subtext behind most of the Chinese characters in these stories. On the one hand, they are brave and relentless. On the other, they are often slow-witted, distant, comical, or all three at once. Even the Flying Tigers occasionally demean them, as when pilot Maverick Brannigan yells at the base's Chinese laborers: "Bend yore backs, y' sawed-off runts. Git those planes under cover 'fore we have the whole Jap Air Force shooting at us!" ("The Flying Tigers," 1943d, p. 52). Such remarks are not common in the fictional world of the comic book stories, but their very presence in one case is symptomatic of an underlying sense of disdain that permeates most of these stories. Despite the courage and tenacity allowed to many of the Chinese characters, then, readers could hardly have seen them as equal to their heroic American allies.

In the end, when one considers them as a group, the Chinese characters in the various Flying Tigers narratives generally serve neither as heroes nor as villains. Instead, they become the rough equivalent of sidekicks in the fight against evil. Just as Batman and Captain America alternately mentored and bailed out Robin and Bucky elsewhere in the comic book world, so too do the Flying Tigers serve as supervisory heroes for what effectively become their junior Chinese sidekicks. In retrospect, the implied message is both condescending and insulting. Not only does it position the Americans as superior to their exotic and mysterious Chinese allies in intellect, reliability, and competence, but it also suggests that the Chinese are childlike and require instruction from foreigners. Despite the vital role of the real-world Chinese in the prosecution of the war, these cartoon Chinese characters are relegated by the American comic book industry to a minor supporting role in the defense of their own homeland.

Conclusion: Glimpsing the Cold War in the East

In this chapter I have tried to establish that the WWII-era comic book story lines that related the legend of the Flying Tigers did so in a rather traditional manner, at least as far as the comic book industry was concerned. Since that industry's emergence in the 1930s, the comic book world had frequently embraced a repetitive character pattern in which heroes fought villains, with sidekicks aiding the heroic cause—if only in unpredictable and less efficient ways. The adaptation of such an underlying narrative blueprint to stories about the Pacific theater, of course, tended to reposition the historical experience of the actual Flying Tigers and their peers into one that was more suitable for the mythic structures of the comic book world. From a commercial point of view, this approach makes sense. After all, the industry could not have survived if it failed to sell issues. Thus, it had every reason to fashion its China-based stories using narrative formulas that had proven to be attractive to readers in the past.

Looking back, however, those formulas and the cultural images that they sketched in the Flying Tigers stories serve as a curious harbinger of the conflicted political situation that would follow WWII in the Pacific arena. For its part, Japan's first task was to face its humiliating and crushing defeat. Not long afterward, though, the dreaded former enemy had made a quick and remarkable transformation into an American ally (Dower, 1986). The United States and Japan were not equal players in this new relationship, to be sure. As Robert MacDougall observes, "the once-fearsome enemy" had only managed to become "an imitative ally, a clever and charming pet" (1999, p. 66). To return to the character roles discussed above, it was as if the villain, shamed in defeat, had decided to embrace the role of a sidekick.

Meanwhile, the role of China had also transformed, but in the opposite direction. In the aftermath of the war, the Communists decisively wrested control from Chiang's Nationalists, establishing the People's Republic of China in 1949. Even before that point, however, "the Japanese and the Chinese had already changed places" in the minds of many residents of the United States (Dower, 1986, p. 309). Soon the Chinese people had "inherited most of the old, monolithic, inherently totalitarian raiments the Japanese were shedding," becoming, at least to American eyes, "the newest incarnation of the yellow peril" (Dower, 1986, p. 309). It was a seemingly effortless transition for many in the Unites States. Comic book fans, for their part, must have been particularly well-suited to grasping what amounted to a transformation from sidekick to villain. After all, as many of them had seen back in 1942, Gotham City's revered district attorney, Harvey Dent, had quickly shifted from hero into the archvillain Two-Face after being disfigured by acid. So it was that China and Japan seemed to easily switch narrative roles in the American imagination after the war.

Of course, China's dramatic transformation might not have been all that surprising to those who had read the China-centric comic book stories of WWII. If, indeed, the Chinese were courageous and stalwart, as those stories had implied, those were traits that were not incompatible with the qualities of an enemy. At the same time, the negative characteristics of the comic book Chinese, such as their untrustworthiness and their generally inferior intellect, could easily be useful in describing an enemy. Simply put, the Flying Tigers story lines had established the Chinese as a kind of contemptible and erratic sidekick, not a fellow hero. The shift from that kind of mysterious, tenuous ally into a feared villain was, it would seem, not too hard for many readers to imagine.

Still, even if these comic book story lines tacitly provided a glimpse of the Cold War conflicts to come, it is important to remember that their creators were primarily concerned with their immediate situation, not the distant future. The saga of the Flying Tigers was a huge psychological boost in the United States at an early point in the war (Janda, 2005), and so it was natural for the comic book industry to embrace that saga, at least for commercial reasons. At the same time, the comic books also undeniably served an ideological purpose, creating for many young Americans an unexpectedly tension-filled view of the Pacific theater and its fascinating cultural players. That potential glimpse of the Cold War, then, was surely incidental. Even so, it serves as an intriguing commentary on the visual and political implications of the simple comic book in a time of war.

Notes

— The author is grateful for the help of Ms. Xiaoqin Zhou, who contributed a lot in translating part of the Chinese manuscript.

1. To this day, the 23rd Fighter Group, a successor unit to the Flying Tigers, continues to use the grinning tiger shark mouths on its A-10s; each aircraft's two-letter identifier is FT, another homage to Chennault's WWII unit (Eisel, 2009).

2. Scholars continue to debate the actual military effectiveness of the Flying Tigers in the context of the Pacific theater. For contrasting views, see Cohen (2009) and Janda (2005).

3. Throughout, I refer to the Japanese characters using male pronouns, since no female Japanese characters appear in the Flying Tigers story lines.

References

Alsford, M. (2006). *Heroes and villains*. Waco, TX: Baylor University Press.

Barry, D., & Ulmer, A. (1943). Introducing the sensational Tiger Squadron in China. In *New Blue Beetle* (pp. 32–43). (No. 20). Holyoke, MA: Holyoke.

Carnahan, W. (1942). The flying tigers. In *War heroes* (pp. 1–6). (No. 2). New York, NY: Dell.

Chennault of the Fourteenth Air Force. (1943, December 6). *Time*, cover.

Chinese Hero No. 1: Chiang Kai-shek. (1941). In *True Comics* (pp. 43–52). (Vol. 1, no. 4). New York, NY: Parents' Institute.

Cohen, W. (2009). *America's response to China: A history of Sino-American relations* (5th ed.). New York, NY: Columbia University Press.

Correll, J. T. (2009, October). Over the hump to China. *Air Force Magazine*, 68–71.

Dower, J. W. (1986). *War without mercy: Race & power in the Pacific war*. New York, NY: Pantheon Books.

Eisel, B. (2009). *The Flying Tigers: Chennault's American Volunteer Group in China*. Washington, DC: GPO.

Elleman, B. A. (2002). *Wilson and China: A revised history of the Shandong question*. Armonk, NY: M. E. Sharpe.

The Flying Tigers. (1943a). In *Air ace comics* (pp. 3–12). (Vol. 1, no. 9). New York, NY: Street & Smith.

The Flying Tigers. (1943b). In *Air ace comics* (pp. 5–12). (Vol. 1, no. 10). New York, NY: Street & Smith.

The Flying Tigers. (1943c). In *Air ace comics* (pp. 25–34). (Vol. 1, no. 11). New York, NY: Street & Smith.

The Flying Tigers. (1943d). In *Air ace comics* (pp. 51–60). (Vol. 1, no. 12). New York, NY: Street & Smith.

The Flying Tigers. (1944). In *Air ace comics* (pp. 35–45). (Vol. 2, no. 2). New York, NY: Street & Smith.

Flying Tigers in Burma. (1942, March 30). *Life*, 27-30.

Frillman, P., & Peck, G. (1968). *China: The remembered life*. Boston, MA: Houghton Mifflin.

Gabilliet, J. (2010). *Of comics and men: A cultural history of American comic books*. Jackson: University Press of Mississippi. (Original work published 2005)

Ge, S. (2001). Kongzhong Feihu: Dierci Shijie Dazhan Zhong de Zhongguo Kongjun Meiguo Zhiyuandui (The Flying Tigers: Volunteers of the U.S. Air Force in WWII). *Huaxia Renwen Dili (Journal of Chinese Cultural Geography), 3*, 12–45.

General Chennault: From the Flying Tigers to the 14th Air Force. (1943, March 22). *Newsweek*, cover.

General Chennault in China. (1942, August 10). *Life,* cover.

Grainger, E. (Producer), & Miller, D. (Director). (1942). *Flying Tigers* [Motion picture]. United States: Republic Pictures.

The Green Turtle. (1944). In *Blazing comics* (pp. 1–9). New York, NY: Rewl.

Haulman, D. (1993). *The high road to Tokyo: The AAF in the Asiatic-Pacific theater*. Washington, DC: Center for Air Force History.

Hotz, R. B., Paxton, G. L., Neale, R. H., & Dupouy, P. S. (1943). *With General Chennault: The story of the Flying Tigers*. New York, NY: Coward-McCann.

In the name of sky victories, Tigers—welcome to my book! (1943). In *Air ace comics* (p. 2). (Vol. 1, no. 9). New York, NY: Street & Smith.

Janda, L. (2005). "Renegades, Mavericks, and Ruffians": The Experience of the "Flying Tigers." In T. C. Dowling (Ed.), *Personal perspectives: World War II* (pp. 81–96). Santa Barbara, CA: ABC-Clio.

Klinkowitz, J. (1999). *With the Tigers over China, 1941-1942*. Lexington: University Press of Kentucky.

Lary, D. (2007). *China's Republic*. Cambridge, UK: Cambridge University Press.

MacDougall, R. (1999). Red, brown and yellow perils: Images of the American enemy in the 1940s and 1950s. *Journal of Popular Culture, 32*(4), 59–75.

Mims, S., & Shenton, E. (1943). *Chennault of the Flying Tigers*. Philadelphia, PA: Macrae-Smith-Company.

Minutes of meeting held at Ambassador Hurley's home, No. 2 Chialing Village. (1945, August 30). Typescript. Albert C. Wedermeyer Papers (Box 87, Folder 4). Hoover Institution Archives, Palo Alto, CA.

Moreira, R. (1943). G2: The case of Cantow Poppy. In *National Comics* (pp. 32–40). (No. 30). Buffalo, NY: Comic Magazines.

Murray C. (2011). *Champions of the oppressed: Superhero comics, popular culture, and propaganda in America during World War II.* Cresskill, NJ: Hampton.

Perret, G. (1993). *Winged victory: The Army Air Forces in World War II.* New York, NY: Random House.

Samson, J. (2012). *The Flying Tiger: The true story of General Claire Chennault and the U.S. 14th Air Force in China.* Guilford, CT: Lyons.

Smith, R. (1943). Capt. Spin Shaw. In *Feature comics* (pp. 35-39). (No. 70). Buffalo, NY: Comic Favorites.

Tanner, H. M. (2009). *China: A history.* Indianapolis: Hackett.

West, D. (1942). Flying Tiger. In *Wings Comics* (pp. 16-21). (No. 24). New York, NY: Wings.

Whelan, R. (1942). *The Flying Tigers: The story of the American Volunteer Group.* New York, NY: Viking Press.

Wing Lee. (1943a). In *Blue Beetle* (pp. 45–54). (No. 23). Holyoke, MA: Holyoke.

Wing Lee: Boy patriot of China. (1943b). In *New Blue Beetle* (pp. 34–43). (No. 22). Holyoke, MA: Holyoke.

Wing Lee: Boy patriot of China, and the Flying Tigers. (1943c). In *New Blue Beetle* (pp. 34-43). (No. 21). Holyoke, MA: Holyoke.

Wright, B. W. (2003). *Comic book nation: The Transformation of Youth Culture in America.* Baltimore, MD: Johns Hopkins University Press.

Xia, Y. (2005). Yingjiu Meiguo Feixingyuan (Rescuing American Air Force flyers). *Fujian Zhibu Shenghuo (Journal of the Fujian Branch of the Communist Party of China), 6,* 37-38.

Yu, Q. (2009). Wo he Meiguo Feixingyuan de Yiduan Wangshi (A Record between a Flying Tiger soldier and I). *Wenshi Yuekan (Journal of Culture and History), 1,* 65.

Zhang, J. (2003). Yingjiu Meiguo Feixingyuan (Rescuing American Air Force flyers). In Z. Chen (Ed.), *Lushan Laoxiangce (The Old Album at Mountain Lu)* (pp. 87–92). Nanchang, China: Jiangxi Art Press.

Zhao, Y. (2011). Dongjiang Column soldiers ventured on rescuing American Flying Tiger members. *Source Magazine (Yuan Liu),* no. 13, 75–76.

★★ 3 ★★

Boys on the Battlefield

Kid Combatants as Propaganda in World War II-Era Comic Books

Jon Judy and Brad Palmer

Given the shared goals of private and state propagandists, it was only natural that comic book creators from the WWII era would produce narratives that echoed the government's agenda (or what they thought that agenda should be), and they often used propagandistic techniques to do so. For example, one of the most popular genres of comic books, the kid sidekick story, often echoed governmental agendas and popular national myths during this era. Child sidekicks were faithful fighting companions to superheroes, serving as proxies for young readers and giving them someone with whom to identify (Savage, 1990, p. 6). The best known of these kid heroes, of course, is Robin, the boy wonder who fought beside Batman.

In the last few decades, the child sidekick trope has been deconstructed to present a more modern idea of the kinds of adults who would allow children to risk their lives as vigilantes. Most notably, Frank Miller (1997) tackled the Batman and Robin dynamic in *The Dark Knight Returns*, and Rick Veitch (2009) examined the hero–sidekick relationship in general, generic ways in *Brat Pack*. These texts were gritty, realistic depictions of the hero–kid relationship, or at least as realistic as a superhero comic can be. In particular, the authors considered the reckless irresponsibility and mental instability of the kind of person who would encourage a child to fight crime, including the implied sexual kinks of such a relationship.[1]

Regardless of how the trope looks to modern eyes, however, the sidekick became an undeniably popular phenomenon on the eve of WWII. After the introduction of Robin, adult superheroes with kid sidekicks were "very nearly de rigueur in the medium during the 1940s" (Savage, 1990, p. 6). As comic narratives routinely placed children on the figurative frontlines of a war against crime, it was perhaps a natural consequence that, in a time of war, the narratives placed children on *literal* frontlines in stories of *actual* war. And so a subgenre of kid combatant stories emerged. If the child super-hero gave young readers the opportunity to experience adventures alongside their heroes, and to engage in an even more direct form of wish fulfillment than they experienced in the pages of other superhero comics, the sidekick trope's shift to a military theme sent the subtle yet indisputable message that the form of young boys' wishes should be changing. In these stories, in other words, children were told that instead of wishing to fly, they should be wishing to fight.[2]

This chapter offers a narrative analysis of a selection of comic books within the sidekick subgenre of WWII, identifying propagandistic characteristics and using social cognitive theory as a guiding perspective with which to identify ways these comic books can be viewed as teaching tools, encouraging readers to enlist when they could. Because of the nature of the subject matter, the chap-ter's methodology is admittedly haphazard. Comic books of this era normally featured several stories in each month's issue, and there is no comprehensive, searchable database that would allow one to isolate all stories within the sub-genre of interest. Consequently, the authors have perused a number of comic books from the era to find relevant stories, but there was no particular pattern to this perusal. Because of the contemporary popularity these story lines en-joyed during the 1940s (and their ease of availability in reprinted collections today), this chapter focuses on Captain America, his sidekick Bucky Barnes, and the Young Allies.[3]

While there are numerous examples of this comic book subgenre,[4] per-haps the most salient of the kid combatants were Bucky and his team, the Young Allies.[5] Bucky first emerged as the kid sidekick of Captain America, the superhero who, on the cover of his 1941 first issue, socked Adolf Hitler him-self (Dell'orto, Wright, & Brevoort, 1998, p. 1). Bucky was a regular child whose "dream is fulfilled as he fights side by side with Captain America against vicious elements who seek to overthrow the U.S. Government!" (Dell'orto et al., 1998, p. 19). In so doing, he became a proxy for young readers. Eventually, Bucky went on to lead a team of boys, the Young Allies.

The Allies had a base/clubhouse where they ran drills and trained to be sol-diers. They also occasionally found themselves chasing spies and undertaking dangerous missions behind enemy lines. The group was apparently intended to represent a cross-section of American boys. They were clearly derivative of the Dead End Kids, a popular group of boy actors who appeared in the play-turned-movie *Dead End* and its sequels (Hulburd, Goldwyn, & Wyler, 2005). One Ally was even identified as "formerly a Dead-End kid" (Sedlmeier, 2009, p. 11). Like the Kids, the Allies comprised a collection of stereotypes—the smart kid, the overweight kid, the tough kid, and so on—and therefore both groups appear to have embraced an inclusive philosophy. Still, the Allies did the Kids one better in that their group actually included a child of color, albeit a crudely stereotyped African American boy named Whitewash. The other members of the team were Toro, the sidekick of the superhero Human Torch; Knuckles, a clichéd tough guy from Brooklyn; Tubby, the overweight kid; and Jefferson Worthington Sandervilt, boy genius and product of high society. Of this team, Toro was the only character with superhuman abilities; the other teammates were normal boys, like the readers themselves.

Social Cognitive Theory

A good beginning point for examining the propaganda impact of kid sidekicks is Albert Bandura's social cognitive theory (1986). His theory suggests that "humans can learn through observation without the need for imitation; learning could be either direct or indirect (vicarious) in that one could learn through observing others' behaviors and the consequences of those behaviors" (Gibson, 2004, p. 195). This theory is suitable for studying media effects, as one can view a media product, such as a comic book, as demonstrating behaviors (Baran & Davis, 2003). Media audiences can "acquire symbolic representations of the behavior, and these 'pictures' provide them with information on which to base their own subsequent behavior" (Baran & Davis,,2003, p. 193). So a child who reads a comic book about children fighting Nazis and being rewarded for doing so might not necessarily try to join the armed forces to imitate the character; the child would, however, learn related appropriate behaviors that they could imitate, such as eventual enlistment.

Social cognitive theory describes four component processes that govern observational learning from media. First, one must be exposed to the media and attend to it. Second, one must be capable of encoding and remembering the observed events, including "both constructing the representation and cognitively and enactively rehearsing it" (Harris, 2009, p. 33). Third, one must be able to translate the observations into appropriate action (assuming the individuals have the ability to act appropriately). Finally, motivation must develop from internal or external means to encourage the behavior.

These components made the comic book genre an ideal medium for influencing children. In the WWII era, the booklets were cheap, plentiful, and written in accessible language, with exciting visuals that could easily capture a child's attention. The simple, repetitive themes made stories, characters, and situations easy to remember and grasp. Of course, readers could not mimic the superhuman strength and agility of the acts of Captain America. Yet characters like Bucky, the Boy Commandos, Airboy, and most of the Young Allies had no powers, which made their actions at least appear to be achievable.

Applying Social Cognitive Theory to Comic Books

Since the sidekick is a child, and therefore similar to most of the genre's home-front readers, the praise the hero offers in these comic books frames the sidekick's actions as acceptable. After all, the hero or guardian is an adult, a figure of authority, and an admirably framed figure as well. The superhero's behavior could, then, become more acceptable and positively charged to young readers, who might view the superhero as the sidekick's role model, and the sidekick as their own role model. In one adventure, for example, Captain America encourages his sidekick, saying "Atta boy, Bucky! You'll make a good soldier yet!" (Dell'orto et al., 1998, p. 19). If one accepts that Bucky was the readers' proxy, it is easy to see how children might interpret such a message.[6] Some of the Captain America and Young Allies stories considered here emerged prior to the entry of the United States into the war. They are nonetheless relevant to the discussion, as they used propaganda techniques to advocate American involvement in the war. Captain America co-creator Joe Simon said that he and Jack Kirby created that character because "the opponents to the war were all quite well organized. We wanted to have our say too." The partners, he concluded, "felt very good about making a political statement" (as cited in Wright, 2001, p. 36). Of course, it is one thing to use propaganda to encourage American involvement in a war and another to use propaganda to encourage martial attitudes in children. Therefore, this chapter includes the ways these stories used propaganda techniques that would have encouraged a perception among young readers that war is a fun, safe, desirable pursuit—regardless of whether the stories predated U.S. entry into the war. Six specific themes are particularly relevant, as discussed in the following sections.

War Is Fun

One recurring theme of the kid combatant stories is that war is fun and game-like. Bucky often shows his enthusiasm during fights with the enemy by excitingly shouting things like "Yahoo!" (Dell'orto et al., 1998, p. 109), "Wahoo!" (Dell'orto et al., 1998, p. 146), and "Hot diggety! A machine gun!" (Dell'orto et al., 1998, p. 147). The Young Allies use "Yahoo!" as a rallying cry during battle (Sedlmeier, 2009, p. 26; see Figure 3.1). This attitude is encouraged by Bucky's primary authority figure and his role model. "Let's go out to look for more trouble and adventure," Captain America prompts at one point. Bucky replies, "Lead the way, Cap!" (Dell'orto et al., 1998, p. 62).

The idea that war is fun emerges outside of battle, too. In an issue where Private Steve Rogers (Captain America's secret identity) and Bucky are assigned to guard duty, Bucky exclaims, "Boy! A real military mission wait'll I tell the Sentinels of Liberty!" (Sedelmeier, 2008,, p. 71). Despite Bucky's experience in countless battles alongside Captain America, Bucky is so excited to be doing basic guard duty that he cannot wait to tell his friends (Sedelmeier, 2008, p. 71).

In one of the many instances in which Cap has to free Bucky from Axis abductors, the boy does not express fear of being hurt by his aggressors or gratitude at being freed, but rather eagerness to further face the dangers of fighting. "C'mon, Cap!" he urges. "Turn me loose so I can get in on the fun!" (Dell'orto et al., 1998, p. 90). Indeed, fighting is far more appealing than both the tedium of a boy's everyday life and the normal amusements of childhood. "Aw, these exams give me a headache. I wish we were out hunting crooks!" he complains to Captain America (Dell'orto et al., 1998, p. 129), and he makes the same complaint about a school field trip to a museum (Dell'orto et al., 1998, p. 132). During another fight, Bucky says, "This is more fun than the circus, Cap!" (Dell'orto et al., 1998, p. 194). Killing is not framed as taking lives or as a dangerous activity, but rather as a game. "What's the score, Bucky?" Toro asks his friend, who has been shooting down planes with an anti-aircraft gun. "Eight Nazi bombers," he replies with a smile (Sedlmeier, 2009, p. 27). The effect of all this is a message that violence and fighting are not to be eschewed, but rather enjoyed. The idea that war is a game certainly defies common sense, and therefore the framing of battle as enjoyable is an attempt to appeal to audiences viscerally rather than logically—a defining characteristic of propaganda (Littlejohn & Foss, 2009).

War Is Masculine

Beyond being fun, kid combatant stories frame war as a positive pursuit for boys because it is an endeavor that is exciting, courageous, and therefore manly. Bucky and his team "plunge into a breath-taking adventure which may result in the loss of their very lives," but such recklessness leads to "a real action-crammed, thrill-a-minute yarn!!" (Sedlmeier, 2009, p. 3). The fear of physical harm is to be overcome, and foolhardy courage is to be applauded, as when the "frightened but determined youngsters" take on gun-toting Nazis with evil intent, armed only with their courage and patriotism (Sedlmeier, 2009, p. 9). Even when the cause is lost, it is important to display courage, as when Bucky is outnumbered by members of a hit squad, and "like a true soldier, Bucky goes down

Figure 3.1: Bucky and the Allies demonstrate how fun war is (Sedlmeier, 2009, p. 27).

fighting even as he's overpowered by weight of numbers!" (Sedlmeier, 2009, p. 88). During one adventure, Captain America questions Bucky before they leap into action: "Think you can handle a man's job . . . Bucky, m'lad?" Bucky answers, "Sure I can—What do you think I am—a baby?" (Dell'orto et al., 1998, p. 19). Failing to engage danger with bravado is unmanly, something of which to be ashamed. "He must be a sissy," Tubby declares when he sees that a British spy had the gall to faint after being tortured. The spy, upon recovering, also sees this as a cause for remorse: "I'd like to thank you young chaps . . . excuse me for fainting!" (Sedlmeier, 2009, p. 11).

In their first adventure, there are two additional instances of the word *sissy* being applied to Young Allies who are regarded as behaving cowardly. In one case, some of the boys are dismissed as "sissies" (Sedlmeier, 2009, p. 17) for being reluctant to pursue enemy soldiers into a cemetery at night, as though the situation and setting were not fearsome enough already. Later, when an Ally does not stoically tolerate the meager conditions they endure as stowaways in pursuit of Nazis, he is derided as "Ya sissy!" (Sedlmeier, 2009, p. 23). In both instances the errant Ally is being derided as cowardly and/or effeminate, a charge that reinforced the importance of the masculine traits of courage and stoicism in a context of espionage, killing, and adventure.

In fact, the entire first Young Allies story has at its center a telling bit of gender bending. The mission involves the boys' efforts at safely escorting—and at times rescuing—a British spy on a vital mission. From the first, there are clues foreshadowing something unusual about this operative (known only as Agent Zero), clues that seem to point to his unmanliness. One Nazi refers to him as a "pretty boy" (Sedlmeier, 2009, p. 5). At another point, Zero responds to a torture threat by exclaiming, "No! Don't! Help!" (Sedlmeier, 2009, p. 6), and he later laments, under interrogation, "Oh . . . I—I—can't hold out much longer!" (Sedlmeier, 2009, p. 59). As noted earlier, this kind of response to torture has been framed in the story as unmanly; for a character presented as a brave opponent of totalitarianism and fascism, this portrayal seems odd. Similarly, in a revealing moment, Agent Zero insists that the Allies exercise improved hygiene, to which one of the boys responds, "Hey! Lay off! Sometimes you act just like a woman, Agent Zero!" (Sedlmeier, 2009, p. 55). If the Allies are framed as admirable role models for their readers, and they do not approve of what they see as Zero's feminine behavior, then the implication is that unmanly behavior is inappropriate. The message is that readers should adhere to socially defined gender roles, which for males includes becoming a soldier.

Readers later find that Agent Zero is in fact a woman in disguise. She explains to the boys that "while men do the fighting on the battlefield, we women do our part, too!" She then rewards Bucky with a kiss, an act of affection she "wanted to do for a long time." Bucky receives her kiss with a protest of "Aw-w-w, g-gosh—Agent Zero—cut it out!!!" Yet his smile belies his protest; he enjoys her affections, even if it is unmanly for him to show it. Zero next addresses the rest of the Allies, saying "I'd like to thank all you boys! You've served democracy like true soldiers!" (Sedlmeier, 2009, p. 61). The boys' risky behavior, then, comes across not as foolhardy but rather as patriotic and courageous—and such actions are rewarded with female affection and approval. Women are allowed to participate in danger with the men, but the story line suggests that their innate weakness and anal retentiveness lead to unseemly shows of fear and to unhealthy fixations on hygiene. Thus, traditional gender roles are reinforced through the Young Allies' story lines: women are subordinate and weaker, while men should be stoic and fearless. There is also the added message that applying these gender roles to war results in accolades and affection for men. Boys should be soldiers, as soldiers get the girls and the glory.

To underscore this point, the team's fourth adventure depicts their handling of both physical and emotional pain when Knuckles is shot through the arm while swimming away from a Nazi ship. Although Bucky is alarmed—"Knuckles . . . you're wounded!"—Knuckles handles the pain appropriately: "Don't mind me! What'cha tink I am, a sissy! I can still swim! Let's get dat guy! C'mon!" (Sedlmeier, 2009, p. 220). Yet as tough as Knuckles is, he appears later to be killed by an explosion, and while the Allies and their friend, government-agent Betty Ross, mourn his passing, they do so in an appropriate way: "*Manfully* [emphasis added], the boys and Betty hold back tears . . . of anguish at Knuckle's [*sic*] loss! Instead of tears comes a burning resolve" (Sedlmeier, 2009, p. 225).

In this way, readers are told that being a man means suppressing emotions and embracing the fight. Later, at a memorial service for Knuckles, readers learn what admiration one can expect for living such a life. "It was a brave thing which Knuckles did," says the captain of the ship on which the Allies are sailing. "His own personal safety was forgotten in his concern for his country and his friend! We salute Knuckles O'Toole, a real American and a real man!" (Sedlmeier, 2009, p. 228). At this point, Whitewash, Bucky, and Betty appear to be looking out at the reader, as though speaking directly to the boys of America (see Figure 3.2). "Did—did yo' hear that?" Whitewash asks. "A-a-a real American!" says Bucky. "And a real man!" (Sedlmeier, 2009, p. 228) adds Betty, putting the coda on the lesson: Be manly and reckless in the face of danger and death, and place country and friend above yourself. This lesson is emphasized by portraying the characters as though they were speaking directly to the readers, many of whom would one day be soldiers. The kid combatant stories thus use another propagandistic technique that would encourage the war effort: an illogical appeal to one's desire to be socially accepted (Littlejohn & Foss, 2009). In this case, that means to be perceived as manly.

War Is Safe

Eventually, of course, Knuckles turns up alive and well. This is only one example of the way readers were encouraged to see warfare as danger-free, something from which there was nothing to fear (or at least nothing serious). Upon seeing that the Young Allies are being pursued by armed Nazis who had already tortured one enemy, Tubby exclaims, "They'll beat us up!" (Sedlmeier, 2009, p. 8), not "They'll kill us!" As their adventure concludes and Captain America learns that Bucky and the other boys had been risking their lives in an international battle of espionage and murder, Cap does not scold or warn his sidekick but

Figure 3.2: The Allies break the fourth wall to emphasize how
to be patriotic and masculine (Sedlmeier, 2009, p. 228).

instead dismisses it all as innocent mischief: "Bucky! You young scalawag!"
(Sedlmeier, 2009, p. 60). In another Captain America adventure, where the Sentinels of Liberty eventually get involved fighting Nazis, there is a hidden group
of Nazis who "had been beating up innocent people who refused to join their
ranks and destroying their homes" (Sedlmeier, 2009, p. 31). Captain America
and the Sentinels, in other words, are faced with Nazi spies who cause terror
but do not kill.

Perhaps for this reason, the kid combatants are never scared or concerned
for their own wellbeing. Instead, they are concerned with proving themselves to
their heroes or not missing out on the action. In one adventure both Hermann
Goering and Hitler run at Captain America and Bucky while arguing over
which of them will attack Bucky (the assumed easier target) and which will
attack Captain America. Bucky charges heedlessly at them, saying, "Let's not
argue boys, you can both have me!" (Dell'orto et al., 1998, p. 14). In one Young
Allies story the boys are caught sneaking into a Nazi camp. The guards line
them up to take them to prison and demand they call themselves "Yankee pigs."
The Allies meet this situation with anger and disgust, and, despite being outnumbered, they attack (Sedlmeier, 2009, p. 37).

One reason not to fear the dangers of war is the ineptitude of the enemy. In
their first adventure, the Young Allies deter a group of Nazis with the use of
fake wooden guns. Later, while in occupied France, they are confronted and

questioned by a German officer. They respond with nonsense and argot: "Aw, go lay an egg!"; "Parley voo-wee-wee"; "Ah'm not hep to yo' jibe!"; "Ixnay ackincray Ucklesnay" (Sedlmeier, 2009, p. 29). Rather than arrest the band of boys, this representative of the super race concludes that they are just incomprehensible Frenchmen and walks away. Later, after having sneaked into Berlin, the gang encounters Hitler himself, who smiles and pats Bucky on the head, dismissing them as "nice Chermun boyz" (Sedlmeier, 2009, p. 29, p. 35). So the Führer himself is not competent enough to detect an enemy when he sees one, even when one is wearing a mask, another is wearing an underwear-like costume, and yet another is a black child in the middle of wartime Berlin. The implication is clear: if the German leader is so incompetent and stupid, what is there to fear from the Nazis?

But of course the Nazis were a real threat, as the entire world was aware. This weakness in the enemy is so absurd that it can in no way be construed as a serious attempt at realistically depicting the Nazis. Still, the fact remains that this mockery is characteristic of propaganda. It is pleasing to deride one's enemy, to reduce what is fearful to objects of ridicule. Furthermore, believing one faces an incompetent foe means one is superior to one's enemy. Accordingly, enemies are commonly depicted in propaganda as inferior in all ways (Pavia, 1994). It is hard to conceive of an enemy who would embody those traits more than do the Young Allies' foes.

War Is a Normal Responsibility

The kid combatant stories also normalize the war effort, reminding readers that the home front is just as involved in the war as the military, and that they have duties to fulfill. The Allies practice maneuvers in preparation for what is assumed to be a looming invasion. Even for children, idleness is inappropriate; everyone should be preparing for war. After the Young Allies have watched an ally agent die from his fatal, Nazi-inflicted wounds, they are not traumatized but instead are eager to charge into the fray. It is their responsibility, and when Bucky speaks to his friends, it would not be much of a leap for young readers to see him as speaking to them. "Young Allies are you ready to do your duty for America and civilization?" he asks them, and the implicit message to readers is that they should be getting ready, too (Sedlmeier, 2009, p. 21). In another adventure, where the Sentinels of Liberty aid Captain America in defeating a gang of thugs, he thanks them by directing his praise at the readers: "And let me thank you too for helping, Sentinels of Liberty all through our great and glorious land! All boys and girls are sentinels of liberty whether they wear the badge or not. America is safe while its boys and girls believe in its creed!" (Sedlmeier, 2008, p. 84).

In several instances, warfare is correlated with responsibilities. "I've studied guns!" Bucky tells his team, as though preparing for war is akin to schoolwork. "I know how to operate one! Whaddya say we do our bit for democracy, fellas?" (Sedlmeier, 2009, p. 26). Beyond emphasizing the importance of taking an active role in the war effort, vignettes such as these suggest that one is honor-bound to make that active role a combative one. In this view, it is not abnormal to risk one's life and to kill. Instead, it is an appropriate, normalized duty, one to which children should aspire. Indeed, war is exciting, rewarding, and normal, not an activity to be avoided. Nor should the more mundane parts of war be cause for complaint or dissatisfaction. As Private Steve Rogers finds himself spending the night in a holding cell as punishment for pranks against the sergeant that he did not commit, he listens to the complaints of a soldier who is fed up with his responsibilities and with being pushed around by the army. Rogers thinks to himself: "That guy, Clodd, looks like a typical whiner! He's poison for the Army" (Sedlmeier, 2008, p. 221).

War Is Normalizing Violence

A final theme is violence framed as normal, and even attractive, behavior. Seeing a sidekick engage in or witness violent behavior and accept it with nonchalance or even relief sends the message that it is normal behavior and should be treated as such. The artifacts repeatedly reinforce this message, such as a story in which Captain America punches the Red Skull into a river. The heroes look for him to resurface, until Bucky remembers Red Skull cannot swim. They assume he drowned, and Bucky meets this realization with relief: "Oh well, good riddance! The world is better off without him—" (Sedlmeier, 2008, p. 149). Captain America agrees, saying, "I guess you're right Bucky" (Sedlmeier, 2008, p. 149). Another image depicts Bucky mowing down several Nazi sailors with a machine gun. In the background Toro propels one of the sailors from his position atop the U-boat on which they are fighting, presumably to his death. The rest of the team is also in the background, scrambling to join the fray. The caption extols the virtues of this situation, framing the Allies as "not heeding the terrible danger which confronts them on all sides," but instead being "fearless" (Sedlmeier, 2009, p. 22). In a later depiction of this battle, the machine-gunning Bucky exclaims, "Here's how Yankees do it! Yahoo!" as he kills his foes (Sedlmeier, 2009, p. 26). Rather than being disturbed by the death all around them, his teammates cheer him on. Later, they are seen grinning widely as they are each awarded "a distinguished service medal" (Sedlmeier, 2009, p. 26). Dealing death is not disturbing and also results in rewards. This rewarded violence is especially noteworthy as media depictions of positive outcomes presented as a consequence of violence are more likely to lead to imitation of the act (Harris, 2009, p. 272). A mere page after earning their medals, as though spurred on by their recognition, the boys take to an anti-aircraft gun and shoot down Nazi planes, lamenting that the count reached only eight planes downed when the enemy retreated: "They left just when I wuz gettin' warmed up!" (Sedlmeier, 2009, p. 27).

Conclusion

By all accounts, and as is evidenced by the reprintings and spin-offs they created, the Young Allies and the Boy Commandos were tremendous successes for their publishers. Although they may have been the most popular examples, they were far from the only children in comic book narratives to pick up guns and fight. None of these children ever seemed to get hurt, other than receiving bumps and bruises, which always disappeared in a frame or two. Certainly they never feared death. To children of the time, these stories could have been of tremendous comfort, reducing the fears induced by blackouts, drills, and absent loved ones to easily digestible, comforting narratives. The enemy is no danger, these comic books said. They are stupid and incompetent. Besides, war is fun.

Yet as the war drew to a close, so did many war comics. They may have been the victims of changing tastes and fads, an indication of the mercurial tastes of the public, but it is tempting to attribute their demise to the end of the war. *Young Allies* was discontinued in 1946, *Boy Commandos* in 1949. It was as though the public were temporarily uninterested in stories of combat, and there was no pressing need to produce new soldiers. Some war comics continued, however, and during the Korean conflict the comic book *G.I. Joe* mirrored some of the propagandistic techniques noted in this chapter (Wright, 2001, p. 114). But for the most part, the characters of comics turned their backs on war, still preaching manliness, still teaching violence, still advocating a belief in America's inherent rightness—but no longer dressing their stories in camouflage.

Notes

1. This predatory subtext is similar to a subtext Fredric Wertham noted in his infamous *Seduction of the Innocent*. Over the decades, comic book fans have derided the doctor for his identification of the domestic life of the Batman–Robin team as like a "wish dream of two homosexuals living together" (1954, p. 190). While one can refute Wertham's confluence of pedophilia with homosexuality, his underlying point is still valid if one removes the homophobia of his day from the equation: the kind of grown man who would play dress-up with a little boy and encourage that boy to engage in potentially lethal actions is not stable, and one can clearly read predatory, sexual subtexts into such a story.

2. To be sure, the observation that World War II–era comic books could be seen as indoctrinating or enlistment-inducing propaganda pieces is not unprecedented. Scott (2007) asserted that propaganda in these comic books could take the complexities of the war and reduce them to the level of the child reader, "so that when the time came children would help in the war effort" (p. 328).

3. The stories of the Boy Commandos, also created by Bucky creators Jack Kirby and Joe Simon, are filled with examples and stories that fit the kid combatant genre and serve as more evidence of its prominence. However, the Boy Commandos will be further examined in the chapter by Katsion.

4. For another prominent example of this subgenre from the same creators of the Young Allies, see the chapter "Everyone Can Help," by Wilt in this volume.

5. Another example of this kind of comic is the story of the *Albatross*, a privateer boat, which appeared in *Military Comics*. The *Albatross* was captained by an adult, but his fighting, shooting officers were all little boys (Phillips, 2000, p. 60).

6. To clarify, the claim here is not of a causal relationship between these comic books and readers' attitudes toward war, but rather for a *possible* causal relationship. One cannot prove intent of comic book authors to help increase enlistment, nor is there data to prove the effects of such an intent if it could be demonstrated. However, one can still apply social cognitive theory to the study of this material, making the assumption that the apparent attempts to persuade and the popularity of the medium would make this a probable example of social learning.

References

Bandura, A. (1986). *Social foundations of thought and action: A social cognitive theory*. Englewood Cliffs, NJ: Prentice Hall.

Baran, S. J., & Davis, D. K. (2003). *Mass communication theory: Foundations, ferment, and future* (3rd ed.). Belmont, CA: Wadsworth/Thomson Learning.

Castiglia, P. (2003, April). Archie does his part. In *Comic Book Marketplace* (pp. 36–41). (Vol. 3, no. 101). Lutherville-Timonium, MD: Gemstone.

Dell'orto, S., Wright, G., & Brevoort, T. (Eds.). (1998). *Captain America: The classic years*. New York, NY: Marvel Comics.

Dittmer, J. (2007). "America is safe while its boys and girls believe in its creeds!": Captain America and American identity prior to World War 2. *Environment and Planning D: Society and Space, 25*, 401–423. doi: 10.1068/d1905

Gibson, S. K. (2004). "Social learning (cognitive) theory and implications for human resource development." *Advances in Developing Human Resources, 6*, 193–210.

Haridakis, P. M., Hugenberg, B. S., & Wearden, S. T. (2009). Introduction: The impact of war on communication theory, research, and the field of communication. In P. M. Haridakis, B. S. Hugenberg, & S. T. Wearden (Eds.), *War and media* (pp. 3–22). Jefferson, NC: McFarland.

Harris, R. J. (2009). *A cognitive psychology of mass communication* (5th ed.). New York, NY: Routledge.

Hulburd, M., Goldwyn, S.(Producers), & Wyler, W. (Director). (2005). *Dead end* [Motion picture]. United States: MGM.

Kimble, J. J., & Goodnow, T. (2009). "You boys and girls can be the Minute Men of today": Narrative possibility and normative appeal in the U.S. Treasury's 1942 *War Victory Comics*. In P. M. Haridakis, B. S. Hugenberg, & S. T. Wearden (Eds.), *War and media* (pp. 112–125). Jefferson, NC: McFarland.

Littlejohn, S. W., & Foss, K. A. (Eds.). (2009). *Encyclopedia of communication theory*. Los Angeles, CA: Sage. Retrieved from http://rave.ohiolink.edu/ebooks/ebc/9781412959377

Miller, F. (1997). *The Dark Knight returns*. New York, NY: DC Comics.

Murray, C. (2000). *Pop*aganda: Superhero comics and propaganda in World War Two. In A. Magnussen & H. Christiansen (Eds.), *Comics & culture: Analytical and theoretical approaches to comics* (pp. 141–156). Copenhagen, Denmark: Museum Tusculanum Press.

Nelson, P. B. (1988). From subhuman to superhuman: Ethnic characters in the comics. *Nemo, 28*, 9–11.

Nybakken, S. (Ed.). (2010). Boy Commandos *by Joe Simon and Jack Kirby*. (Vol. 1). New York, NY: DC Comics.

Pavia, N. (1994). Racism in Japanese and U.S. wartime propaganda. *Historian, 56*, 671–684.

Phillips, A. (Ed.). (1941/2000). Q-Boat (pp. 56–64). In *Military Comics (Millennium Edition)*. (No. 35). New York, NY: DC Comics.

Savage, W. M. Jr. (1990). *Comic books and America: 1945-1954*. Norman: University of Oklahoma Press.

Schumacher, M. (2010). *Will Eisner: A dreamer's life in comics*. New York, NY: Bloomsbury USA.

Scott, C. (2007). Written in red, white, and blue: A comparison of comic book propaganda from World War II and September 11. *The Journal of Popular Culture, 40*, 325–343.

Sedlmeier, C. (2008) (Ed.). *Golden Age Captain America*. New York, NY: Marvel.

Sedlmeier, C. (2009) (Ed.). *Marvel masterworks: Golden Age Young Allies. Volume 1*. New York, NY: Marvel.

Sharma, R. (2009). Drawn-out battles: Exploring war-related messages in animated cartoons. In P. M. Haridakis, B. S. Hugenberg, & S. T. Wearden (Eds.), *War and media* (pp. 75–89). Jefferson, NC: McFarland.

Veitch, R. (2009). *Brat pack*. West Townshend, VT: King Hell.

Wertham, F. (1954). *Seduction of the innocent*. New York, NY: Rinehart.

Wright, B. W. (2001). *Comic book nation: The transformation of youth culture in America*. Baltimore, MD: Johns Hopkins University Press.

Yronwode, C., & Mullaney, D. (1987). (Eds.) House advertisement. In *Air Fighters Classics* (p. 56). (Vol. 1.). Forestville, CA: Eclipse.

★★ 4 ★★

The *Boy Commandos* Comic Book as Equipment for Living

The Comic Book Form as Propaganda

John R. Katsion

Nothing did more to destroy a home-front child's sense of security than the death of a father or brother. But sudden departures and long absences also resulted in fears of abandonment. Because of the war, many home-front girls and boys suffered a premature loss of invulnerability. All else paled beside this fact (Tuttle, 1993, p. 48).

Childhood should be carefree, but the lives of U.S. children during WWII were often filled with moments of extreme fear. Huddled around the family radio, they would hear the nightly bulletins of progress in the war, and many of them wondered if beloved uncles, brothers and even fathers would ever return home again. How could they cope? How could they hope to make sense of the turmoil surrounding them?

One way children in the WWII era coped was by immersing themselves in the lives of fictional characters from the popular culture of the time. One place these youthful role models could be found was in popular kid gang comic books. The previous chapter lays out an excellent argument for the ways that kid sidekicks, or kid gangs, were used as propaganda during WWII. This chapter will add to the sidekick discussion by revealing how the comic book *form*, from the perspective of the audiences receiving these texts, was the perfect vehicle through which to propagandize Americans, particularly America's children. This chapter will analyze a popular sidekick comic of the time known as the *Boy Commandos*, as this series is an excellent example of the sidekick/ kid gang genre.[1] To begin, we need a way to look at how popular culture works as a form of persuasion, and to do this we will borrow from the ideas of Barry Brummett and his work in the rhetoric of popular culture, and it is his work that we turn to next.

Barry Brummett and the Social Function of Rhetoric

Brummett (1991) calls rhetoric "the social function that influences and manages meaning" (p. xii). With this definition, Brummett (1991) moves the rhetorical challenge from the speaker to the agent receiving the text: "I would move the site of struggle from the text, which is merely product, to the logics that create texts, and to choices among and awareness of those logics and how they position us as subjects" (p. 89). So Brummett would be interested in looking not so much at the producers and creators of these comics, but instead at how a reader might use that particular edition, or a character in the story, to make sense of their world. And what things do people typically need to make sense of on a daily basis? Some of them need to make sense of their lot in life, or their last argument with their wife, or whether their candidate of choice will win the next election, or if they can get their neighbor to turn down his radio when he barbecues. And here we should add that people in 1941 America, both young and old, were trying to make sense of the growing specter of war looming ever larger in their daily world. In other words, people have a lot of different concerns to make sense of, and Brummett sees these concerns falling on a continuum.[2] Brummett's redefinition of rhetoric and its functions and manifestations are important to understand, but equally important to assimilate for this study is Brummett's notion of "bits."

A bit is "an event, an object, a person, in short, any experience of sensations that we perceive as a unit," and Brummett (1991) views people as agents "moving through a world of discontinuous and chaotic signs, a mélange of bits" (77). As the person moves through this confusion, some of the bits are at any given time brought out of chaos and put into a coherent order, a mosaic of meaning. He sees the agent placing these bits within a mosaic, which is simply a way of ordering various bits into a message. So when someone read the latest edition of the *Boy Commandos,* and then turned on the radio and heard the nightly news, and then saw a fleeting glimpse of a newspaper blaring a headline as they walked through the streets, these are all examples of "bits" to Brummett.

And what Brummett wants is for critics using his approach to show how people could have glued these "bits" together into a mosaic, or some type of coherent meaning to help them with various types of problems.

Brummett (1991) then wants the critic of popular culture to find the homology that holds the bits of the mosaic together. A good way to think of a homology is to envision it as "formal glue holding the actual, perceived components of a mosaic together" (p. 87). Emphasizing the connections, rather than differences, between the bits, he goes on to say that to "construct a mosaic, to find meaning in experience, to order part of life is therefore to find a homology that sees the constituent texts, contexts, and subjects as formally linked" (Brummett, 1991, p. 87). To find that glue, or homology, the following three things need to be established: the content of the text(s), the medium conveying the text(s), and the history of the agent receiving the text(s).

Finally, Brummett (1991) uses Kenneth Burke's concept of "equipment for living" to help establish the homology by suggesting that people use texts to help them deal with their daily problems. Brummett sees agents constructing mosaics so as to help them order their personal and public lives; to make coherence of the mess of "bits" they find themselves in every day. So the homology that glues a mosaic together equips the person to answer questions and solve problems; it provides the agent "equipment for living." To begin establishing that homology in the case of the *Boy Commandos* comic book series, it is important initially to understand the context of the artifacts themselves.

Context of the *Boy Commandos*

The cultural context of the readers and creators of these comic books has been dealt with in earlier chapters, and we need not go into great detail here. Suffice it to say that the cultural context of the average American reader in 1941 was one that was marked by a constant, pervasive fear that impacted both children and adults. At the same time, comic book writers and artists—whether they were directly influenced by the government or by their own ethnic backgrounds and political leanings—were interested in using their comics as a vehicle for teaching young readers about the danger of Nazi oppression and the justice of the American cause. This pair of contextual factors establishes a solid basis for addressing the next important area, which is the actual content of the comic books themselves. To uncover this content, a description of the characters and the overarching stories they inhabited is given, followed by an analysis using the ideas of Burke and Brummett to better examine the form of the story lines themselves.

Characters of the *Boy Commandos*

The Boy Commandos were led by Captain Rip Carter. Carter led a squadron of elite commandos into battle, and he also had charge over his squadron's mascots, the so-called Boy Commandos. Always depicted wearing his military uniform or his combat fatigues, he had black hair and fit the classic, chiseled, male stereotype.

Carter's charges made up the comic book's young heroes, or sidekicks. Pierre Chavard was a black-haired orphan from France, who usually wore a uniform or combat fatigues. His dialogue was written with what, in the comic book world, passed for a French accent.

Alfy Twidgett was from England. He was shorter than his fellow commandos, and slightly chubby. Twidgett ended up being the foil for much of the physical humor in the comic book and was clearly not as good-looking as the other kids. Like Chavard, he generally wore uniforms and fatigues.

Jan Haasen was a stereotypically blond orphan from the Netherlands, whose strength was being a fierce fighter. His hair was in a longer style, perhaps fitting the creators' mental image of what someone from Holland might look like. However, he was a tough character that was often seen fighting in various adventures; like most of the others, he mainly wore a uniform.

Finally, there was Brooklyn, a rough street kid from New York who led the boys and was the toughest of them all. He was the only member of the gang who did not wear a uniform; instead, he wore a red bowler hat, a green turtleneck shirt, and brown pants. Even when he did wear combat fatigues, he still wore his red bowler hat and turtleneck shirt. He was not as handsome as the other characters but had a chubby, tough-looking face. He was also the only character who had an object that he carried with him into battle: a violin case.

Basic Story Lines in the *Boy Commandos*

The overarching story lines in the comic book series mainly involved traveling to Europe and Asia so that the young commandos could assist their adult counterparts in the fight against the enemy. As Captain Carter led his unit into battle, the kids joined alongside, sometimes even leading the charge against the Germans or the Japanese. Often, the commandos liberated innocent Europeans, Russians, and Chinese. In looking at the basic messages of these comic books, the themes that emerge are: war is fun, war is a masculine pursuit, war is safe, war is predetermined, war is your responsibility, and violence is normal. Here, however, it is instructive to focus on the *form* of the comic book, as well as how that form could help to propel these messages. Here again the work of Burke and Brummett proves fruitful.

Writing in *A Grammar of Motives* (1945), Burke speaks of the need people have in conversation to find vocabularies that are "faithful reflections of reality" (p. 59). In so doing, he believes, they come up with words that are selective of the reality they are experiencing. So, in a field of study like physics, or chemistry, the people populating these areas invent grammars or terminologies to reflect selectively the reality they are talking about. They create a *representative anecdote*, which Burke (1945) describes as "a form in conformity with which the vocabulary is constructed" (p. 59). Brummett (1984) sums up this concept of the representative anecdote:

> Burke argues that to treat discourse as if it were the enactment of a plot represents (and thus, *reveals*) the essence of that discourse. . . . And therefore, one key Burkean method stemming from his dramatistic metaphor is his insight that the content or "terminology" of whole discourses or groups of discourses will imply, or seem to be based upon, a *representative anecdote*. (p. 163)

A representative anecdote, then, acts as a hub that "grounds several motives of the discourse" (p. 163).

Brummett (1984) further clarifies Burke's concept of the representative anecdote for the rhetorical critic when he notes that it "is a dramatic form which underlies the content, or the specific vocabulary, of discourse" (p. 163). This concept transfers well to the comic form. Drama is both verbal and visual but does not need to be spoken to have effect. The art of the mime is an excellent and apt example of the power to tell stories, or dramas, visually. As Brummett (1984) advises, "the critic in search of an anecdote must therefore exercise his or her powers of abstraction to detect a form or pattern which is a plot, a story line, immanent within the content of the discourse and able to represent the discourse" (p. 163). Brummett (1991) goes on to clarify two features that a representative anecdote must have: it must be *representative*, and it must be *in story form* (pp. 149–150).

To be representative, the anecdote must become a "microcosm of a more complex set of signs. It must essentialize or metonymize elements of a whole discourse into a single representative form that describes the whole discourse" (Brummett, 1991, p. 149). At the same time, the anecdote must "be in story form, the structure of a narrative." Brummett (1991) goes on to say that "the critic should be able to state the narrative form abstractly, and that statement then serves as the critical vocabulary, set of coordinates, or calculus which . . . allows the critic to analyze the discourse(s) or mosaic" (p. 149).

The content underlying the stories in the *Boy Commandos* comic books followed a consistent pattern: a person or a group of persons embarks on a quest to kill a dangerous entity. The quest is fraught with peril, but through bravery, sacrifice, and action, the person(s) arrive(s) at their final destination and succeed in killing the dangerous entity. For this study, this pattern will be called the *righteous-quest* representative anecdote.

This particular representative anecdote appeared in the very first issue of the *Boy Commandos*. The story opens with a German officer receiving a cryptic note that states that "the Commandos are Coming" (Simon & Kirby, 2010, p. 12). The note is given to him by another officer, who then tells him to take the commandos seriously, launching into a story about them. In this tale-within-a-tale, readers meet "a cynical, disheveled fellow—a man without faith," whose name is Leon LaFarge (Simon & Kirby, 2010, p. 12). He is a lawyer who defended a French resistance fighter against the Nazis and set him free. The grateful resistance fighter then tried to thank him, but LaFarge pushed him away, as he felt like an outcast in French society; indeed, he did not stand behind the French resistance cause. The lawyer left France and headed to England, where he met Captain Carter's Boy Commandos, who happen to be returning from a raid on the Nazis in France. At first, LaFarge refuses to help, but then when he sees the money he could make, he decides to join the Commandos and give them needed intelligence about the layout of the towns and countryside. As he goes on raids with the Commandos, he begins to see their bravery and their acts of selflessness. He eventually finds that the French resistance leader he helped earlier is about to be shot in Calais. So he and the Commandos raid the enemy and save the life of the very man he once despised. Ironically, as the story comes to an end, readers find that the lieutenant who tells this Nazi officer the story is in fact LaFarge himself. He then kills the Nazi, which brings the story to an end.

All of the elements of the *righteous-quest* representative anecdote are present in this story. The Boy Commandos embarked on a journey, fraught with peril, to sacrifice themselves for the good of someone else and in order to destroy a dangerous enemy. LaFarge also went on a personal journey: from one who did not care and thought only for himself, to arrive at the point where he was willing to give his life for another. Later, in a story titled "The Treachery of Osuki," the term "righteous" is actually used. In this story the boys are about to be killed by a Japanese soldier, but minutes before they are to be executed, they make a desperate plea for help on the radio, and, "as is often the case for the righteous, fate is on their side" (Simon & Kirby, 2010, p. 65); their plea is heard by none other than their leader, Captain Rip Carter, who dispatches commandos and saves them from certain death.

It is important to point out how closely this representative anecdote, and these stories, models Kenneth Burke's guilt–redemption cycle. In Burke's view of guilt and redemption, a moral agent begins by making a free choice between either the *yes* of order or the *no* of disorder (as cited in Gusfield, 1989, p. 287). Since society is constructed along a hierarchical order, choosing either one will lead to feelings of guilt, and thus the need for redemption: "If order, then guilt; if guilt, then need for redemption" (Gusfield, 1989, p. 280). Guilt causes the agent to be polluted, in need of purification, which then leads to the amplified need for someone to take the guilt—"the sacrificial animal upon whose back the burden of these evils is ritualistically loaded" (Burke, 1967, pp. 39–40). Burke further stresses that, with the sacrifice, either the *kill* of the sacrifice is emphasized, or the *sacrifice* of the kill is stressed (as cited in Gusfield, 1989, p. 298). So, for one, killing the scapegoat is the sacrifice; for the other, the allowing of oneself to be killed is the sacrifice.

In the *Boy Commandos* stories, one can see the *kill* of the sacrifice emphasized with the group journey, and the *sacrifice* of oneself being emphasized in the personal journey. In the previous story, LaFarge killed the Nazi major and, by killing him, completed the guilt–redemption cycle. By choosing to give himself up for the life of the French resistance leader, he learned to sacrifice himself by being killed. In the end, LaFarge is not killed; he instead disappeared, never to be seen again. Symbolically, however, he killed and sacrificed his old self to be renewed in the life of the new self.

Some might argue that a scapegoat is chosen because of its purity—to be, in Old Testament terms, a lamb "without blemish" (Exodus 12:5 King James Version). Yet Burke offers a different take on the scapegoat concept. He writes that the scapegoat is worthy to be chosen as the sacrifice in three ways: *legalistically* (it has broken some laws and needs to be punished), *fatalistically* (some omen, some sign that points to the future sacrifice), and *poetically* (in other words, this person is too good for this world, the perfect sacrifice) (as cited in Gusfield, 1989, pp. 294–295). Within the pages of the *Boy Commandos*, the Nazis and the Japanese were depicted as legalistically worthy of death. In one telling moment, Brooklyn looked down at a dead Japanese soldier and said, "I'll bet the chief also learned that a good Jap is a dead Jap" (Simon & Kirby, 2010, p. 72). In this story the Boy Commandos showed humanitarian goodwill and saved the Japanese soldier's life, only to later have that same soldier turn on them. The animalist-looking Japanese soldier rallied with a band of once-peaceful people who, because of his influence, were now warlike and foolishly sided with him in an attempt to slay the Commandos. In the end the Japanese soldier was shown to be pure evil, and the Boy Commandos killed him in battle. Meanwhile, like the Japanese, the Germans were portrayed as evil individuals in many of the story lines as well. In one issue, the "moronic," "detestable" "Nazi plague" was contrasted with the "hardy," "kind," and "courageous" Russian peasants they were mercilessly destroying (pp. 74–76). Clearly, the Japanese and Nazis were worthy scapegoats because of the atrocities, the crimes, and the laws they continually broke.

What is also interesting about these story lines is their use of time. Many of the story lines began in a previous time period, where some famous figure of the past predicted the coming of a group of great warriors, or where an enemy of freedom today is shown to have existed long before the present. A story called "Heroes Never Die" is a good example of this. Captain Carter and the boys are fighting in China when they come across an old native who knows them all by name and who tells them about previous American freedom fighters who liberated his people centuries before (Simon & Kirby, 2010, pp. 124–135). This development ties well into the *righteous quest* representative anecdote, because it grounds the present conflict within an eternal quest. It insinuates, that this quest has always gone on, and heroes will continue to walk its path. This use of time helps to connect the Boy Commandos' present with the past and also lends itself to a predictive element: as the story has unfolded before, so it will unfold today, and, as in the past, the quest will come to a victorious end.

In the end what better form to place propaganda messages like "war is fun" or "war is masculine" within than the righteous-quest representative anecdote. By also placing these themes within the guilt–redemption cycle, one can begin to see the powerful form propaganda can take within the pages of a simple comic book. The *context* is characterized by a common fear and urges to fight the Nazis in both the comics' creators and the audience, while in the *content* the main ideas are conveyed through the representative anecdote of America on a righteous crusade. The *medium* used to convey these messages of propaganda, the comic book itself, must now be analyzed.

The Medium of the *Boy Commandos*

Much has already been said in previous chapters about the power of the comic book form and how it worked as a vehicle to draw their readers into its world. This section does not rehash those ideas but looks at some detailed examples from the *Boy Commandos*, specifically the ideas of simplicity, closure, and depictions of the hero and the enemy.

In what Scott McCloud (1993) calls "amplification through simplification" (p. 30), the simplicity of form in a cartoon allows a reader to insert himself or herself into the action. So when a child saw the atrocities being committed by the Axis powers upon the various characters in these stories, or when one saw the various children fighting Nazis or Japanese soldiers, he or she experienced it more fully than if viewing this same story through a text–based form. In the *Boy Commandos*, the artists drew the background military airplanes and ships with a high level of realistic precision, while the characters fighting on those backgrounds were less realistic and more simplified. To McCloud (1993) this is an example of how comic books allowed readers to *see* the battle, and to *see* the conflict, but then the simplified characters inhabiting these detailed landscapes allowed the reader to *be* a Boy Commando (p. 43).

The promise of action was one of the key attractions of the *Boy Commandos* series, and that focus on action by the artist Jack Kirby, became another avenue through which to propagandize the agents receiving these texts. Not surprisingly, Kirby was a groundbreaking artist in his ability to illustrate action through frame after frame. He pushed the boundaries of the art form using what McCloud (1993) calls closure to convey the energy and, ultimately, the emotion of each scene. As Goulart (2000) puts it, "his characters moved— sometimes the panels couldn't contain them—and when they slugged each other, you felt it" (p. 125).

Finally, one of the outcomes of domestic propaganda was to produce in the audience a world that saw America, and by extension Americans, as the peaceful protagonist in this conflict, and the enemy as the evil antagonist. Arguably, that world could be seen in the ways the characters were depicted in the *Boy Commandos*: the men were handsome and chiseled, the women thin and glamorous. For example, Captain Carter has broad shoulders and the classic all-American endomorphic torso. The women, when they were seen, were kind, gentle mothers or little girls that needed protection and help.

In developing the image of the antagonist in the story, the producers and writers of propaganda messages choose to either demonize or dehumanize the enemy (Kimble, 2005, p. 209). In creating a dehumanized enemy, the propagandist treats the antagonists in the story as if they were animals or monsters, "irrational creature[s] or infestation[s] lacking both subjectivity and rationality" (Kimble, 2005, p. 210). In the *Boy Commandos*, the villains were often dehumanized, appearing animalistic, especially the depictions of the Japanese who took on a monstrous, nonhuman form. The Germans also often had apelike or ratlike features and spoke in guttural, ignorant ways. Both depictions conveyed to readers that their opponents were nowhere near as human, or humane, as the Allies. The best example of this phenomenon from the *Boy Commandos* is in a story titled "Nine Lives for Victory," where the commandos catch a German spy who literally looks more rat than human (Simon & Kirby, 2010, p. 247).

In the end, the medium itself conveyed the message of action and promise in the American cause. Readers were drawn into the story and found themselves in the middle of the action as they connected with the characters. They felt the action and were energized to fight. Also, the way these comics depicted the Americans and Allies versus the Axis characters would have encouraged readers to see the promise and the high moral purpose of the Allied cause.

Homology of Hope

As mentioned above, Brummett wants the critic to find a mosaic—a homology—that glues the textual context, content and medium together. This homology, he believes, acts as a form of equipment for living to the audience when dealing with some perceived problem.

The first important question to ask is this: what function did these comic books serve, and on what part of Brummett's continuum—exigent, quotidian, implicative—would the audience have used them? Remember, this study is concerned with how the *audience* could have used these comic books. The creators of these comics had an interventionist manifestation and thus had an interventionist aim. The audience, on the other hand, was made up mainly of children who would not have had the ability or the status in society to speak out or to intervene actively in their surroundings, as well as the many GI's who read them to pass the time before their next call to arms, perhaps mainly seeing them as a way to relive popular culture from their youth. I see the children and adults reading these comics *appropriating* these texts to deal with their daily concerns over war and the tough conditions of their lives. These comic books would therefore have fallen into the quotidian function for most of their readership and would thus have had an appropriational manifestation.

Therefore, the second question to answer is into what mosaic, or homology, could these bits be placed to provide an answer? The homology that seems to tie these three areas together is a *homology of hope*. The context of fear surrounding the writers and the audiences, combined with the content of being on righteous crusade and a medium that pushes the reader to action, can be formed into such a homology.

A homology of hope would have been a powerful answer to the problems facing Americans in 1941. This homology would have encouraged the children reading these comics to keep up the watch for enemy agents and to participate in the scrap metal drives in their community. This homology of hope would have provided needed motivation for the many GI's reading these comic books in their barracks before heading out on a mission. At its most basic, the homology of hope would have allowed the children and their state-side parents to endure the pain and insecurity of having loved ones being deployed to places far from home. Therefore, it should be seen that as a form through which to propagandize Americans both home and abroad, the homology of hope constructed by context, content, and medium would have provided the perfect vehicle within which to send such a message.

Conclusion

From this study of a comic book series, the force of the comic itself becomes apparent. Notice the power that must be inherent in this form of propaganda when it ends up becoming the very equipment one uses for dealing with one's daily problems, when the very appropriational form the propaganda takes bears the irresistible power to draw in a reader and give the promise of hope. American children and the broader audiences who read these comic books wanted to believe that the people they loved and depended upon were fighting in a just war for a righteous cause, and these comic books told the readers exactly that. The audience also wanted to believe that the enemy was truly horrific and needed to be fought on every front; again, these comic books delivered that very message. Ultimately, the booklets created that picture through the lens of hope: the enemy is evil, our cause is just, and in the end we will win if we take care of one another—*so push on in hope.*

The power of the comic book form is also evident in the very content of the story lines, as well as in the medium of the comic strip itself. In terms of the content, it is apparent that the righteous-cause representative anecdote would have been the perfect vehicle through which to place propaganda and its corresponding messages. The story begins with the need to kill the scapegoat represented by the villain of the Axis powers. The story then continues with heroic endeavors of the children and adults on righteous quest, who through trials and danger learned the importance of self-sacrifice and in the end, sacrificed their old selfish lives to be reborn anew, ended up being a very powerful story in which to place a propaganda message.

Also evident in this study is the power of the medium of the comic book itself. Highlighting the potency of closure and amplification through simplification, McCloud has shown that comic books can be a uniquely strong form of propaganda. For instance, the chiseled-looking men or the horrific foes were simplified characters, justifying action in a complex situation. Yet ultimately, the depiction of the children would have wooed both young and old toward the Allied cause. They were illustrated as cute street kids or chubby innocents; they were depicted as the ordinary kid-next-door. This strategy would have allowed young and old to invest themselves in these characters. Indeed, the GI that fought overseas, in reading these comics, could have seen the son he left behind and could have found motivation to fight; the young children picking up this comic from their friend's collection could have found themselves in the action and, for the moment, filled with hope.

In the end this study has shown that the kid gang comic book was a compelling medium, which served as a vehicle through which to model behavior and attitudes to children as well as adults. As this chapter began by showing the difficult lot of many children growing up during this time period, it ends with a realization of the power of hope contained in these comic books, and what that would have meant for their audiences. In a story titled "The Knights Wore Khaki," the boys discover an old man who tells them a fairy tale about a peaceful land being invaded by an evil tyrant. He does not end the story, though; he instead leaves the kids wondering what will happen, asking them:

> What are fairy tales? They may be actual events recorded by an imaginative people ... even history presented in a colorful manner! Mine is such a book. . . . I have presented it in such a way since its theme is so fantastic . . . [and] so diabolical, that it could have been conceived only by a madman . . . and none would believe it as fact! I hope to find mighty warriors of great courage and daring to write the last chapter. (Simon & Kirby, 2010, p. 239)

The old man's story beautifully echoes the *righteous quest*. His last question is a wonderful example of the power of the homology of hope offered by these comic books. In effect, he asked the reader a series of pertinent questions: Will you be a mighty warrior? Will you show great courage and help to write the last chapter? The message underlying these questions must have given hope to the child who no longer had a father at home, and to the GI who missed his family. It asked the reader to join the quest and to help write the victorious ending.

Notes

1. This analysis will be limited to the comic editions found in the *Boy Commandos* (vol. 1) (Simon & Kirby, 2010). The comic editions found in this collection serve here as a representative selection and will be more than adequate to demonstrate how the form of these comics provided the perfect vehicle for the act of propaganda.

2. These are the exigent, quotidian, and implicative functions. Imagine them on a continuum, with the exigent at the left end, the quotidian in the middle, and the implicative at the right end. Each function also has a corresponding way it manifests itself: the exigent has an interventionist manifestation, the quotidian an appropriational manifestation, and the implicative a conditional manifestation. So in relation to the examples given earlier, worrying about whether your political candidate will win, or wondering how to get your neighbor to stop playing loud music, that would be an exigent function and it would require you to intervene in the situation. You will have to go talk to your neighbor or campaign on behalf of your candidate.

The quotidian function is the area that deals with the daily, often trivial, concerns of life. These kinds of anxieties "do not take the form of peak crises . . . but do involve long-term concerns as well as momentary choices." These are not explicit answers to pressing needs, as with the exigent function, but rather they are rhetorical tools to help people deal with daily, perfunctory problems and choices. And within the quotidian function, a certain appropriational manifestation is in process when people appropriate phrases, slogans, songs, or texts that are already available in the society within which the agent is acting. So when you are down about your life not being where you would want it to be at the age you are, you might listen to a song to cheer you up, or that is when the storyline of a television show might speak to you.

On the far right side of the continuum, the implicative function deals with meanings taken for granted, meanings that are so woven into the fabric of our lives that we never question them. This function manifests itself conditionally. Conditional rhetoric "is embodied in the basic values, grammatical categories, fundamental assumptions, and rules of thought and language that are conditions for, and are implied by, rhetoric's other manifestations" (Brummett, 1991, 38–45).

References

Brummett, B. (1984). Burke's representative anecdote as a method in media criticism. *Critical Studies in Mass Communication, 1,* 161–176.

Brummett, B. (1991). *Rhetorical dimensions of popular culture.* Tuscaloosa: University of Alabama Press.

Brummett, B. (2004). *Rhetorical homologies: Form, culture, experience.* Tuscaloosa: University of Alabama Press.

Brummett, B. (2006). Rhetorical homologies in Walter Benjamin, *The Ring,* and Capital. *Rhetoric Society Quarterly, 36,* 449–469.

Burke, K. (1945). *A grammar of motives.* New York, NY: Prentice-Hall.

Burke, K. (1967). *The philosophy of literary form: Studies in symbolic action.* Baton Rouge: Louisiana State University Press.

Goulart, R. (2000). *Comic book culture: An illustrated history.* Portland, OR: Collectors.

Gusfield, J. R. (Ed.) (1989). *Kenneth Burke: On symbols and society.* Chicago, IL: University of Chicago Press.

Howell, T. (1997). The Writer's War Board. Historian: *A Journal of History 59,* 795–813.

Jowett, G. S., & O'Donnell, V. (1986). *Propaganda and persuasion.* Thousand Oaks, CA: Sage.

Kennedy, D. M. (1999). *Freedom from fear: The American people in depression and war, 1929–1945.* New York, NY: Oxford University Press.

Kimble, J. J. (2006). *Mobilizing the home front: War bonds and domestic propaganda.* College Station: Texas A & M University Press.

Lee, S. (2009). *Marvel masterworks: Golden Age Young Allies* (Vol. 1): New York, NY: Marvel.

MacKenzie, D. W. (2006). Depression, Great. In M. Odekon (Ed.), *Encyclopedia of world poverty* (Vol. 1, pp. 250–254). Thousand Oaks, CA: Sage Reference.

McCloud, S. (1993). *Understanding comics: The invisible art.* New York, NY: HarperPerennial.

Pilcher, T., & Brooks, B. (2005). *The essential guide to world comics.* London, UK: Collins & Brown.

Scott, C. (2007). Written in red, white, and blue: A comparison of comic book propaganda from World War II and September 11. *Journal of Popular Culture, 40,* 325–343.

Scott, C. (2011). *Comics and conflict: War and patriotically themed comics in American cultural history from World War II through the Iraq War* (Doctoral dissertation). Available from ProQuest Dissertations and Theses database. (UMI NO. 3473332)

Simon, J., & Kirby, J. (2010). *The Boy Commandos* (Vol. 1). New York, NY: DC Comics.

Tuttle, W. M. (1993). *Daddy's Gone to War: The Second World War in the lives of America's children*. New York, NY: Oxford University Press.

Whitfield, S. J. (2004). Companion to 20th-century America. Retrieved from http://search.ebscohost.com.ezproxy.liberty.edu:2048/login.aspx?direct=true&db=nlebk&AN=108698&site=ehost-live&scope=site

Winkler, A. M. (1978). *The politics of propaganda: The Office of War Information, 1942–1945*. New Haven, CT: Yale University Press.

Wright, B. W. (2003). *Comic book nation : The transformation of youth culture in America*. Baltimore, MD: Johns Hopkins University Press.

Wynn, N. A. (1996). The "good war": The Second World War and postwar American society. *Journal of Contemporary History*, 31, 463–482.

★★ 5 ★★

Uncle Sam Wants You

Uncle Sam Comic Books as World War II Propaganda

Travis L. Cox

During WWI civilians could see the image of Uncle Sam nearly everywhere. Millions of copies of James Montgomery Flagg's famous poster—depicting a stern-looking Uncle Sam pointing at his audience and stating "I WANT YOU"—were distributed around the country as a recruiting tool for the U.S. Army (Capozzola, 2008, p. 4). Although portrayals of Uncle Sam had appeared during the War of 1812 (Cull, Culbert, & Welch, 2003, p. 403) and the Civil War (Ketchum, 1959, p. 82), Flagg's widespread depiction of the character helped establish Uncle Sam as a national symbol. The poster itself is arguably "the most famous image to come out of World War I" (Ross, 1996, p. 251).

Historically, the character of Uncle Sam was based on Samuel Wilson, a meat packer from Troy, New York, who provided the army with food during the War of 1812. Since the letters *US* on the side of Wilson's meat crates shared the initials of Uncle Sam, Wilson's well-known nickname, the army began referring to the food as "Uncle Sam's," and the expression gradually became connected to the protection and support of the United States (Ketchum, 1959, p. 39). Although the name eventually came to be synonymous with the United States, it was not until the Civil War that the modern visual representation of Uncle Sam developed.

Cartoonist Thomas Nast, best known for his introduction of the elephant as the visual representation of the Republican Party, is credited with the first representation of Uncle Sam as a tall, lean character with a small beard (a portrayal believed to be modeled somewhat after President Lincoln [Cull et al., 2003, p. 262]). This characterization of Uncle Sam became popular and soon made its way into both pro- and anti-American political cartoons. Capozzola (2008) explains that as a result of the widespread use of Uncle Sam's image, the figure became "one of the most iconic images in American politics, even a visual metaphor for America itself" (p. 4). By the time Flagg's famous recruitment poster was developed, Uncle Sam had already been established in the public eye as a symbol of the United States, which made the use of his image an effective "staple of propaganda" in WWI (Cull et al., 2003, p. 403).

The advent of the modern comic book in the late 1930s provided a new venue for this familiar character to aid his country in a time of need. In the years leading up to WWII, many well-known comic book heroes, including Superman, Wonder Woman, and Captain America, began appearing in stories focused on wartime scenarios (Fuchs & Reitberger, 1971/1972, p. 103). In the midst of this surge of war-related comic books, Will Eisner (best known for his popular comic book superhero the Spirit) created a superhero based on Uncle Sam to be a new champion against the forces of evil. Since the symbol was already recognized across the country as a representation of the United States itself, the transition of Uncle Sam from political image to personified superhero supporting the values of America was an obvious choice. With powers like super strength and speed, it fell on Uncle Sam to come to the aid of the nation and principles he himself represented.

However, unlike Flagg's earlier image, which was explicitly designed to encourage Americans to support the army, the propagandistic messages in Eisner's *Uncle Sam* comic books were less explicit. If propaganda is understood as involving the intentional transfer of ideas and/or behavior from the propagandist to a desired audience, it is easy to see how Flagg's poster, with its specific instruction to American citizens, involved a transfer of ideas and was therefore an instrument of propaganda. On the other hand, while the later comic book superhero fighting various antagonists arguably functioned as propaganda as well, the less explicit transfer of ideas that were conveyed through that character's visualized actions had to be interpreted by the audience—increasing the complexity of how these messages where being communicated and subsequently adopted by comic book readers.

This examination of *Uncle Sam* thus provides a systematic approach to understanding how Eisner's comic book series functioned as a form of propaganda before and during WWII. In order to establish Eisner's comic book as propaganda, it is necessary to examine the motivation behind *Uncle Sam*. An understanding of the motives undergirding the development of the series enables closer scrutiny of the ideas that were being transferred to its audience and how they were being presented. Burke's (1945) dramatistic pentad provides a helpful methodological approach to gaining a better understanding of these motives. From Burke's perspective, an analysis of five specific elements within any rhetorical act reveals the motives behind that act. As he writes, "any complete statement about motives will offer some kind of answer to these questions: what was done (act), when or where it was done (scene), who did it (agent), how he did it (agency), and why (purpose)" (Burke, 1945, p. xv). This chapter supports the assertion that Eisner's use of this comic book constituted a form of wartime propaganda, by first explaining Burke's pentad, then by examining agency, scene, agent, act, and purpose as they were presented by Eisner in the *Uncle Sam* series in order to influence readers.

Burke's Pentad

In their survey of the varied perceptions of propaganda over the last century, Cull, Culbert, and Welch (2003) contend that there is a consensus that propaganda is "both conscious and deliberate" (p. 318). This intentional characteristic implies that there is some sort of motivational force that encourages the development of a specific propaganda artifact. This force is quite similar to Burke's conception of motive. In this respect, the opening of Burke's (1945) *Grammar of Motives* asks a pertinent question: "What is involved, when we say what people are doing and why they are doing it?" (p. xv). To answer this question, Burke established the pentad as a systematic way to investigate and evaluate motives. Benoit's (1996) analysis of Burke's conception of motive explains that it is "an internal state or drive that functions to create or impel action" (p. 67). This internal drive can be seen as the motive behind the intentional development of propaganda. Therefore, the use of Burke's pentad has the ability to provide insight into the possible propagandistic motives behind *Uncle Sam*.

From Burke's perspective, an understanding of the five elements of act, scene, agent, agency, and purpose reveals the motives behind the action. Rountree (2001) elaborates that "each of these questions must be considered in any *fully rounded* statement of motives because ... statements that disregard one or more of them are 'partial' accounts and not as fully rounded as they could be" (p. 4). Hence, in order to develop a complete understanding of Eisner's propagandistic motives in his creation of *Uncle Sam*, this investigation explores the use of all five of Burke's pentadic elements in the comic book series.

In addition, Burke (1945) explains that the individual elements of the pentad work together to reinforce one another through "ratios" (p. xv). He argues that there are 10 basic ratios that might develop as particular pentadic elements are emphasized within discourse. As Meisenbach (2008) writes, "while the pentadic terms usually refer to distinct ideas, they are most usefully assessed in relationship to one another" (p. 5). Beyond simply understanding the use of the various individual pentadic elements, then, it is valuable in developing a consistent perception of motive to observe which elements are emphasized and used together to influence how the pentad is being presented as a whole.

As a result, this analysis of *Uncle Sam* begins by contending that the character of Uncle Sam takes on the role of agency. Looking at the character of Uncle Sam as a form of agency allows one to see how all five of the pentadic elements work together within the series to form a consistent message for readers. Moreover, Eisner's focus on an agency–purpose ratio throughout the series clarifies its use as a form of propaganda.

The remainder of this chapter examines a survey of *Uncle Sam* comics, ranging from the series' prewar introduction in July 1940 through its conclusion in 1944. The analysis scrutinizes the character's regular appearances in *National Comics* as well as his own short-lived series, *Uncle Sam Quarterly*. In order to identify the pentadic elements that emerged from nearly 50 individual issues, I examine specific examples of agency, scene, agent, act, and purpose as well as more general consistencies that appear throughout the entirety of the *Uncle Sam* wartime comic books.

Pentadic Elements in *Uncle Sam*

Although Uncle Sam faced a wide variety of foes in a number of locations, a large majority of the storylines followed a predictable pattern that betrayed consistencies in the underlying pentadic elements. The typical *Uncle Sam* story line opens with some evil plot being developed by an enemy to attack either the United States or an Allied nation. Through a series of events, Uncle Sam stumbles onto the plot, forcing him (and his sidekick, Buddy) to jump into action to stop the enemy from succeeding. In his effort to defend freedom and democracy from the villains, Uncle Sam often calls upon soldiers or average citizens to aid him in his endeavor, inevitably leading to eventual triumph. While the specific pentadic elements changed from issue to issue, this stable set of events created an important consistency in establishing Eisner's propagandistic message.

Uncle Sam as *Agency*

Looking at the character of Uncle Sam himself is helpful in understanding how this consistency developed throughout the series. As the title character, not only was Uncle Sam the only character to appear in every issue, but he had a dramatic influence on the other elements of the pentad as well. At first glance, it might appear that he is the principal agent in the comic book. However, closer analysis reveals that the role Uncle Sam played in this series is more closely connected with *agency*. While one could argue that the agency used to defeat the various counteragents included legislation and weapons, from a broader perspective it seems evident that the primary agency was Uncle Sam himself. True, Uncle Sam did his share of fighting the enemy. Yet, unlike many of the other superheroes who appeared in home-front comic books, Uncle Sam was a relatively nonviolent entity who was forced into combat when it became necessary to defend the places and ideals that were part of him.

Despite the fact that Uncle Sam's backstory established that the figure had appeared in numerous wars, it is evident by his attitude that he preferred less violent solutions. While counteragents were often shown using murder and other nefarious tactics to impose their will, Uncle Sam regularly tried to avoid using lethal force. This use of nonlethal justice is significant, because it was consistent with his concern for democracy. Uncle Sam did not simply beat foes, as did other superheroes. Indeed, many issues ended with the enemy being handed over to the police or military so that they could go through the democratic process of justice—further emphasizing the character's principles.

Additionally, it is clear from his actions as a form of agency that Uncle Sam rarely sought out fights. In typical storylines, the superhero and Buddy were minding their own business, often fishing (Eisner, 1940d; Eisner, 1941b; Eisner, 1941h) or walking through the forest (Eisner, 1942c) and enjoying their freedom, when they stumbled upon some new threat that forced them into action. These scenes clearly tried to emphasize that Uncle Sam was America's *uncle*, not America's *soldier*. In his discussion of the use of the image of Uncle Sam during wartime, Capozzola (2008) explains that "his silly hat and ill-fitting suit suggest that Uncle Sam doesn't usually do this. He reassures viewers that war is not America's lifeblood; the nation, like its uncle, would rather be doing something else" (p. 5). The familial relation of Uncle Sam emerged in many scenes. When Buddy first meets Uncle Sam, for example, he asks, "Whose uncle are you?" Uncle Sam replies, "Everyone's uncle . . . every American boy is my nephew" (Eisner, 1940a, p. 4). This nonviolent, familial characterization of Uncle Sam was important in showing how he functioned as agency to guide other agents throughout the various storylines.

When discussing Uncle Sam as a form of agency, it is important to remember that he was not an actual person, but rather the personified spirit of America. He was not some combatant who survived throughout the centuries, continually fighting enemies. Instead, the comic book Uncle Sam was a being who appeared in America's times of need in order to provide support. Similar to images of Uncle Sam in *National Comics* #1 (Eisner, 1940a; see Figure 5.1) appearing in various historical wars that involved the United States, *National Comics* #5 (Eisner, 1940e) printed a historical flashback showing Uncle Sam as the "great invisible force" that lent Americans a hand when needed (p. 2). Eisner graphically shows Uncle Sam taking over the body of a man who needs to defend his town from antidemocratic enemies. By controlling the man's actions, Uncle Sam literally becomes the agency this particular agent needs in order to defeat the counteragents. While this scene is the most extreme example of the superhero functioning as agency, the manifestation of Uncle Sam in other issues of the comic book functioned in a similar way.

In many episodes, Uncle Sam established himself as agency by facilitating Americans with the means to defend themselves. When Uncle Sam and Buddy found themselves stumbling upon some evil plot, they were forced to take action, often by warning the right sources so they could receive support. As a result, it was very rare for Uncle Sam to take on counteragents alone. Typically, Buddy was there to round up agents whom Uncle Sam could encourage or rally to the cause. In *National Comics* #7 (Eisner, 1941b), for instance, Uncle Sam and Buddy discover that a European dictator is sending underwater tanks to invade the United States. Instead of fighting the tanks head-on, Uncle Sam rushes back to shore to rally a group of fishermen to help fight even as Buddy runs to warn the Coast Guard. Uncle Sam gathers the fishermen and explains, "This country is in danger of immediate invasion . . . I'll need every last one of you to help me!" The fishermen enthusiastically respond, "We're with you, Sam!" (Eisner, 1941b, p. 3). Following this exchange, images of the fishermen defending their country with fishing nets and spears against the armed invaders appear alongside Uncle Sam throwing punches. When the enemy seems to be too strong, Uncle Sam provides the fishermen with access to one of the enemy tanks to allow them to continue their defense until the Coast Guard arrives and finishes off the enemy. Although Uncle Sam physically fights alongside the agents with his super powers in this story, it is his initial role as agency, providing warning of the attack—and his ability to facilitate his side's continued involvement—that leads to victory against the enemy. By always seeming to be in the right place at the right time, then, Uncle Sam's warnings and assistance became the means through which the various allies were able defend the United States and the principles of freedom and democracy.

Uncle Sam's role as agency was also reinforced through his connection with other famous American spirits. In several issues, the superhero communicated with figures such as George Washington (Eisner, 1942c), Simon Bolivar (Eisner, 1942c), and Teddy Roosevelt (Eisner, 1941l), looking for guidance on how to best lead the people to defend the United States. This type of interaction with

Figure 5.1: National Comics #1. The agency of Uncle Sam can be seen throughout American history (Eisner, 1940a, p. 1).

other spiritual beings established the commonalities Uncle Sam had with other invisible forces in aiding the nation. However, unlike these other spiritual aides, Uncle Sam was not a real historical figure, but a personification of the country itself, as well as an embodiment of the principles of freedom and democracy. This connection motivated Uncle Sam to embrace the role of agency, showing home-front citizens what they should be fighting for and providing them with the ability to defend the principles that were important to them. As a result, these scenes reinforced the perception that Uncle Sam was less of an agent responsible for actual defense and more of a guiding spirit warning, encouraging, and facilitating Americans to defend themselves. The consistency in the role that Uncle Sam played as agency, however, is even more evident when looking at how he shaped the use of scene.

The United States as Scene

The opening scene of *Uncle Sam* (Eisner, 1940a) displayed a proud-looking Uncle Sam marching through the United States in various historical moments, including the American War of Independence and the Civil War. From the beginning, it was clear that Uncle Sam was the personification of the nation. and its ideals or, as the comic book suggested, the "spirit" of America (Eisner, 1940a, p. 1). As a result, this initial imagery indicated that since Uncle Sam was present, the *scene* of *Uncle Sam* would primarily take place within the nation he represented. Rather than an offensive force in a global conflict, then, he was shown as a defender of the United States through the places he chose to protect.

The story line of the first issue emphasized this domestic scene through the use of a stylized location akin to *The Grapes of Wrath*, with poor Americans traveling through the Dust Bowl toward the hope of California (Eisner, 1940a). Right away, the audience is viewing the United States during the Great Depression through images of families walking and driving through the desert and gathering in camps along the way. Readers familiar with Steinbeck's popular novel (which was published the previous year) would have immediately recognized this scenic choice and likely empathized with the difficulties these Americans were facing. However, while this setting choice presented an obstacle to overcome, more importantly it also presented an America that was open and free, allowing citizens to move where they pleased.

As the story continues, scenes of the spacious American Southwest are quickly contrasted with the stark, unfriendly interior of a stone fortress nearby that a group of power-hungry enemies is using as a base. Linking the imagery of the enemy with a hidden underground fortress full of prisons and machines disconnects the villains from the open territory aboveground, where Uncle

Sam's American citizens have dominion. When the character Buddy escapes by running out into the open desert, he eventually meets Uncle Sam, who seems to materialize out of the American countryside. The use of scene here is rooted in the United States, and, consequently, there is little wonder that Uncle Sam is already present to function as agency and to facilitate the protection of the place he represents. In fact, a similar use of scene—associating Americans and Uncle Sam with recognizable regions of the United States while enemies are shown in concealed and confined locations—emerged in many other *Uncle Sam* issues.

Through the course of its brief run, the scenic choices in *Uncle Sam* provided a relatively comprehensive look at the continental United States Small midwestern towns (Eisner, 1940e; Eisner, 1941d; Eisner, 1941h), industrial factories (Eisner, 1940b; Eisner, 1941f; Eisner, 1941i), forested countryside (Eisner, 1941c), military bases (Eisner, 1941g; Eisner, 1941j), and large cities (Eisner, 1942d) were all depicted as important elements of the nation, each deserving of support and protection. While specific locations were often unidentified, the story lines and visual images made it clear that these scenes were taking place within the continental United States. Additionally, since part of Uncle Sam's role was to defend the principles of freedom and democracy, it is not surprising that many scenes took place inside the U.S. Capitol building (e.g., Eisner, 1940b; Eisner, 1941a) and the White House (Eisner, 1941i). In particular, the floor of the U.S. Senate became a recurring scene, allowing various agents to fight against internal threats with legislation. All of these domestic scene choices from throughout the country were significant through their connection to Uncle Sam and the people who lived there, aiding him in overcoming various dangers.

In order to provide further defense of the nation, the scene of *Uncle Sam* expanded occasionally to include story lines that took place at sea. While not an actual part of Uncle Sam's continental persona, the Pacific Ocean (and, in rare cases, the Atlantic Ocean) were evidently important symbolic barriers between the United States and various foreign powers. However, oceans became powerful settings, because they are difficult to defend and have the ability to be breached by enemies. Even before the bombing of Pearl Harbor, Uncle Sam appeared in various scenes on enemy vessels, including floating islands (Eisner, 1940d), submarines (Eisner, 1940f), and underwater tanks (Eisner, 1941b). In particular, the scene in *National Comics* #18 (Eisner, 1941m; see Figure 5.2) gained notoriety for featuring foreign invaders bombing Pearl Harbor *before* the actual attack. Even though these scenes were at sea, the enemy's target was still the United States. As a result, Uncle Sam was able to provide agency by helping warn other agents about these threats and aiding them in the defense of their homeland, making his presence understandable.

Figure 5.2: National Comics #18. Uncle Sam comic visualizes Pearl Harbor attack before the actual Japanese invasion takes place (Eisner, 1941m, p. 1).

While a majority of *Uncle Sam*'s story lines took place within the United States, it is important to note that on occasion the character did come to the defense of several foreign locations. Although Uncle Sam never crossed the Atlantic Ocean into Europe or Africa, he did make appearances in the Philippines (Eisner, 1940c), the Soviet Union (Eisner, 1943b), Brazil (Eisner, 1942c), Mexico (Eisner, 1942e), and Panama (Eisner, 1941l). Initially, these unusual scenes in foreign locations seem to contradict the role that Uncle Sam played as the agency of U.S. defense. However, each of the issues reassured readers that coming to the aid of foreign regions was itself a form of defense for the United States, not to mention a means of preserving the principles of freedom and democracy that Uncle Sam and Americans were fighting for.

Whether foreign or domestic, then, Eisner's use of scene drew a sharp contrast between the locations that Uncle Sam and his many allies occupied and the locations that the enemies that appeared throughout the comic book series used. While the protagonists seemed to favor the freedom of outdoor scenes and unrestricted locations in towns and cities throughout the United States, scenes featuring counter-agents were consistently presented in a very different manner. Overwhelmingly, in fact, America's enemies found themselves in very confined locations. In various *Uncle Sam* issues, the enemies made extensive use of hidden fortresses and hideouts (Eisner, 1940a; Eisner, 1941i; Eisner, 1942f; Eisner, 1943a), small offices (Eisner, 1940b; Eisner, 1941d), submarines (Eisner, 1940f), tanks (Eisner, 1941g), basements (Eisner, 1941e), mines (Eisner, 1941h), train cars (Eisner, 1941j), and even isolated floating islands (Eisner, 1940d). Regardless of the geographic location of these scenes, they all located the enemy in places where freedom was significantly restricted. This lack of freedom and the inability to move around as they pleased created a significant contrast between enemy locations and the United States,—where Uncle Sam allowed his compatriots the opportunity to enjoy their freedom. With the scene firmly established in the United States (or, on occasion, in Allied nations), various agents and counter-agents would appear to either work with or against Uncle Sam.

Agents and Counter-Agents in *Uncle Sam*

In examining the pentadic use of *agent* in *Uncle Sam*, it is essential to begin with the series' enemies as a means of understanding why Uncle Sam had to intervene as a form of agency on behalf of other agents in defending the scenes he was connected to. Since these enemies created the problems that the agent or agents needed to solve, Burke's (1945) term "counter-agent" (p. xx) is useful in describing their pentadic role. As Fuchs and Reitberger (1971/1972) explain, the use of the "super villain" as a staple of comic books did not fully develop until after WWII (p. 105). As a result, most counter-agents found in early comic books took the form of more realistic enemies and organizations. *Uncle Sam* followed this early trend by presenting different counter-agents in each issue. Even though some particular enemy-organization names appeared in multiple story lines (such as the Purple Shirts and Black Legion), the actual counter-agents themselves continuously changed. In fact, the lack of a singular counter-agent was actually important to Uncle Sam's purpose. Uncle Sam did not just materialize to fight the Axis powers. Instead, he addressed a wide range of other enemies and organizations, each threatening freedom and democracy from either within or without the United States.

The comic book series made it clear that the country had more than one enemy; since Uncle Sam was responsible for defending the nation he was therefore forced to provide agency to deal with a variety of counter-agents. Throughout the series, corrupt government officials (Eisner, 1941a; Eisner, 1941d), greedy factory owners (Eisner, 1940b; Eisner, 1941f), racketeers (Eisner, 1941d; Eisner, 1943a), foreign spies (Eisner, 1941e; Eisner, 1941k), and multiple German- and Asian-looking dictators (Eisner, 1940a; Eisner, 1940c; Eisner, 1941i; Eisner, 1942a) schemed to harm the United States or its foundational principles in some way. Additionally, most of these counter-agents also had their own contingent of personal followers to carry out their sinister plans. All of these counter-agents were important, because they each became enemies of the very American way of life that Uncle Sam sought to protect.

Eisner's depiction of these counter-agents was often rooted in stereotypes. Enemies resembling Germans were depicted in recognizable brown shirts or black, Nazi-stylized uniforms—including peaked hats and jodhpurs. High-ranking villains also sported a monocle or Hitler-like mustache. In addition to their visual representation, the use of names such as *Fritz* and *Von Stuhl*— as well as their fractured English—left little doubt about whom they were intended to represent. For example, in *National Comics* #25 (Eisner, 1942e), German thugs wearing Nazi uniforms attempt to capture a senator. Their words are comically stereotypical, as they avow that "ve mean bizness" and "ve vill take the senator to der chief" (Eisner, 1942e, pp. 2–3). Asian counter-agents received similar treatment, with stereotypically slanted eyes, Fu Manchu facial hair, and buck teeth (e.g., Eisner, 1940c; Eisner, 1942b). Of course, domestic enemies were harder to identify by image and language alone. However, many of them did wear recognizable gangster and thug attire, including bowler hats and suits.

It is interesting to note that the only actual living person to have made an appearance in *Uncle Sam* was the counter-agent Adolf Hitler. He first appeared in a scene commenting about the importance of a particular operation to sabotage U.S. oil shipments in issue #26 (Eisner, 1942f). Later, he delivered a speech threatening his enemies with "Mongrel Men" (Eisner, 1942a). While pre-war counter-agents typically were labeled ambiguously as the "Purple Shirts" (Eisner, 1940a) or, more often, the "Black Legion" (Eisner, 1940e; Eisner, 1941i), shortly after the United States entered the war, enemies labeling themselves as Nazis began to appear in *Uncle Sam*.

With all of these counter-agents threatening the United States, it fell to Uncle Sam to be the agency by warning other agents to protect their home and the freedom and democracy it represents. As the title of the comic books suggested, the superhero Uncle Sam was featured as the main protagonist throughout the series. However, the use of agent in *Uncle Sam* established that average Americans were just as important to the defense of their country as a character with superhuman abilities. As mentioned previously, in *National Comics* #1 (Eisner, 1940a), Uncle Sam first appears to a young boy named Buddy Smith, whose father was just murdered by a group of counter-agents. Buddy quickly becomes a co-agent by helping Uncle Sam defeat the Purple Shirts, who are trying to manipulate poor Americans into accepting a dictatorship. As a result of this first encounter, a connection is formed and Buddy becomes Uncle Sam's sidekick, appearing in nearly every issue of *Uncle Sam*.

Buddy soon took a direct role in much of the action by thwarting the various plots of the counter-agents. Despite Uncle Sam's warnings to stay out of the battles, Buddy almost always found a way to throw a well-needed punch or to alert other agents about a looming threat. For example, when a German spy tries to take Buddy as a hostage aboard a submarine, he quickly jumps into action, stealing their guns and forcing the enemy to fire on their own ships; he saves many navy ships as a result (Eisner, 1941k). In Scott's (2007) discussion of the importance of Bucky Barnes to *Captain America* comics, he argues that the inclusion of a young character "gave readers a chance to insert themselves into the action presented in the comic book" (p. 334). As with Bucky, Buddy's role as a co-agent offered young readers someone they could relate to. While Uncle Sam was a super-powered representation of the United States, in many ways Buddy represented average Americans who did not quite understand why enemies were attacking them—but who were willing to lend a hand to defend the nation if necessary.

This focus on the influence that an average person without super powers could have against threats to the nation becomes even more significant when looking at the other allies that come to the aid of Uncle Sam. Uncle Sam might have been the superhero, but in many scenes, average citizens took on the role of agent to defend their country. In *National Comics* #1 (Eisner, 1940a), for instance, Uncle Sam's main role is not to physically attack the power-hungry Purple Shirts; it is to vocally rally the American people to stand up against the dictatorship's ideals. After his rousing speech, many citizens begin shouting support, such as "I'm with Uncle Sam," as they begin fighting back against the enemy (Eisner, 1940a, p. 8). In the scenes that follow, there are several images that show American agents fighting the enemy. "Staunchly," adds the text, "the Americans stand off the attack" (Eisner, 1940a, p. 8). As the fight draws to a close, then, it is not Uncle Sam who claims victory, but average American citizens who raise the American flag. Indeed, in virtually every issue of *Uncle Sam*, everyday human agents appeared to lend a hand to defend their country.

U.S. military forces made several appearances as the agents defending their country as well, but they were joined at times by senators (Eisner, 1940b; Eisner, 1942e), fishermen (Eisner, 1941b), scientists (Eisner, 1941i), and reporters (Eisner, 1940b). Sometimes these agents were even able to intervene on behalf of Americans in ways that Uncle Sam could not. In one particular story, thugs are threatening and attacking townspeople on their way to vote, forcing many of them to return to their homes for protection. Regardless of how hard Uncle Sam tries to convince them that they need to vote and that it is their right as free Americans, the people are too frightened to leave their houses. At that point, co-agent Buddy finds a group of young men playing baseball and convinces them to escort the people to the polls. These boys thus become the agents of the story, helping the townspeople and fighting back the thugs to defend democracy. Therefore, although Uncle Sam might have been the superhero, he was generally *not* the agent responsible for the actions that stopped the counter-agents. Rather, he served as the *agency* that encouraged and allowed the true agents to fight for the American way of life.

Act and Purpose in *Uncle Sam*

On the surface, *act* and *purpose* appeared to change in each issue of *Uncle Sam*. As previously established, *Uncle Sam* provided a wide variety of domestic and allied scene locations as well as various types of agents. With so many diverse agents and counter-agents appearing in all sorts of identifiable settings, it makes sense that *Uncle Sam* would also have required a variety of acts to serve a range of purposes as well. As a result, agents were called upon by Uncle Sam to take action in various ways: infiltrating and capturing hidden fortresses (Eisner, 1940a), fighting back invading forces (Eisner, 1940d; Eisner, 1940f; Eisner, 1941b), tracking down and capturing spies (Eisner, 1941c; Eisner, 1941e; Eisner, 1942f), defeating various gangsters and other thugs (Eisner, 1941d; Eisner, 1942d; Eisner, 1943a), and a wide range of other acts. Not surprisingly, a majority of the acts in *Uncle Sam* involved the use of physical violence. Whether it was beating counter-agents into submission so that they could be arrested or turning the enemies' own weapons against them, agents—with Uncle Sam's agency and Buddy's help—became very resourceful in doing what was necessary to protect their country.

Just as the acts that emerged from the many *Uncle Sam* stories were varied, it would have additionally made sense for the *purposes* behind those acts to change as well. When considered separately, the act of agents fighting their way through an enemy fortress for the purpose of stopping the spread of dictatorship and the act of a reporter exposing corruption in Congress for the purpose of preserving legislation appear to have little in common. However, while the specific action in each story was different, from a broader perspective they were united because they were both products of Uncle Sam's agency. Upon closer inspection, it becomes clear the continued presence of Uncle Sam as agency provides a summative purpose for the varied acts that take place.

Uncle Sam, as the personification and spirit of America providing the agency for his agents, was the enabling force that gave all of these varied acts a consistent purpose of defending the United States and the principles of freedom and democracy. From this perspective, a group of fishermen beating back an invading force of foreign military was just as significant as a factory owner realizing he needed to provide additional aid for his workers (since their actions all contributed toward Uncle Sam's summative defensive purpose). Uncle Sam's purpose was reinforced at the end of nearly every issue through an additional image of Uncle Sam either talking with Buddy or looking out at the reader to explain the importance of defending democracy and freedom. For example, in *National Comics* #4 (Eisner, 1940d), after Uncle Sam and Buddy let the navy chase away a group of invaders, there is a scene showing the two characters sitting in front of a sunset. Buddy states, "Gosh, Uncle, they sure made quick work of those foreigners," causing Uncle Sam to respond, "And the same goes for anyone who tries to come here to disturb our peaceful democracy" (Eisner, 1940d, p. 9). These typical scenes explicitly establish the consistent purpose that was being presented to readers. As a result, *Uncle Sam* was not a collection of stories about various agents doing various acts for various purposes. Instead, it was about Americans and their Allies doing whatever acts were necessary in order to defend their nation and the principles it stood for, united by a common purpose that was symbolized and facilitated by a singular character. Without Uncle Sam there to provide agency, the use of purpose, as well as the other pentadic elements, would have lost its consistency.

Ratios

To further clarify the consistency underlying the rhetorical message in *Uncle Sam*, it is valuable to look at the use of ratios in the comic book series as well.

From the perspective of the pentad, it would make sense for most propaganda appeals to adopt an act-agent ratio in order to encourage the target audience to recognize their connection to the agent and, as a result, to want to take action by adopting the intended idea or behavior. For example, in Flagg's WWI Uncle Sam recruitment poster, the message emanated from a recognizable agent who explicitly told the audience to take the action of joining the army. Although the purpose for joining the army (that is, defending the United States) was also present to a degree, the main focus in the poster was clearly on the agents *taking* action, not thinking about why they should.

However, unlike many forms of prewar and wartime propaganda, the *Uncle Sam* series avoided the use of an act-agency ratio in favor of an alternative ratio more appropriate for a comic book featuring a personified superhero. Even though the role of agent in the story lines was essential to the actual defense of the United States, it would be a mistake to argue that agents were the main focus. Fundamentally, *Uncle Sam* was a superhero comic book series, and, hence, the character was the primary element in the story. Therefore, since Uncle Sam can be seen as the agency that shaped the other four pentadic elements within the world of the comic book, agency was clearly one of the ratio elements being emphasized by Eisner. Due to Uncle Sam's predominance, it is also easy to see how his personification established a consistent scene set in the United States, or locations that were associated with his ideals, as well as influencing what types of agents were being used to perform the acts necessary to defend that scene. This influence of agency was repeated everywhere in the series, through warning agents about potential threats and giving them the ability to complete their acts.

The consistency that Uncle Sam's agency developed with these pentadic elements helped establish the underlying purpose as well. Repeatedly, Uncle Sam reminded readers that the purpose of everything that was going on in the war was to protect democracy and freedom by defending the United States and, when necessary, its Allies. As previously mentioned, this consistent purpose was often made explicit in the final frame of many issues through Uncle Sam's statements like, "It is the duty of good citizens to be ever on the lookout for enemies of your country and mine" (Eisner, 1941g, p. 9), and tag messages about the future issues, including, "Uncle Sam fights for democracy again" (Eisner, 1941e, p. 9). Such scenes were common in the series, continually allowing Uncle Sam to reinforce his purpose of defending the United States and its principles by reflecting on the agency he provided to the agents of the story.

Therefore, due to Uncle Sam's predominant role, the pentadic ratio of agency-purpose stands out as the primary emphasis in the comic book series. Burke (1945) suggests that an agency-purpose ratio is common when the focus of a rhetorical act is on the means to an end. This type of ratio worked well in the comic book series, because Uncle Sam was continually forced to find ways to adapt the agency he provided to satisfy his purpose. Regardless of his superhuman abilities, Uncle Sam's presence as a personified spirit of America continually communicated that the nation and democracy needed protection—and that, with Uncle Sam's help, protection was possible.[1]

Conclusion

This analysis suggests that Eisner's motivation behind the development of *Uncle Sam* led to a consistent message that stressed both agency and purpose. While Eisner never publicly stated that *Uncle Sam* comic books were trying to send propagandistic ideals, the repetition of the message throughout the series encourages the perception that he wanted readers to be aware of this message. Continually presenting readers with the idea that their country and principles were in danger—and then showing them that it was possible to overcome that danger—might well have been a potent appeal for a wartime audience. Moreover, if propaganda is in fact the transfer of ideas from the propagandist to a desired audience, then such an appeal thus constituted a propagandistic message. While this message did not explicitly tell readers to take action, its ideological influence was probably just as important. In his discussion of the role that comic books might play as a form of propaganda, Scott (2007) comments that "while the definition of propaganda is associated with government groups, in the case of comic books, the form of propaganda was to simply promote a viewpoint" (p. 326). From this perspective, although *Uncle Sam* might not have had the direct influence that more behavioral forms of prewar and wartime propaganda might have possessed, Burke's pentad establishes that Eisner's viewpoint throughout the series formed its own unique kind of propaganda.

From its outward appearance, then, *Uncle Sam* was just another comic book series about a superhero fighting crime. However, there was significantly more going on within the pages of this comic book series than just stories about defeating villains. By using Burke's pentad as a systematic approach to analyzing *Uncle Sam*, this analysis exposes important elements about Eisner's particular message. Establishing Uncle Sam as agency allowed him to develop a level of constancy in the other pentadic elements, forming a foundation for his message. Uncle Sam's manifestation as the personification of the United States played a significant role in shaping the predominantly domestic use of scene and agent that was repeated throughout the series. In addition, despite the fact that individual acts within the series were occasionally carried out for varying purposes, Uncle Sam's presence also established the perception that all of the acts contributed to the consistent, unified purpose of defending the nation and its principles. As a result, Uncle Sam allowed Eisner to present his ideas through an agency-purpose ratio, an approach that was arguably an effective form of propaganda for his readers.

This conclusion is significant, because it reveals *how* the *Uncle Sam* series functioned as a form of wartime propaganda. In addition, it demonstrates that Burke's pentad is useful in understanding the nature of propaganda. Instead of simply labeling pieces of communication as propaganda, it is valuable to have a way to evaluate how propagandists communicate messages to their audience. While it is beyond the scope of this study to draw conclusions about the use of other comic books being used as prewar and wartime propaganda in WWII, further exploration of the pentadic elements in other comic books might provide insight into alternative ways propaganda emerges in this medium. Additionally, it would also be valuable to explore the continued use of the character of Uncle Sam as a source of propaganda. Although predominantly associated with both world wars—just like the character in Eisner's comic book series— versions of Uncle Sam seem to reappear whenever the United States is threatened, often in the form of political cartoons, but even as a reemergent comic book superhero in 1970 and 2005. Regardless of what form he takes, however, it is clear that Uncle Sam has become a recognizable American image that will continue to play a role as long as he is needed. As Ketchum (1959) explains, "Uncle Sam is the personal, human embodiment of the U.S.A. Presidents enter and depart, but Uncle Sam goes on indefinitely" (p. 1).

Notes

1. There were some occasions when Eisner's message shifted to address the importance of agents, as when Uncle Sam states, "I alone cannot fight sinister forces undermining our democracy! All true Americans must help" (Eisner, *National Comics*, November 1940, p. 9). However, these particularly agent-centered moments were few and far between.

References

Benoit, W. (1996). A note on Burke on "motive." *Rhetoric Society Quarterly, 26*(2), 67–79.

Burke, K. (1945). *A grammar of motives.* Berkeley: University of California Press.

Capozzola, C. (2008). *Uncle Sam wants you: World War I and the making of the modern American citizen.* New York, NY: Oxford University Press.

Cull, N. J., Culbert, D., & Welch, D. (2003). *Propaganda and mass persuasion: A historical encyclopedia, 1500 to the present.* Santa Barbara, CA: ABC-CLIO.

Eisner, W. (1940a, July). Uncle Sam. In *National Comics* (pp. 1–9). (Vol. 1). New York, NY: Quality Comics.

Eisner, W. (1940b, August). Uncle Sam. In *National Comics* (pp. 1–9). (Vol. 2). New York, NY: Quality Comics.

Eisner, W. (1940c, September). Uncle Sam. In *National Comics* (pp. 1–9). (Vol. 3). New York, NY: Quality Comics.

Eisner, W. (1940d, October). Uncle Sam. In *National Comics* (pp. 1–9). (Vol. 4). New York, NY: Quality Comics.

Eisner, W. (1940e, November). Uncle Sam. In *National Comics* (pp. 1–9). (Vol. 5). New York, NY: Quality Comics.

Eisner, W. (1940f, December). Uncle Sam. In *National Comics* (pp. 1–9). (Vol. 6). New York, NY: Quality Comics.

Eisner, W. (1941a, Autumn). Forged faces. In *Uncle Sam quarterly* (pp. 1–14). (Vol. 1). New York, NY: Quality Comics.

Eisner, W. (1941b, January). Uncle Sam. In *National Comics* (pp. 1–9). (Vol. 7). New York, NY: Quality Comics.

Eisner, W. (1941c, February). Uncle Sam. In *National Comics* (pp. 1–9). (Vol. 8). New York, NY: Quality Comics.

Eisner, W. (1941d, March). Uncle Sam. In *National Comics* (pp. 1–9). (Vol. 9). New York, NY: Quality Comics.

Eisner, W. (1941e, April). Uncle Sam. In *National Comics* (pp. 1–9). (Vol. 10). New York, NY: Quality Comics.

Eisner, W. (1941f, May). Uncle Sam. In *National Comics* (pp. 1–9). (Vol. 11). New York, NY: Quality Comics.

Eisner, W. (1941g, June). Uncle Sam. In *National Comics* (pp. 1–9). (Vol. 12). New York, NY: Quality Comics.

Eisner, W. (1941h, July). Uncle Sam. In *National Comics* (pp. 1–9). (Vol. 13). New York, NY: Quality Comics.

Eisner, W. (1941i, August). Uncle Sam. In *National Comics* (pp. 1–9). (Vol. 14). New York, NY: Quality Comics.

Eisner, W. (1941j, September). Uncle Sam. In *National Comics* (pp. 1–9). (Vol. 15). New York, NY: Quality Comics.

Eisner, W. (1941k, October). Uncle Sam. In *National Comics* (pp. 1–9). (Vol. 16). New York, NY: Quality Comics.

Eisner, W. (1941l, November). Uncle Sam. In *National Comics* (pp. 1–9). (Vol. 17). New York, NY: Quality Comics.

Eisner, W. (1941m, December). Uncle Sam. In *National Comics* (pp. 1–9). (Vol. 18). New York, NY: Quality Comics.

Eisner, W. (1942a, Autumn). Mongrel men. In *Uncle Sam quarterly* (pp. 1–14). (Vol. 4). New York, NY: Quality Comics.

Eisner, W. (1942b, Autumn). Odakim the fierce. In *Uncle Sam quarterly* (pp. 32--41). (Vol. 4). New York, NY: Quality Comics.

Eisner, W. (1942c, February). Uncle Sam. In *National Comics* (pp. 1–9). (Vol. 20). New York, NY: Quality Comics.

Eisner, W. (1942d, April). Uncle Sam. In *National Comics* (pp. 1–9). (Vol. 22). New York, NY: Quality Comics.

Eisner, W. (1942e, July). Uncle Sam. In *National Comics* (pp. 1–9). (Vol. 25). New York, NY: Quality Comics.

Eisner, W. (1942f, August). Uncle Sam. In *National Comics* (pp. 1–9). (Vol. 26). New York, NY: Quality Comics.

Eisner, W. (1943a, April). Uncle Sam. In *National Comics* (pp. 1–9). (Vol. 34). New York, NY: Quality Comics.

Eisner, W. (1943b, June). Uncle Sam. In *National Comics* (pp. 1–9). (Vol. 36). New York, NY: Quality Comics.

Fuchs, W., & Reitberger, R. (1972). *Comics: Anatomy of a mass medium.* (N. Fowler, Trans.). Boston, MA: Little, Brown. (Original work published 1971)

Ketchum, A. (1959). *Uncle Sam: The man and the legend.* New York, NY: Hill and Wang.

Meisenbach, R. J. (2008). "They allowed": Pentadic mapping of women's maternity leave discourse as organizational rhetoric. *Communication Monographs, 75,* 1–25.

Ross, S. H. (1996). *Propaganda for war: How the U.S. was conditioned to fight the Great War of 1914–1918.* Jefferson, NC: McFarland.

Rountree, C. (2001). Instantiating "the Law" and its dissents in *Korematsu v. United States*: A dramatistic analysis of judicial discourse. *Quarterly Journal of Speech, 87,* 1–24.

Scott, C. (2007, April). Written in red, white, and blue: A comparison of comic book propaganda from World War II and September 11. Journal of Popular Culture, 40, 325–343.

★★ 6 ★★

Superman as Allegory

Examining the Isolationist/Interventionist Dilemma in U.S. Foreign Policy Prior to Pearl Harbor

Trischa Goodnow

In Harry Brod's 2012 work *Superman Is Jewish?: How Comic Book Superheroes Came to Serve Truth, Justice, and the Jewish-American Way*, he contends that the Jewish creators of Superman desired to "counter the notion that strength or manliness and Jewishness are incompatible." Brod posits that Clark Kent and Superman represented the perceived weakness of Jews and the true nature of Jews as strong. He spends a great deal of time laying out the argument that Superman is the true being and Clark Kent is just a facade.

In this chapter I argue an alternative position to Brod's. I argue here that the Clark Kent/Superman duality can be considered as an allegory for American isolationism versus American interventionism, with Clark representing the former and Superman the latter. The allegory is extended with the character of Lois Lane representing Europe. By situating comic book Superman within the dimensions of a political allegory, the reader comes to a greater understanding of the Jewish position in regard to American policy in Europe and toward the war prior to Pearl Harbor. "Maybe this was the strangest thing of all: that the Jews were eager for battle, the Jews who had never trusted governments or militaries and had always tried to keep their sons away from the front were rooting for Roosevelt to get us over there and spit in Hitler's eye" (Jones, 2004,

p. 162). Additionally, Dittmer (2007) argues, "This aversion to the Nazis and to isolationism was especially visible among the creators of the comics, who were almost uniformly Jewish and liberal (p. 80).

This chapter seeks to examine the allegorical dimensions of the *Superman* comic series as represented by the two personae of Superman (Clark Kent/ Superman) serving as a warning of isolationist/interventionist policies of the United States in the prewar years. To understand this argument, I will first briefly explain the concept of allegory; then consider the climate into which Clark Kent/Superman was born, along with his history; and then examine three story lines that illustrate the isolationist/interventionist dichotomy before finally drawing implications from this analysis.

The specific comics chosen for analysis in this chapter appeared before the U.S. entrance into World War II. *Superman Vol. 1, #1* was chosen because it is the first comic book and establishes the allegorical dimensions of the series. The consecutive books *Action Comics #22* and *#23* were chosen because in these story lines, Superman intervenes in a war between fictional nations that mirror the conflict in Europe. Finally, *Superman Vol. 1, #8* takes a different tack and considers fifth columnists in the United States.[1] These three comic books represent the different approaches Superman's creators took in attempting to influence perceptions of U.S. foreign policy. Most often Superman is considered in the whole. Consequently, by examining specific storylines, the allegorical dimensions of the comic book can be fully explored.

Allegory

Allegory is a literary trope that conveys a story that operates on two levels. The first level is the fictional story, while the second level is "real." Van Dyke (1985) explains that "the words and meanings in allegory correspond not antithetically, as in irony, but on parallel planes (p. 26). The secondary level is related to reveal a moral or prediction. To conduct an allegorical analysis, the critic first describes the context in which the allegory is found. Then different aspects of the narrative are related to the real situation to which they refer. Finally, the moral and/or prediction of the allegory is determined.

The most famous allegory is L. Frank Baum's novel *The Wizard of Oz* as examined by Littlefield (1964). Each part of the story related to the political situation in the United States in the late 1800s. During this time some members of Congress wished to convert to a silver standard from the gold standard (Dorothy's original shoes were silver—changed to the more visually appealing ruby for the movie version—and they walked on the yellow brick road: gold). William Jennings Bryan was considered a blowhard with nothing behind his threats and hence was represented by the Cowardly Lion. The Scarecrow was representative of the Midwestern farmer who was "made to feel dumb by the great Midwestern drought of the 1890s and low crop prices" (Thomas, 1989, p. 52). Baum used these characters and situations to warn of the dangers of Eastern political hegemony. These are but a few examples of how a fanciful story can send a strong message about the real world.

Other scholars have used the allegorical form to examine hypothetical stories to warn of actual political danger (see for example, Coffey 2014, Hantke 2012). Perhaps most relevant to this analysis is Knapp's (1996) analysis of another comic that sought to warn of the dangers of Communism. Knapp examined the *Rocky and Bullwinkle* animated television series as an allegorical warning of the dangers of Soviet domination in the late 1950s and early 1960s. Rocky, Bullwinkle, Boris, and Natasha represented the two sides of the Cold War—the United States and the Soviet Union. Individual story lines depicted the fight of good against evil, with good always winning out. In this way, *Rocky and Bullwinkle* offered encouragement to U.S. citizens that the United States would prevail over the Soviet Union.

Given these parameters, we can turn to the political culture into which Clark Kent and Superman made their appearance in the late 1930s.

Political Climate

During the 1930s the United States was pulling itself out of the Great Depression, where the country and its citizens were struggling to gain economic footing. Dealing with its own issues, the country adopted an isolationist policy where it would stay out of other countries' affairs. Theoretically this would enable the United States to focus on its issues and save its financial resources for domestic needs. Organizations such as America First advocated that the U.S. government and citizens focus their attention on domestic issues. As Europe found itself facing Hitler's rise to power and his desire to conquer and control Europe, the United States chose to turn a blind eye, at least initially. The debate over isolationism versus interventionism is chronicled in great detail in Olson's 2013 account *Those Angry Days: Roosevelt, Lindbergh, and America's Fight over World War II.*

As Olson (2013) points out, Americans were caught between the repercussions of U.S. involvement in World War I and the need to assist in Britain's survival and the moral imperative to stop Hitler. Blower (2014), however, argues that isolationism versus interventionism created a false dichotomy, contending, "Binaries simply cannot encompass the confounding issues Americans faced during these years nor properly illuminate the solutions they entertained" (p. 353). This was true, according to Blower, because not intervening was a form of intervention, as it weighted the conflict for one side by not participating. Indeed, in the prewar years American opinions about how much to remain isolated or how much to intervene ran the gamut.

Jewish groups, particularly, were caught in the policy dilemma. Olson's (2013) work recounts the conflict between President Roosevelt and airman Charles Lindbergh. FDR knew that U.S. involvement in Europe was inevitable, so he asked Congress to repeal the Neutrality Act in early 1939. In November of that year, he asked Congress to approve the Pittman Bill, which would enable the United States to sell arms for cash ("American Isolationism," n.d.). Lindbergh was decidedly anti-intervention and was FDR's staunchest opposition in the direction the United States should go (Olson 2013).

Within the United States, not all citizens or groups were happy with the isolationist policy. Jewish groups, who were aware of Hitler's targeting of Jews, wanted the United States to intervene, as they saw Hitler's policies as a direct threat not only to their families but to the freedoms they enjoyed in the United States. Lindbergh identified American Jews as war agitators and believed that involvement in the European conflict would only incite "a violent outbreak of anti-Semitism in the country" (Olson 2013). Jewish Americans recognizing the potential pitfalls of U.S. involvement in Europe "were inclined to go along with the idea of keeping a low profile, especially with regard to the war."

Into this fray came the comic book heroes. Superman's creators were Jewish. Jerry Siegel, the artist, and Joe Shuster, the writer, both were of the stock of European Jewry and lived in Jewish neighborhoods in Cleveland, Ohio (Ricca, 2013). Consequently, it is not surprising that they could use the comic form to warn readers of the dangers of U.S. policies. Siegel and Shuster's Jewish influence has been discussed at length elsewhere (Brod 2012).

That Superman's origin is biblical in nature is undisputed. His name from Krypton was Kal-El; in Hebrew *El* means God, and *Kal* represents voice and vessel. Tye (2013) contends that "together they suggest that the alien superbaby was not just a Jew but a very special one." Brod (2012) contends that the Superman/Clark Kent duality sought to recreate the Jewish stereotype with "the superman who is real, and the alter ego, Clark Kent, who is fictitious." Given this understanding of how Superman can be interpreted, as Brod does, through a Jewish lens, it is reasonable to extend this interpretation to revision the American foreign policy over isolationism or interventionism as the two sides of Superman—weak and strong.

The Basic Characters of the Allegory: Clark Kent/Superman/Lois Lane

The comic book that introduced the characters of Clark Kent, Superman, and Lois Lane laid the groundwork for the interventionist leanings of their creators. However, before examining the story-line examples that depicted the conflict between isolationist and interventionist policies, an analysis of the characters who portrayed the various perspectives in the coming World War II arena is appropriate. The most important characters are, of course, Clark Kent, Lois Lane, and Superman.

Clark Kent and Superman are two sides of the same person. In two pages of strips, *Superman* #1 explains that a scientist from the doomed planet Krypton places his infant son in a rocket ship bound in the direction of Earth. An elderly couple finds the baby and takes him to an orphanage, but they decide to adopt and raise him. They name the baby Clark and soon discover his unusual strength, encouraging him to hide it until it can be used for humanity. After his parents' death, he decides to use his strength and other unusual talents to benefit mankind. Realizing that he would have advance notice of dangerous situations, Clark decides to try to become a reporter at the *Daily Star* (the name was later changed to the *Daily Planet*). Hence, Clark's alter-ego Superman is born. As the stories progress, it is clear that Clark, in order to maintain his anonymity as Superman, must project an ineffectual image. This is evident whenever Clark finds himself or Lois in a dangerous situation. Clark avoids conflict and literally runs from danger. Superman, on the other hand, rises to the challenge of danger. While Superman never initiates conflict, he is quick to respond. Because of his superior strength and speed, he is able to vanquish his opponents.

Perhaps this perspective is most evident in this question by some skeptics: If Superman was so powerful, why didn't he just join up and stop the war? Indeed, Siegel and Shuster did address this conflict by having Clark attempt to enlist. Unfortunately, during his eye test, he forgot and used another of his powers—his x-ray vision—and read the chart in the next exam room. Hence, Superman was relegated to the home front. Because of his failure to enlist, Superman became a symbol of home-front patriotism, encouraging citizens that doing their bit stateside was just as heroic as fighting on the frontlines (Weldon 2013). In this way, the interventionist position was justified as a reactive position rather than a proactive one.

Given the political climate at the time, these characters can be correlated to the major actors in the coming war. A common story line that illustrated this was Lois and Clark chasing a story that inevitably involved bad guys who would put Lois, and sometimes Clark, in peril. Clark would either avoid confrontation or prove ineffective in fighting back. Clark would disappear and Superman would show up to save the day. Superman usually does this by showing his superior strength and intellect. Lois praises Superman and wishes Clark could be more like the Man of Steel. That Clark and Superman were the same person is telling. After all, the U.S. policy of isolationism proved ineffective in stopping Hitler's march through Europe. Granted, that was the whole point of isolationist policy. However, when danger was lurking as a worldwide threat, isolationism avoided the conflict completely. Only with intervention could the threat be tamed.

The elements of the allegory begin with these characters. Clark Kent represented isolationists, who chose to avoid interfering in conflicts with which they were not directly involved. U.S. policy at the time of the publication of the first *Superman* was one of neutrality, even as major actors in the government (namely FDR) were laying the groundwork for the U.S. entrance into the war. Superman, conversely, understood that his superior strength and intelligence could be the only thing to prevent tragic outcomes in the dangerous situations in which he chose to engage.

Lois Lane, while independent and smart, often found herself in situations from which she could not extract herself without help. Lois Lane plays the part of Europe. It was becoming increasingly clear to FDR that Britain and its allies would not be able to defeat the Axis powers on their own. The Allies needed the help of a strong savior—the United States. Both Clark Kent and Superman express both affection and concern for Lois. However, their methods of expression and protection vary. Clark admonishes her to avoid dangerous situations, while Superman actively saves her when she is in danger. Likewise, isolationists in the United States, such as Charles Lindbergh, argued that a German-controlled Europe wouldn't be a disaster. Rather, European allies would be better off avoiding war with Germany. Alternatively, U.S. interventionists believed that it was in the U.S. interest to aid Europe to prevent a German takeover.

This allegorical interpretation is further supported with an analysis of specific story lines. While the majority of story lines dealt with the criminal element, occasionally the comic book dealt directly with war, sometimes a fictional conflict and at other times World War II specifically. Three separate storylines are examined here to further the argument of Superman as allegory.

Superman, Volume 1, #1 (June 1939)

Superman #1 introduced the world to Clark Kent, his alter ego, Superman, and the object of affection for both, Lois Lane. This first comic book contains a series of 11 interconnecting episodes that establish the characters, their strengths and weaknesses, and their essential characteristics. Amongst the various story lines that see Clark tackling stories to win the reporter job is Siegel and Shuster's first foray into establishing Clark and Superman's perspectives on armed combat.

The basic story line finds Clark hired as a reporter for the *Daily Star*. After saving a woman minutes from execution for the murder of Jack Kennedy, reports of the Man of Steel begin to surface, and Clark is put on the Superman beat. Gathering his courage he asks Lois Lane out, and they go to a nightclub. A thug breaks into their dance and challenges Clark to a fight over Lois saying, "Fight . . . you weak-livered pole-cat." Clark responds, "Really – I have no desire to do so" (Siegel, 1938, p. 12). Hence, even when antagonized, Clark remains out of the fray. When Lois is kidnapped by the thug, Superman comes to her rescue. Superman recognizes that his strength should be used to make sure that justice and right prevail. These early stances of both Clark Kent and Superman neatly reflect the perspectives of isolationists and interventionists, respectively.

The next day, Lois Lane gives Clark the cold shoulder, and he is assigned to cover the war in the fictional South American country of San Monté. Instead of going to South America, Clark goes to Washington, D.C., and uncovers a corrupt senator who is working with a munitions manufacturer to promote the war in San Monté. Lois also is then assigned to cover the war, giving the reporting a feminine touch. On board a steamer heading toward South America, Lois is set up as a spy, caught, and sentenced to execution the following morning. Superman is, of course, there in the nick of time and rescues Lois.

It can be noted that there are three scheduled executions of innocent people that Superman saves just in time in this first comic book. Since stories of the persecution of Jews in Europe—including the November 1938 Kristallnacht— had already started to surface, it is reasonable to suggest that Siegel and Shuster were advocating for the strong United States to come to the rescue of helpless European Jews before time ran out.

After rescuing Lois, Superman takes on a merciless aviator who is bombarding a camp and destroys the plane, saving the troops. He then takes the commanders of the opposing sides and demands that if they want to fight, they do it themselves. The commanders decide that they don't know why they're fighting and end the war. While this may seem like an antiwar stance (and it is), it can also be interpreted as an admonition against war for unreasonable reasons. This was 1938, after all. While the United States had avoided involvement in the European conflict, it continued to expand its economic interests in Latin America ("American Isolationism"). Consequently, it was deemed acceptable for the U.S. to intervene in South American affairs while maintaining distance from the European situation.

The broader point, however, is that Superman gets drawn into the situation and uses force to ensure that good prevails over evil. Alternatively, Clark stays in the background and avoids conflict, preferring to allow bullies and thugs to prevail at the peril of losing Lois's respect and interest. Hence, the United States was justified in participating in South American issues while avoiding Europe.

The comic book then turns to stories that concern a corrupt football team throwing a game so that a thug wins a bet. Superman intervenes to ensure that the game is played fairly. This sounds like an admonition that a stronger force needs to intervene to ensure the outcome is just.

In this first comic book, the parameters are set: Clark acts only out of self-interest, as does the United States. Superman, the strong United States, never initiates, only intervenes. Lois needs the protection of her stronger ally, as Europe and European Jews need the protection of the United States. The allegory is established.

Action Comics #22 (March 1940) and #23 (April 1940)

The #22 issue of *Action Comics*, created before the U.S. entrance into the war, is oddly prescient and clearly advocates for intervention in the war. The comic begins by explaining that the "armed battalions of *Toran* unexpectedly swoop down upon a lesser nation, *Galonia*" (Siegel and Shuster, 1998, p. 24). Here the comic book sets up the helpless-nation story. Clark continues his nonaggression stance, while Superman intervenes to save the day.

Clark Kent and Lois Lane are sent to cover the war as correspondents. Clark ponders on the steamer, "So once again the world is being flung into a terrible conflagration! How senseless!" (Siegel and Shuster, 1998, p. 25). On board the steamer is a well-known foreign actress, Lita Laverne. Clark interferes in an assassination attempt on Lita, and she befriends him, inviting him to a reception at her manor when they reach shore. Clark is turned away from learning any information at the foreign ministry, where Lita snubs him. So, Lois and Clark go to Lita's reception, and she is quite friendly to Clark and gets him alone. Here they have this exchange:

Lita: And now that we're alone—tell me all about yourself!
Clark: There's not much to say I—
Lita: Then tell me about the great nations. Do you think they are in sympathy with *Toran's* invasion of *Galonia*?
Clark: (" . . . now she's getting down to business! . . .")
Clark: The democracies are definitely opposed to aggressor nations. — Any more questions? (Siegel and Shuster, 1998, p. 28)

Lita then leaves to find someone else from whom to seek information. At the same time, the city is bombed. Clark, in response to the bombing, adheres to "his false attitude of cowardliness" (Siegel and Shuster, 1998, p. 29) and dives for cover. He quickly changes into his Superman costume and in a three-page battle eliminates the bombing planes. As he does so, he spies Lita entering the foreign ministry, and he overhears her talking with a military official. She states, "And so you see, if the neutral liner *Calcutta* was to be torpedoed by our enemy, the sympathy of the world would be on our side." The official responds, "I've already followed your suggestion in [*sic*] dispatched orders to submarine Y-263.—In fifteen minutes the *Calcutta* will be at the bottom of the ocean" (Siegel and Shuster, 1998, p. 34). Superman saves the liner and interrupts the Toranium War Council. He forces the officer to admit that he and Lolita had plotted to destroy the *Calcutta*, and justice is served. Thus, *Action Comics* #22 ends.

In this comic book the allegory is continued. The differences between Clark Kent and Superman and the elements of the allegory are highlighted here. While it is Clark that stops Lita from being assassinated, there are warnings for isolationists. Clark only interrupts the attempt; he does not engage in any retaliation. In fact, by stopping the assassination attempt, he helps the enemy, since Lita is a spy. This could be a warning that repealing the Neutrality Act would not be enough and could, in fact, aid the enemy by not fully engaging in the conflict.

Though Clark expresses dismay at the world being involved in all-out war, he equivocates when he suggests that "democracies are definitely opposed to aggressor nations." Consequently, much like some isolationists, Clark understands the dilemma of not intervening. Hence, Clark illustrates the idea that war is distasteful but in some situations necessary. The question was whether participation was necessary at that point.

That Lita and the military officer plot to engage a neutral country is interesting, since this was nearly two and a half years before the Japanese attack on Pearl Harbor. The idea that the United States could be specifically drawn into the war by an assault from an aggressor nation was not without precedent. There was a little-remembered attack on the U.S. gunboat the *Panay* on the Yangtze River in China on December 12, 1937. "So why did the Japanese attack? Spark [documentary director Nick Sparks] says the chaos in Nanking created an opportunity for renegade factions within the Japanese army who wanted the United States and China to 'get into an active conflict so that the Japanese could once and for all drive the United States out of China'" (Robbins, 2007). Consequently, this story line suggests that in terms of the conflict in Europe, to which Japan was sympathetic, engaging a neutral country was desirable.

In *Action Comics* #23, Superman stops the attack, implying that the United States should intervene before other nations are drawn into the war. The idea is furthered in the next episode in the comic book. In the next installment, Lois is rendered unconscious when a shell explodes near where she and Clark are walking. Clark carries her to safety, changes into Superman, and hurls the shells back at the bombers to destroy them. As he changes back into Clark, he states, "If there's anything I particularly despise, it's the destruction of helpless civilians" (Siegel and Shuster, 1998, p. 39). After Lois awakens they meet with a general who tells them that a truce will take place shortly. However, the truce isn't honored by Galonia, and the battle resumes. When confronted, the Galonian general says it was a mistake and certainly not on purpose. Clark suspects his treachery and, as Superman, follows him to a mountain.

Deep within the mountain, the general speaks with a talking slab of rock, later revealed as Luthor. When he leaves, Superman confronts the general, who confesses, "Momentarily a squadron of unidentified planes are to invade and bombard a nearby neutral country. Luthor's plan is to engulf the entire continent in bloody warfare" (Siegel and Shuster, 1998, p. 42). Before the general can answer Superman's question about who Luthor is, the face in the slab reappears and kills the general with a laser. Superman is able to withstand the laser, which then collapses the mountain. Superman escapes from the mountain and stops the bombardment. Surely, the slab's intent to conquer the entire continent echoes Hitler's plan to control all of Europe.

In an attempt to stop Clark from reporting on the story, Lois is kidnapped. Superman allows himself to be taken to rescue her. Luthor confronts Superman. When Superman asks him what kind of creature Luthor is, he responds, "Just an ordinary man – but with th' brain of a super-genius! With scientific miracles at my fingertips, I'm preparing to make myself supreme master of th' world. My plan? To send the nations of the earth at each other's throats, so that when they are sufficiently weakened, I can step in and assume charge!" (Siegel and Shuster, 1998, p. 47). This statement by Luthor could easily have been made by Adolf Hitler as he was committing experiments in the camps, and his goal was to take over Europe, perhaps the world.

After defeating Luthor's efforts to destroy him, Superman takes Luthor and Lois back to the city. Immediately he eliminates both the dirigible that was designed to destroy the city and, with it, Luthor. The two warring countries reach a truce. Clark returns to the *Daily Planet* with the scoop while a worker exclaims, "And he appears to be such a meek, shy person!" (Siegel and Shuster, 1998, p. 50).

The elements in this part of the story line certainly have allegorical dimensions related to the German aggression in Europe. Luthor is representative of Hitler and his plans for Europe. Initially, Hitler intended to invade Russia, with Japan attacking from the East and Germany from the West. However, when England would reach a peace agreement, Hitler was forced to reach a pact to take over Poland. Early in 1939 Hitler's plan to take over Poland forced England and France to declare war on Germany and thus to start World War II (Warlimont, 1991).

The fact that the comic book ends with a description of Clark as meek and shy could imply that though the United States had maintained an isolationist policy, the potential was there for the country to aid the European nations. Lois is used as an easily captured victim who must rely on Superman's help. Europe, too, was easily falling to Germany with Czechoslovakia, which was annexed, being the first domino to fall. The episodes that begin and end this story line further the creators' advocacy of intervention.

Superman, Volume 1, #8 (January/February 1941)

This Superman comic begins with Clark observing someone outside his window watching his home. Before he can, as Superman, confront the stalker, Frank Martin with the anti-espionage service shows up at his door. He tells Clark that a boat carrying the leader of a fifth-columnist movement is arriving, and he wants Clark to investigate. Clark agrees. After Martin leaves, Superman follows the stalker, who is now following Martin. It turns out the man is Martin's assistant Carlton, and Superman is relieved. He then flies to the waterfront to see what is happening with the boat.

He observes the sailors from the boat entering a warehouse, where the man in charge, Reibel, pays the men for distributing subversive material. They complain about the amount, but the man replies, "No complaints. On the day the United States is conquered you will receive rewards beyond your highest dreams!" (Siegel and Shuster, 1990, p. 228). Overhearing the plan, Superman vows to teach the sailors "respect for the country they're seeking to destroy!" (Siegel and Shuster, 1990, p. 228).

The sailors pledge to undermine the United States. Superman breaks up the meeting by throwing a huge box through the wall. He takes a list of all of the subversives from the leader, whereupon Reibel threatens to shoot Superman. However, Superman takes the gun and not only threatens to but fires it. But since the Man of Steel is faster than a speeding bullet, he stops the bullet from hitting the leader. Assuming Reibel and the sailors will be sufficiently scared into giving up their subversive ways, Superman as Clark arranges to turn over the list to Martin from the anti-espionage service. As Clark arrives at the office, he hears a shot. Carlton, Martin's assistant, has shot him. Clark confronts him, but Carlton tosses the gun at Clark just as the police arrive. The police search Clark, who pleads his innocence, and discover the list of subversives. Carlton explains that Martin was about to expose Clark and the other subversives, and the police arrest him.

Since Clark is Superman, he is able to escape by leaping in a flash onto a girder. He then goes to the warehouse, where the leader Reibel is leaving. Superman follows him as he boards a plane with other subversive leaders. The plane lands in a valley, where Superman proclaims from a mountaintop, "In the valley below, a scene that might well be laid in Europe . . ." (Siegel and Shuster, 1990, p. 232). Superman surmises that the plan is to attack from the rear while the military defends the coast against potential invasion. Reibel is reporting to his commander, Sagdorf. He discusses that they confronted a "super-strong man, a veritable one man army." Sagdorf doesn't believe him and orders him to make contact with Carlton. When the tent is empty, Superman begins to break into the safe, which holds the leader's files.

His attempt is interrupted by a guard and then more troopers, but he disposes of them all quickly. Superman then destroys a phalanx of planes and a hangar holding more. As he ponders how to destroy a munitions plant without killing citizens in a nearby neighborhood, Sagdorf approaches and orders one of his men to shoot Superman, who, of course, dodges the bullet. The bullet hits and destroys the munitions plant, with Superman the only survivor.

The only task left is to clear his name. To do this, he returns to the Federal Building and confronts Carlton. With gun in hand, Clark promises to make Carlton confess and takes him to the offices of the *Daily Planet*. At the Planet, Lois admits that she can't believe that Clark is a fifth columnist. Clark and Carlton arrive, and Clark threatens to shoot Carlton if he doesn't confess. With Clark counting down from three until he shoots, Carlton confesses, even as Lois advises that the confession won't hold up in court. Clark points out that the detail in his confession will convince the authorities. The episode ends when Lois asks, "Supposing Carlton hadn't confessed would you really have shot him?" Clark responds, "That's a little thought you can puzzle over for the rest of your days, my dear!" (Siegel and Shuster, 1990, p. 238).

This comic book appears nearly three years after the first Superman entry into the comics fold. The strategy of the creators had changed. While early allegories sought to explain the threat to the United States by showing how foreign conflicts impact the country, this comic book seeks to address the direct threat *within* the United States. Persico (2002) suggests that in 1939 President's Roosevelt's fears of "a secret and silent invasion by fifth columnists and saboteurs" allied him with J. Edgar Hoover in order to ferret out such espionage (p. 34). In May 1940 the FBI received "over twenty-nine hundred reports of suspected sabotage" (p. 65). The September 1, 1940, *New York Times* warned of the dangers of fifth columnists, stating that there existed "in this country a Nazi Fifth Column, one million strong, which is occupying strategic spots—factories, offices, educational institutions—working and waiting to break down our industrial machine as well as our psychological defenses" ("Fifth Columnists, 1940). Consequently, the threat within the borders of the United States was considered real. Siegel and Shuster used Superman to further warn of the dangers of fifth columnists.

There are several subtle hints that the fifth columnists are really about the potential for German fifth columnists in the United States. Early in the story line, when Superman breaks up the meeting of the newly paid sailors, the brown-suited leader gives a Hitler salute with his hand raised, palm facing out. There are no other overt references to Nazism, but this reference is clear. In addition, the name Sagdorf surely references a German surname. *Dorf* in German means "village" and is a common German surname suffix. Reibel is also a common German surname.

When Superman observes the valley with planes and troops, he suggests that this is a scene that could take place in Europe. Thus, he is warning that what happened in Germany's takeover in Europe could happen in the United States. Persico (2002) suggests that FDR felt that "the swift collapse of France, the Low Countries, and Norway could be explained only by fifth column subversives operating from within" (p. 65). With over a quarter million U.S. residents of German origin, the fifth-column threat was all too real.

If we accept the premise that Lois Lane represents Europe, it is no coincidence that she does not appear until the final page of the comic book. After all, fifth columnists were a domestic issue. The statement that Lois makes and the question she asks are telling, however. She can't believe that Clark would be a fifth columnist. Given that Clark represents the isolationist position, it makes sense. If the United States were to stay out of the war, fifth columnists would be antithetical to that goal. Further, when she questions whether Clark would have shot Carlton had he not confessed, it seems to imply that recognition of fifth columnists might push the isolationist position to a more active intervening position. Certainly, from Europe's perspective the threat of fifth columnists had played a role in their own conflict with Germany. Lois's absence in the comic reveals the domestic situation as Superman's creators saw it.

Implications

Superman during the prewar years clearly reflected Siegel and Shuster's perspective on the U.S. stance on isolation/intervention. Wright (2001) suggests, "Morally repelled by the Nazis, they [comic book artists] expressed their politics in their work" (p. 35). While many authors have considered the propaganda dimensions of *Superman* prior to and during World War II (see, for example, Murray, 2000; Wright 2001), the notion of Superman as allegory has been underanalyzed. This chapter seeks to rectify that. From this analysis several implications can be drawn.

Superman's authors were Jewish and, thus, had a vested interest in the U.S. involvement or lack thereof in Europe. There were two primary stances in the United States prior to World War II: isolationist or interventionist. The policy of isolation made sense for many, as it was a European war. Citizens needed to be aware of their own interests in the conflict before they could be convinced of the necessity of intervening in the war. Hence, *Superman* #1 establishes that the moral imperative is to aid weaker nations. In *Action Comics* #22 and *Action Comics* #23, not only is the threat of Hitler to the United States established, but the merits of thwarting him are proposed. Finally, in *Superman* #8, if the threat overseas isn't enough, the public needs to be aware also that there might be fifth columnists operating within the United States, making America vulnerable to foreign attack. Consequently, prewar Superman advocates for a shift in foreign policy. Other than these three comics, there were other episodes that advocated for American intervention. For example, "The Dukalia Spy Ring" examines how a naval officer was working for the nation of Dukalia, which wishes to take over the United States (Siegel and Shuster, 1997).

After Pearl Harbor and the U.S. entrance into World War II, the focus of the comic shifted. Rather than dealing with fictional foreign nations, Superman concentrated his energies on crime in the United States. On occasion, though, Superman dealt with the Nazi threat directly. For example, in *Superman* #25 he thwarts the efforts of Henkel, the leader of the 101% American committee (Siegel and Shuster, 2006). This comic is replete with Nazi symbolism (swastikas and chants of "Heil Hitler"). Siegel and Shuster used their comic book to advocate their stance prior to World War II, and after the U.S. entrance into the war, the comic shifted into the typical story line they would follow until the present day (good versus evil).

Given that the creators used Superman to demonstrate the necessity of U.S. entrance into the war, Siegel and Shuster found a convenient way to inform average citizens of the dangers of an isolationist policy. Consequently, the value of popular culture as a way to espouse political stances cannot be discounted. Certainly, there have been a number of analyses of popular culture artifacts and their influence on political opinion (see, for example, Conners, 2005; Street, 2004; Van Zoonen, 2005). World War II, however, found popular culture serving the interests of the government in getting citizens involved in the war effort. Since the creators had begun the comic with political overtones, that the comic would continue its war stance after Pearl Harbor was no surprise.

The notion of allegory is one that is often underutilized in academic scholarship. As the early Superman comics illustrate, however, it is a useful way to espouse a political view without being overt. Siegel and Shuster clearly had a vested interest in the U.S. involvement in Europe. Much has been written about the Jewish influence in early comic books (see, for example, Fingeroth, 2007; Weinstein, 2009; Witek, 1989). These analyses, however, focus more on the Jewish culture and its influence than on the Jewish perspective on what U.S. participation in the war would involve. As a result, looking at a specific comic book and the literal and figurative interpretations of Superman reveals a more directed perspective on U.S. participation in the war.

Finally, the fact that a comic book could offer direction toward U.S. foreign policy is itself interesting. That *Superman* was popular was undeniable. If one takes into account the allegorical dimensions of the comic, Siegel and Shuster were at the beginning of a trend that exists to the current day: comics are used as a way to express their creators' take on the political landscape (see, for example, Esren, 2012; Brantner and Lobinger, 2014). Comics are more than just interesting children's stories. They are pulses for the national political culture.

Conclusion

Superman was more than just a character in a hero myth. He was a way for his creators, Siegel and Shuster, to express their political desires. Indeed, the audiences of *Superman*, if perceptive enough, would understand that there was a policy agenda underneath the tales of heroic rescue. Superman and Clark Kent operated as two sides of the American coin, isolationist and interventionist. In the late 1930s, it would be easy for citizens to opt out of participation in the looming world war. However, *Superman* was a harbinger of the dangers of sticking the collective consciousness in the sand. The comic warned of the potential for the calamity that might strike should the United States maintain its isolationist position. As a result, Superman became not just a hero for the ages, but the perfect dichotomy of American policy prior to World War II.

Notes

1. DC Comics, the parent company of the Superman franchise, ran two simultaneous series of Superman comic books, *Superman* and *Action Comics*. *Superman* involved a series of episodes that were often different story lines within the same comic book. *Action Comics* published a single storyline within one book. Hence, *Action Comics #22 and #23* were published before *Superman #8*.

References

American Isolationism in the 1930s - 1937–1945 - Milestones - Office of the Historian. (n.d.). Retrieved from http://history.state.gov/milestones/1937-1945/american-isolationism

Blower, B. L. (2014). From isolationism to neutrality: A new framework for understanding American political culture, 1919–1941. *Diplomatic History, 38*(2), 345-376.

Brantner, C., & Lobinger, K. (2014). Campaign comics: The use of comic books for strategic political communication. *International Journal of Communication, 8*, 27.

Brod, H. (2012). *Superman is Jewish?: How comic book superheroes came to serve truth, justice, and the Jewish-American way.* New York, NY: Free Press.

Coffey, M. (2014). "She is waiting": Political allegory and the specter of secession in Chimamanda Ngozi Adichie's *Half of a Yellow Sun. Research in African Literatures, 45*(2), 63-85.

Conners, J. L. (2005). Visual representations of the 2004 presidential campaign political cartoons and popular culture references. *American Behavioral Scientist, 49*(3), 479-487.

Dittmer, J. (2007). "America is safe while its boys and girls believe in its creeds!": Captain America and American identity prior to World War 2. *Environment and Planning D, 25*(3), 401.

Estren, M. (2012). *A history of underground comics.* Berkeley, CA: Ronin.

Fifth columnists active in America. (1940, September 1). *New York Times (1923-Current File)* Retrieved from http://search.proquest.com/docview/105337465?accountid=13013

Fingeroth, D. (2007). *Disguised as Clark Kent: Jews, comics, and the creation of the superhero.* New York, NY: Bloomsbury Academic.

Hantke, S. (2012). Exit strategies: Narrative closure and political allegory in *Lost* and *Battlestar Galactica. Zeitschrift für Anglistik und Amerikanistik, 60*(4), 375-390.

Jones, G. (2004). *Men of tomorrow: Geeks, gangsters, and the birth of the comic book.* New York, NY: Basic Books.

Knapp, T. (1996, Spring). Popular political culture: Rocky and Bullwinkle and the culture of the Cold War. *Journal of the Northwest Communication Association, 24*, 1–10.

Littlefield, H. M. (1964). *The Wizard of Oz*: Parable on populism. *American Quarterly, 16*, 47–58.

Murray, C. (2000). *Popaganda: Superhero comics and propaganda in World War Two.* In H. C. Christiansen (Ed.). (2000). Comics & culture: Analytical and theoretical approaches to comics. Copenhagen, Denmark: Museum Tusculanum Press.

Olson, L. (2013). *Those angry days: Roosevelt, Lindbergh, and America's fight over World War II, 1939–1941.* New York, NY: Random House.

Persico, J. E. (2002). *Roosevelt's secret war: FDR and World War II espionage.* New York: Random House.

Ricca, B. (2013). *Super Boys: The Amazing Adventures of Jerry Siegel and Joe Shuster---the Creators of Superman.* New York, NY: Macmillan.

Robbins, T. (2007, December 13). A Japanese attack before Pearl Harbor. Retrieved from http://www.npr.org/templates/story/story.php?storyId=17110447

Siegel, J. (1938, Summer). *Superman: The complete stories of the daring exploits of the one and only Superman.* (No. 1). New York, NY: Detective Comics.

Siegel, J., & Shuster, J. (1990). *Superman: Archives (Vol. 2).* New York: DC Comics.

Siegel, J., & Shuster, J. (1997). *Superman: Archives (Vol. 3).* New York: DC Comics.

Siegel, J., & Shuster, J. (2006). *Superman: Archives (Vol. 7)*. New York: DC Comics.

Siegel, J., & J. Shuster (1998). *Superman: The* Action Comics *archives (Vol. 2)*. New York, NY: DC Comics.

Street, J. (2004). Celebrity politicians: Popular culture and political representation. *The British Journal of Politics & International Relations, 6*(4), 435–452.

Thomas, R. (1989). *The ruby slippers of Oz*. Los Angeles, CA: Tale Weaver.

Tye, L. (2012). *Superman: The high-flying history of America's most enduring hero*. New York, NY: Random House.

Van Dyke, C. (1985). *The fiction of truth: Structures of meaning in narrative and dramatic allegory*. Ithaca, NY: Cornell University Press.

Van Zoonen, L. (2005). *Entertaining the citizen: When politics and popular culture converge*. Lanham, MD: Rowman & Littlefield.

Weldon, G. (2013). *Superman: The unauthorized biography*. New York, NY: John Wiley & Sons.

Warlimont, W. (1991). *Inside Hitler's headquarters, 1939–1945*. (Trans. R. H. Barry). Novato, CA: Presidio Press, 1991.

Weinstein, S. (2009). *Up, up, and oy vey: How Jewish history, culture, and values shaped the comic book superhero*. Fort Lee, NJ: Barricade Books.

Witek, J. (1989). *Comic books as history: The narrative art of Jack Jackson, Art Spiegelman, and Harvey Pekar*. Jackson: University Press of Mississippi.

Wright B. (2001). *Comic book nation: The transformation of youth culture in America*. Baltimore, MD: Johns Hopkins University Press.

★★ 7 ★★

Racial Stereotypes and War Propaganda in *Captain America*

Deborah Clark Vance

Four German soldiers fire at Captain America, who deflects a bullet with his shield as he socks Adolf Hitler in the jaw. Hitler appears to be crying out in pain, his mouth wide open, and two of the soldiers' mouths are open as they fire at Captain America, whose face depicts strength and determination. A large television screen in the background shows a soldier blowing up a U.S. munitions factory; a map of the United States is spread open on the floor, and swastikas hang on the walls. Bucky, the young sidekick, appears in an inset, saluting and smiling broadly. These images adorn the cover of the first issue of *Captain America*, which appeared in March 1941, a year before the United States declared war on Germany.

The symbols and story structures in *Captain America* can best be understood within the context of previous propaganda campaigns. By the time the comic book hit the stands, much of its content appeared as cultural truth. Because symbols circulating through cultures help to define and perpetuate them (Barthes, 1982; Blumer, 1969; Burke, 1989; Eco, 1976; Fiske, 2011), such symbol systems—which exist even in comic books—can provide excellent insights into culture (Burke, 1989).

Captain America appeared in a culture that for several decades had been shaping a modern patriotic American identity by perpetuating a system of symbols and codes that originated in propaganda messages. For example, racial stereotypes in the comic emerge from those that were widely circulating a few years earlier, during WWI. These stereotypes in turn had themselves been popularized during an earlier Americanization campaign, launched in 1912 and carried on during the teens by industrialists (who later received support from the government). The racial propaganda originating in the Americanization program nurtured war fervor (Carey, 1997). Thus, in two campaigns, one to Americanize waves of immigrants and the other to mobilize a reluctant population to enter WWI, propagandistic images had worked together in a total environment so that wherever one looked the message was reinforced. By the 1940s these sorts of images had become entrenched in American culture.

Because definitions of propaganda stretch its boundaries to encompass almost all forms of persuasion—after all, every instance of communication is biased in favor of the beliefs and values of a particular group of people (Allen, 2005)—it makes sense to narrow the definition. This chapter draws its definition from Stanley B. Cunningham (2002), viewing *propaganda* as messages that manipulate without one's knowledge or consent. Comic books are, in this respect, a rich source of propaganda messages. Whereas readers are aware when viewing commercial advertisements that someone behind the message wants them to buy something, those readers most likely perceive comic books as innocuous and remain unaware of the propagandistic elements in stories about superheroes fighting evil enemies.

This chapter draws upon the theory of social semiotics to analyze the symbols in the inaugural issue of *Captain America* and interpret what they reveal about the American worldview of 1941. Social semiotics isolates important signs and the system in which they appear, and then looks to the worldview encoded within this system to help understand the culture in which it exists. Dominant culture has power over the way events, history, and policy are broadly interpreted (Fiske, 1989). Those in a dominant culture circulate stories that affirm their belief in themselves and their place in the world, signaling to the out-group its position as well. Such stories—or myths—are recognized by in-group members not as propaganda but as both truthful and natural (Barthes, 1982; Fiske, 1989). Being true does not mean something must exist in reality. By the same token, unreal does not mean something is untrue (Levi-Strauss, 1978), and indeed sometimes a belief can overpower physical evidence. So a comic book character can enshrine dominant U.S. values that ring true for its readers. Whereas propaganda is generally performed without the awareness of its target audience and for reasons that may actually go against their beliefs and desires, its purpose may not be truth but cooperation with its goals, one of which includes altering the reality of its target (Cunningham, 2002).

In order to scrutinize the symbols in *Captain America*, this chapter proceeds through several sections. First it establishes the theoretical connections between culture and myth; then it locates important roots of *Captain America's* ideology in two propaganda movements that arose during the early twentieth century to Americanize immigrants and to convince the public to enter WWI. The analysis then shifts to *Captain America's* first issue itself, establishing that symbols used in that comic in 1941 are rooted in the earlier propaganda campaigns that were designed to encourage immigrants to assimilate as "true" Americans, which had become part of the country's worldview.

Culture and Myth

Because people particularly let down their guard when being entertained, outwardly neutral channels of public communication such as news and entertainment serve as prime vehicles for propaganda (Sproule, 1994). In this way cultural myths—such as that of America's mission to spread democracy around the world—appear in stories and can surreptitiously manipulate those who do not understand their origin or their connection to any particular source. Social and aesthetic phenomena, like the symbols that exist in art and media, do not have inherent meaning but exist in larger systems where each derives meaning from its relationship to others. Moreover, such symbolic messages produce meaning as readers interact with them (Fiske, 1989). Beliefs about a nation's meaning are carried in symbols that circulate through cultural institutions—like family, law, education, and media—which cultural members learn, internalize, and solidify into belief systems, or ideologies. Myths and stories are typical vehicles for ideologies and are used by cultures to explain various aspects of their reality (Barthes, 1982). In fact, such myths and stories have multiple purposes: they serve to inform a culture's sense of itself, to determine its position in the world, and to help its members establish order (Peterson & Horton, 1995); they justify history by making it seem natural, and they make contingent events seem eternal (Barthes, 1982); and they affirm cultural experience, orient ways of life, provide continuity, model behavior, and support and validate the social order. Members of a culture must learn the myths that explain their culture because, in part, those myths embody metaphors that inform the culture's sense of itself, determine its position in the world, justify its history, and help create order among its members (Peterson & Horton, 1995). Myths thus contain values, beliefs, and attitudes that community members generally share, but they also have enough imprecision to allow for individual interpretations (Frentz & Rushing, 1993). Insofar as audiences accept myths as literally true, they also accept the belief system that supports the myths (Burke, 1989).

Just as meaning exists in our minds and is not imposed on us from without, so does culture itself, which can be considered a universe of shared meaning. Symbols contain no absolute, independent meaning but exist in relatively closed cultural systems, relating to and relying on each other for meaning. They are meaningful in context, not in isolation, and work together in systems to form codes that help simplify one's understanding of phenomena (Chandler, 2002). Viewers create meaning as they interact with texts and make connections the text cannot make for them (Barthes, 1982).

Walter Lippmann (1922) coined the term *stereotype* to explain how individuals form opinions based on unconscious images imposed by culture. He argued that most cultural knowledge is mediated, as it comes from secondhand information (such as stories, other people, and news) that people internalize and take for granted. Texts organize symbols according to codes that readers internalize as those codes slip beneath conscious awareness (Chandler, 2002). Lippmann recognized that people respond as strongly to these stereotypes as to actual phenomena. When

> the herd must think for itself, it does so by means of clichés, pat words or images which stand for a whole group of ideas or experiences. . . . By playing upon an old cliché, or manipulating a new one, the propagandist can sometimes swing a whole mass of group emotions. (cited in Bernays, 1928/2000, p. 74)

As stereotypes are shorthand codes, so myths are coded stories containing cultural meanings. Both are symbolic structures that carry cultural ideologies (Barthes, 1982). Myth supports ideological social beliefs (Fiske, 2011). Visual symbols take root after having been implanted by an authoritative source (Lippmann, 1922) and are especially powerful because they can communicate myth economically.

Media rely on cultural myths because such myths communicate meaning that audiences understand and respond to. As community members learn the myths that explain their culture, the extent to which they absorb the underlying ideology becomes apparent in how they describe their experiences through their own discourse (Black, 1970). When myths encourage communal beliefs that do not stand up to scrutiny, they are a type of propaganda (Cunningham, 2002). Comic books carry myths efficiently in their images and narratives. The messages carried by comic book images predominate over and anchor the meaning of the words. The words, in their turn, carry messages via character dialogue, internal monologue, and narration (Costello, 2009).

For its part, *Captain America* can be considered propagandistic when readers unquestioningly consume its myths, thereby assenting to the ideologies contained in them. Comic drawings are iconic images representing character types (Chandler, 2002). Indeed, the comic book superhero genre itself signals a particular meaning: drawings of recognizable stereotypes, characters that embody clear virtue and vice, and a story with a clear moral depict a world where a self-sacrificing individual triumphs over evildoers. In the case of Captain America, these sorts of mythic appeals were rooted in the prior discourse of immigration and WWI.

Immigrants and Race

Theories of racial hierarchy confounded America's attitudes toward immigrants in the early twentieth century. Enormous social changes had occurred with the vast influx of immigrants into the United States during 1890–1910. The eugenics movement (which ultimately influenced Hitler's racial attitudes) was also active in the United States during the interwar period (Crook, 2007). The belief in the notion that people were divided into racial categories led to the stratification of immigrants into inferior races. One's head shape (the so-called cephalic index) was used to identify racial types. Imperfect English could indicate racial inferiority (Jirousek, 2008). The idea of racial hierarchy had become so normalized in the teens that even immigrants referred to themselves through the language of this framework. Eugenicist Charles Davenport's 1911 book warns that values among Southern European immigrants, "with their sense of individualism and ideas of gain," contrast sharply with the early English and later Scandinavians, "with their ideals of community life in the open country, advancement by the sweat of the brow and the uprearing of families in the fear of God and the love of country" (cited in Jirousek, 2008, p. 66). Some expressed fear that the "pioneer breed" of Anglo-Saxon Americans would be overcome by immigrants (Jirousek, 2008, p. 61).

By the turn of the twentieth century, the British stereotyped Germans as "vulgar, arrogant, boorish, warlike, with slavish obedience to authority and an unswerving veneration of all things military" (Storer, 2009, p. 40). Such negative stereotypes lasted throughout the teens and twenties (and can even be found today). In the stories that emerged from these stereotypes, Germans became "dangerous warmongers, savage and aggressive, arrogant and selfish, with no sense of the value of human life, ungentlemanly in the pursuit of war and without mercy towards their defeated enemy" (Storer, 2009, p. 40). When the British were actively propagandizing the American elite before WWI, they included atrocity stories that carried such stereotypes. Lippmann (1922) suggests that presenting people with stereotypes that arouse their prejudices is an effective way to manipulate them. Emotional appeals and simplistic caricatures of the enemy influenced many Americans in this period by arousing fears connected to widely circulating stereotypes.

Race theories undoubtedly influenced U.S. industrial leaders, who sought to squelch radicalism among immigrant workers from countries with socialistic forms of government. Similarly, the federal government worried about the national security problems in worker unrest as the Industrial Workers of the World (IWW) incited immigrants to revolution (Carey, 1997). A pivotal moment unfolded in 1912 at a textile mill in Lawrence, Massachusetts, where 70% to 90% of the employees were foreign-born. After police killed a striker, a group of women and children were fleeing for refuge with out-of-town relatives when police assailed them, beating a pregnant woman unconscious and killing her fetus. The resulting negative publicity led business and industry leaders to implement a campaign to "reeducate" the foreign-born so they could learn the beliefs and values of America that the industrialists shared. Within two years the Americanization campaign was formalized as the Committee for Immigrants in America. The campaign, along with the outbreak of the ensuing 1915 European war, stimulated nationalist feelings.

Although some scholars recognize the WWI period as being the first time governments created propaganda campaigns across all media (Miller, 2004), modern propaganda techniques were tested during the Americanization movement that surfaced in 1912 and continued through 1919 (Carey, 1997). For example, the Committee for Immigrants in America envisioned July 4 as National Americanization Day, a time to join in an expression of unity and faith in America, and planned celebrations throughout the country as a national way to showcase the friendly aims of the government rather than repression, discrimination, and injustices (Hartmann, 1948). To carry through its plans, the committee partnered with such federal departments as Labor and Education, and its goals found their way into government policies. By 1917 the Americanization movement involved a strong foundation of private, municipal, state, and federal support. The wealthy industrialists behind the Americanization campaign channeled their propaganda through business owners, schools, and civic groups to connect with employers of immigrant labor, attempting to convince them that they could pacify the workforce by inducing them to adopt an American identity and embrace capitalist ideology (Hartmann, 1948). Those in positions of power sought ways to assimilate immigrants—as long as they learned proper ways of being American. As the U.S. entry into WWI neared, Americanizing the immigrants soon became a national crusade. For example, former president Theodore Roosevelt and current president Wilson disdained the use of the hyphen (e.g., German-American) to put the motherland ahead of America, an act they considered anti-American (Hartmann, 1948).

From WWI Propaganda to WWII

As Edward Bernays describes it, an invisible government molds the minds of society (cited in Miller, 2004). Propaganda in the United States was initiated by British and German operatives, but it was the British who targeted the ruling elite—who themselves grew to believe that public opinion needed management (Taylor, 1999). To accomplish such management, the Committee for Public Information (CPI) was formed in April 1917 as soon as the United States declared war on Germany. This agency flooded the channels of communication with manipulative messages designed to stir up fear and loyalty as well as to provoke hatred of Germany and of the Germans themselves. By this time, the propaganda efforts of Americanization had been incorporated into various federal agencies. Thus, although a high percentage of people of German descent had immigrated to the United States, anti-German sentiment grew among those with business connections in Europe and among the East Coast upper class (Delwiche, 1994). The two intertwined propaganda campaigns of war preparedness and Americanization led 14 states to target German Americans as convenient scapegoats and to ban the speaking of German in public schools. Further, in New Mexico, a mob accused an immigrant miner of supporting Germany and forced him to kneel before them, kiss the flag, and shout, "To hell with the Kaiser." And in Illinois, a group of zealous patriots accused a German coal miner of hoarding explosives and lynched him; explosives were never found (Delwiche, 1994).

Although getting support for the war from a reluctant populace was its purported goal, the CPI did so by selling the idea of democracy, not war (Miller, 2004), just as selling democracy had been the approach of the Americanizers. Indeed, George Creel (1920) proclaimed that WWI was the first war fought for the idea of democracy rather than for more concrete, less ideological, reasons.

In their work to establish an environment that encompassed all corners of society, the CPI sent pro-war materials into the population. According to Creel (1920), many of its divisions included News Media, Syndicated Features (that solicited novelists, essayists and short story writers), a Division of Civic and Educational Cooperation (that published pamphlets written by academics), and the Division of Pictorial Publicity and the Division of Advertising (both of which used the talents of artists and illustrators).

Some of the most effective propaganda media were posters, with their powerful patriotic symbols designed to arouse emotional reactions in viewers (Lippmann, 1922). Uncle Sam, the Statue of Liberty, the heroic figure of Columbia, the bald eagle, the American flag, stars and stripes, and the colors red white and blue had been used by the Americanizers in typical July Fourth celebrations. Many WWI posters showed women and children as vulnerable and weak, and the soldier as heroic, brave, and strong. The German enemy—the so-called Hun—was depicted as dark, sinister, animal-like and evil and was accompanied by such slogans as "Bleeding Belgium," "The Criminal Kaiser," and "Make the World Safe for Democracy." A typical poster portrayed an aggressive, bayonet-wielding German soldier above the caption "Beat back the Hun with Liberty Bonds" as emotions of hate and fear were redirected toward giving money to the war effort (Delwiche, 1994, p. 4).

Perhaps an even more effective strategy for demonizing Germans and arousing hate was circulating atrocity stories, a method used successfully for centuries. The stereotype of the enemy as demonic constituted a typical approach. As Harold Lasswell (1927/1971) said, "so great are the psychological resistances to war in modern nations that every war must appear to be a war of defense against a menacing, murderous aggressor. There must be no ambiguity about who the public is to hate" (p. 47). Bernays (1928), who directed CPI's efforts in Latin America, later revealed that the CPI used atrocity stories—some of them retreads from previous wars—to inflame sentiments against Germany.

Thus, the CPI had engineered events to change perceptions, using mass psychology to manipulate people (Bernays, 1928/2005). The desired effect was "universal and continuous; and in its sum total it is regimenting the public mind every bit as much as an army regiments the bodies of its soldiers" in order to shape events to influence the public (Bernays, 1928/2005, p. 52). Moreover, by creating an environment where a single message came from multiple channels, the CPI was able to "control and regiment the masses according to our will without their knowing about it" (Bernays, 1928/2005, p. 38). After the War, the Director of the CPI's Foreign Division argued that

> the history of propaganda in the war would scarcely be worthy of consideration here, but for one fact—it did not stop with the armistice. No indeed! The methods invented and tried out in the war were too valuable for the uses of governments, factions, and special interests. (Irwin, 1919)

The formal war propaganda ended when the CPI was disbanded, but not until after the organization propagandized against Bolshevism in 1919, giving Americanizers another push (Hartmann, 1948). Afterward, CPI propagandists went to work for private industry to engineer consumer culture; the extent to which this occurred has yet to be fully scrutinized. Moreover, sociologists, social workers and teachers continued the Americanization process. Although they used such terms as *American way of life, good patriotic American, old-fashioned American values,* and *civic loyalty,* they never actually defined them for the immigrants (Hartmann, 1948).[1]

Besides the massive campaign of business propaganda at the end of WWI, the National Association of Manufacturers launched another propaganda campaign from 1934 to 1939 "to capture American minds for business" (Hartmann, 1948, p. 138). In the same manner used in WWI by the CPI, WWII also quickly became a total war environment (Wilt, 2011). When being confirmed by multiple interrelated messages, ideas based in propaganda are hard to dispel.

Given the breadth and depth of propaganda efforts by business and government during the teens and 1920s, and again by businesses in the 1920s and 1930s, it is unlikely that U.S. culture emerged unaffected. The nationalistic values, beliefs, and practices begun in the teens and carried forward into the war had become part of the American cultural fabric, whose strong threads include how July 4 is observed with flag waving, how wars are fought for democracy, and how public discourse contains antisocialist and anticommunist sentiments in discussions about the economy. A stepping-stone along the way was WWII, when the relatively new comic book medium portrayed these nationalist ideas and stereotypes from earlier decades.

Many comic book writers volunteered for the private War Writers Board (WWB), which was established to promote government policy and discourage profiteering (Scott, 2007). The WWB soon joined forces with the Office of War Information, whose purpose was to coordinate media for the war effort by giving details of the war and preventing images that might demoralize people. Martin Goodman, publisher of *Captain America*, said he started the comic to express his feelings about "what the United States stood for" (C. Goodman, cited in "Martin Goodman," 1982, para. 4). That America stands for freedom and democracy had become a cultural truth with its roots in earlier propaganda campaigns.

Social Semiotic Analysis of *Captain America*'s Inaugural Issue

Hero and villain characters were stereotyped, with villains caricatured as subhuman and heroes as virtuous (Costello, 2009). A superhero has a dual identity. When dressed in his or her costume, the character's identity is fixed as a hero (Costello, 2009). Although The Shield had been the first truly patriotic character, Captain America is the character most associated with patriotism, not to mention the most famous and enduring superhero (Scott, 2007). Introduced in 1941, a year after The Shield, Captain America fought "the enemies of the United States directly, both at home and abroad" (Scott, 2007, p. 334) and upheld American ideals. According to one of its writers, Captain America could be considered the "living symbol of the American dream (White, 2014, p. 144). The work of comic book superheroes was already understood by the time *Captain America* appeared. In the character's inaugural issue, U.S. military leaders joke about how to fight sabotage: "What would you suggest, gentlemen? A character out of the comic books? Perhaps the Human Torch in the army would solve our problem" (Simon & Kirby, 1941/2011, p. 2). *Captain America*'s inaugural issue is concerned with spies engaging in sabotage within the United States, specifically against the defense industry: Captain America encounters German spies seeking to disrupt war production or threatening to invade the United States and establish a dictatorship. In the first story, amid a wave of sabotage that ravages the country, army officers confess to President Roosevelt that spies have infiltrated their ranks. The president informs them of a secret weapon that's being developed. The reader is taken to a curio shop that serves as a front for a secret laboratory, where Professor Reinstein has developed a serum that will transform average men into an army of super-agents. He inoculates his first volunteer, frail Steve Rogers, whose physical and mental abilities quickly become transformed, and Reinstein christens him Captain America. But suddenly a spy from Hitler's Gestapo shouts, "Death to the dogs of democracy!" as he shoots and kills Professor Reinstein and destroys the serum.

The next story features a phony magic act performed by Sando von Krantz and his runty assistant, Omar, who pretend to foresee future events that are actually acts of sabotage planned by the Gestapo that they already know about. Captain America tracks down von Krantz backstage and finds that his Nazi assistants have already captured a beautiful federal agent named Betty Ross, who says she has been investigating the spy ring. When Captain America confronts von Krantz, he reveals that he works for the "Phewrer" and plans "a chain of disasters that will destroy the morale" of the United States (Simon & Kirby, 1941/2011, p. 14).

"Captain America and the Soldiers' Soup" a two-page narrative spread with only two illustrations, is about saboteurs trying to poison army food. The characters' dialogue is written in dialect, which emphasizes the sense of their otherness. In the next story in the issue, Rathcone, a creepy killer with aspirations of becoming the dictator of the United States, has constructed a giant chessboard on which he positions top military leaders, as well as Captain America and Bucky. He then systematically targets and kills the officers before the duo discover his plot.

The last story is the first to have a title, and it introduces a character who will plague Captain America in future issues. "Captain America and the Riddle of the Red Skull" features Mister Maxon of Maxon Aircraft Corporation, who sells aircraft to the military, but of course the planes are rigged to crash. Maxon's alter ego wears a terrifying red skull mask as he confronts his victims—army officers—whom he injects with poison.

By tightly controlling the way a reader interprets events, mon
can be considered propaganda, because they present themselves a;
alternative interpretations (Bakhtin, 1982). As a monologic text, th
of *Captain America* provides no alternative interpretations but steer;
to reach the conclusions desired by the author. It provides little room for a
reader to identify with the villains or to oppose the heroes. Stereotyping can
be construed as a way to steer the reader's perceptions. Ethnic stereotyping was
common in superhero comics (Costello, 2009). This contrasts with a dialogic
text that allows the reader to reach conclusions in any number of ways (Bakhtin,
1982). In this respect, character types and visual images can be scrutinized to
identify textual meanings that may lie outside an author's intent. To locate the
often unintended, underlying meanings in a text, a paradigmatic analysis looks
for polar oppositions (Berger, 2012). Sometimes a sign also derives meaning
from what other signs in the sign system are *not* (Gaines, 2008). As Barthes
contends, codes "fabricate reality in accord with a bourgeois view of the world
and covertly propagate bourgeois values as self-evident" (Chandler, 2002, p.
164). Closely examining the symbols in a text can help a reader uncover the
underlying ideology that can help in understanding a culture's motives and
worldview. Semiotic analysis involves identifying sequences (syntagms) and
types of characteristics (paradigms). The notion of syntagms and paradigms is
confounded when dealing with images (Lemke, 2009). Paradigms often contain
binary oppositions that privilege one side and marginalize the other. By identifying the codes, the analyst can describe the worldview of the text. In this way
a reader can locate and expose codes that serve the purposes of a ruling elite
(Posner, 2011, p. 19). In order to identify the worldview in the inaugural issue of
Captain America, I examined the images and character roles and located the
following polarities in the text.

Beautiful/Ugly

From one's first glance at the cover, it's clear that German and American faces
look different. German faces appear as grimacing and grotesque, with scowling,
squinty, sunken eyes; uneven pointy teeth in their open mouths; underbites and
thick lips; grasping claw-like hands with long fingernails; unkempt hair, hair
brushed upward, or bald heads. They seem like creatures akin to gargoyles. The
first killing in this issue happens as a gnarled bony hand wields the gun that
shoots Dr. Reinstein. Rathcone's sharp pointy teeth and nails, the tight-fitting
glasses that outline his eyes like a raccoon's, and an upturned, piglike nose all
make him look like a subhuman being, ugly and dark. Omar is a bald-headed

dwarf with a monkeylike face. The thugs who grab Bucky are overweight, with thick lips. Contrasting the Germans, Bucky and Captain America are light-haired and attractive, with strong, even features. They move with grace and skill as their uniforms emphasize their strong muscles.

Bravery/Cowardice

Those who fight Captain America and Bucky behave disgracefully. One of the spies whom Captain America confronts tries to run away from him, "half crazed with fear and pain" (Simon & Kirby, 1941/2011, p. 7). On the other hand, the teenage Bucky risks his own well-being when he grabs a lit bomb from Von Krantz's hand and throws it out the window. The German spies lurk in dark, dingy underground hideouts that Captain America and Bucky gallantly penetrate. When Bucky approaches a shabby building and a door slams in his face, he attributes it to the wind. When he heads down a dark stairway, he says to himself, "In moving pictures, these stairways always lead to something exciting!" (Simon & Kirby, 1941/2011, p. 25).

Fair/Crooked

Rather than face his enemies fair and square, Maxon surprises his victims with his red-skull disguise, catching them off guard and injecting them with poison. He treats his assistants meanly, ordering them to rob a bank or he'll kill them. His henchmen themselves don't hide their bloodthirstiness: "I vanted to twist his young neck," says the Strangler (Simon & Kirby, 1941/2011, p. 25). Having lured Bucky into his lair, Rathcone sneaks up and trips him with his cane, rather than confronting him squarely. However, Captain America relies on his strength, not stealth or deceit. Even his enemies admire his skill. A spy observes his speed and says, "Ach! Dot yank iss loaded mit dynamite" (Simon & Kirby, 1941/2011, p. 31.)

Humor/Darkness

One of the remarkable characteristics of the Captain and Bucky is their sense of humor when facing dire circumstances. Having discovered von Krantz and Omar's hideout, Captain America says, "Well, well, if I haven't stumbled into a skunk's nest (Simon & Kirby, 1941/2011, p. 14). When trying to track down Rathcone, Bucky is trapped in a corner and jokes, "My kingdom for a beebee gun (Simon & Kirby, 1941/2011, p. 21). Punching one of Rathcone's henchmen, Captain America says, "Here's a medal you'll have a hard time pawning."

(Simon & Kirby, 1941/2011, p. 21). To get a Nazi to talk, Captain America quips, "Isn't that just too bad? This calls for a tightening of the windpipe" (Simon & Kirby, 1941/2011, p. 22). To the hidden microphone in the ceiling Captain America says, "If I'd know we had an audience, I might've sung a few numbers" (Simon & Kirby, 1941/2011, p. 30). Further, as he knocks a dagger out of a Nazi's hands, he says, "Drop that penknife" (Simon & Kirby, 1941/2011, p. 31), and, "Didn't think that love tap would stop me, did you?" (Simon & Kirby, 1941/2011, p. 32). Captain America and Bucky engage in an easy repartee: "So you disobeyed my order, eh? You little rascal," to which Bucky, referring to the den of spies, replies, "Yeah, but lookit the nice party I crashed" (Simon & Kirby, 1941/2011, p. 39). Against this humor, the Germans are no match. Their speech only describes their desires for domination. Their relationships are hard and uncaring.

Legal/Illegal

Captain America does his job and takes it seriously, following the rules. He is "the nemesis of spies and crooks" (Simon & Kirby, 1941/2011, p. 20), who fights within the system, and with the aid of the U.S. military. The Germans, though, break all rules. Red Skull and Rathcone are psychopathic serial killers. Van Krantz attempts a suicide bombing (Simon & Kirby, 1941/2011, p. 15).

Protection/Treachery

The U.S. government researches in secrecy for the good of the country, careful lest the spies discover their secret intelligence. Captain America and Bucky hide their true nature and also work in order to protect their country and fellow citizens. On the other hand, German saboteurs hide in the upper ranks of the military, allowing them to penetrate into the secrecy of the serum experiment. Their stealth involves slinking and hiding in secrecy to destroy the United States.

Sacrifice/Selfishness

Captain America and Bucky are soldiers who selflessly risk themselves for the safety of the country. Captain America uses his superpowers for the benefit of society. On the other hand, Rathcone aspires to be dictator, Maxon wants to attain the position of minister of U.S. industry promised him by Hitler, and the Red Skull, whose powers were also enhanced by a super-serum experiment, uses his superpowers for self-gain.

Trust/Deceit

The Americans are trusting, even of their stealthy enemies: Bucky follows the Strangler, who tells him he'll lead him to the officer Ellsworth's killer and leads him to Rathcone's lair; Bucky is taken by surprise by Rathcone, who knocks him out; the major unwittingly opens the deadly gift he has received. The Germans' deceit extends also to Sando and Omar's fraudulent magic show, where they "predict" attacks they already know about.

Democracy/Hierarchy

American society is depicted as one of equals, aside from the fact that there is a military hierarchy. But the Germans are shown as having a clear upper and lower class. Sando wears a monocle, has an exaggerated stiff jaw, and sports a pencil-thin mustache. Maxon is bespectacled, with a trim beard and mustache. The Germans' henchmen speak and behave like members of a lower class (saying "dat" for that). They have course features with double chins and thick lips and carry toothpicks between their teeth. Sando and Omar perform in a magic show that would be recognized as working-class entertainment.

Discussion

As the analysis above demonstrates, the war propaganda in the inaugural issue of 1941 *Captain America* uses ethnic stereotypes and concerns about immigrants that were just as prevalent in two earlier propaganda campaigns: Americanization and WWI. The public, insecure about assimilating a large immigrant population, had responded to stereotypes in the teens that were perpetuated through the 1930s and reemerged in *Captain America*. The comic book thus served to solidify and elaborate upon the already vilified stereotype of the German enemy.

The comic book cautions readers to be watchful, because spies and saboteurs inside the country constantly threaten to take it over for their own benefit. Further, the stories center on ethnic stereotypes and nationalistic beliefs, which were rampant in both the earlier Americanization and WWI propaganda campaigns, and tie those stereotypes to the treacherous nature of the German spies. Where the true Americans are iconic images of average white European Americans, the Germans are caricatures, with grotesque features and Teutonic accents.

Pulling together information from the polarities in the text, one can reconstruct a worldview behind the comic book's authors, one that is located in the text's symbol system. The binary oppositions in *Captain America* suggest that Americans and Germans are so different as to be incompatible: they are of different races, and the German race is the inferior one. The text contains no nuance, and very little room for a reader to oppose the preferred reading. Depictions of the Germans as not-American underscores a belief that they cannot possibly have American ideals and values. Polarities between German and American actions and demeanors can be seen as clear antisocial and prosocial categories that constitute the German and American national characters, respectively.

The German stereotypes are firmly rooted in prejudices dating to the age of the Kaiser during WWI (Scott, 2007). The German leaders exhibit an aristocratic demeanor (represented by the monocle), and arrogance toward anyone not of their background. The Germans are depicted as having a strict class system with aristocratic power-hungry leaders and lower-class, dull-witted thugs who do their bidding. Despite their aristocracy, the German national character is apparent in the types of faces that look less than human. Self-centered, bloodthirsty, monomaniacal enemies of democracy, the German enemy is motivated by personal gain. Even the thugs must be bullied and threatened to do the bidding of their evil masters. There is very little room in this monologic text for a reader to see the German characters as anything but evil. Such stereotypes recall the ones that were circulating during the teens.

Contrast the sinister world of the enemy with the United States, whose culture features an upbeat outlook, ease, and friendship, and where people trust each other and cooperate. Joking as they fight, Captain America and Bucky subdue their enemy. Their honest, open manner presents a contrast to the enemy: they are too trusting to suspect the evil motives of the enemy. The heroes' bravery appears in their relaxed manner. Their repartee further indicates their confidence and strength. All of these traits show the heroes to be confident and courageous. As Bucky says, "It's the Captain and I against all enemies of liberty" (Simon & Kirby, 1941/2011, p. 9). The heroes' actions show that they believe in working for the common good by selflessly and courageously fighting for democracy. The enemies of liberty are "the vicious elements who seek to overthrow the U.S. government" (Simon & Kirby, 1941/2011, p. 8.). *Captain America*, then, shows what it means to fight for and to make the world safe for democracy at a time when fear of spies ran rampant in the United States (Scott, 2007).

Conclusion

During two propaganda campaigns in the early twentieth century, ideas were introduced symbolically into U.S. culture to help create a nationalistic identity by upholding as a model the notion of *American* favored by an elite class, and concurrently by presenting a foreign model inimical to this idea. The two models come together and can be seen in the comic book *Captain America*. Both models short-circuit rational thought and rely on stereotype. That Germans are evil appears as a given fact and thereby conceals its ideological nature. Depictions of both German and American characters in *Captain America* adhere closely to the stereotypical views of these nationalities (so-called races) that had circulated during the teens in the two major propaganda campaigns of those years.

Like other mythic heroes, Captain America embodies culturally recognized virtues that enable him to perform extraordinary acts. Thus, he enshrines an ideal that encourages readers by affirming their resolution to unite in upholding American values against a villain who threatens cultural stability. He, too, embodies the ideal characteristics of the so-called pioneer stock who advanced by their own hard work, believed in community life, and taught their children to love God and country (Jirousek, 2008).

As this discussion suggests, propaganda makes its way gradually into the culture, because both propagandist and propagandee are complicit in devaluing higher cognitive values (Cunningham, 2002). These traits make comic books fertile ground for propagandistic messages. That is, people circulate meanings in a culture. Once this circumstance occurs, it is hard to know how and where ideas originated.

Many of the insecurities about aliens were later reincarnated and recirculated for use against the Communists during the Cold War period of the 1950s through the 1980s, and against terrorists from the 1990s until the present. During the discourse of those periods, the enemy is similarly demonized, and America still fights for democracy. As ever, the discourse does not always align with external reality, but internalized beliefs about a shared national identity throughout the dominant culture are strong enough to adapt to an ever-changing external reality. Also, the idea of *keeping America safe for democracy* has become a cliché in the war mentality of the Unites States. This chapter has theorized that propaganda campaigns, designed to blanket the population with similar messages from multiple channels, can be so effective that they become part of the cultural fabric and are difficult—and perhaps impossible—to dislodge.

Notes

1. A close observer might notice that these oft-used terms are rarely if ever defined even today.

References

Allen, D. S. (2005). *Democracy, Inc.* Urbana: University of Illinois Press.

Bakhtin, M. M. (1982). *The dialogic imagination: Four essays.* Austin: University of Texas Press.

Barthes, R. (1982). *A Barthes reader.* New York, NY: Hill and Wang.

Berger, A. A. (2012). *Media analysis techniques* (4th ed.). Los Angeles, CA: Sage.

Bernays, E. (2005). *Propaganda.* New York, NY: Ig. (Original work published 1928)

Black, E. (1970). The second persona. *The Quarterly Journal of Speech, 56,* 109–119.

Blumer, H. (1969). *Symbolic interactionism: Perspective and method.* Englewood Cliffs, NJ: Prentice-Hall.

Burke, K. (1989). *On symbols and society.* Chicago, IL: University of Chicago Press.

Carey, A. (1997). *Taking the risk out of democracy: Corporate propaganda versus freedom and liberty.* Urbana: University of Illinois Press.

Chandler, D. (2002). *Semiotics: The basics.* New York, NY: Routledge.

Costello, Matthew J. (2009). *Secret identity crisis: Comic books and the unmasking of Cold War America.* New York, NY: Continuum.

Creel, G. (1920). *How we advertised America: The first telling of the amazing story of the Committee on Public Information that carried the gospel of Americanism to every corner of the globe.* New York, NY: Harper and Bros.

Crook, P. (2007). *Darwin's coat-tails: Essays on social Darwinism.* New York, NY: Peter Lang.

Cunningham, S. B. (2002). *The idea of propaganda: A reconstruction.* Westport, CT: Praeger.

Delwiche, A. (1994). Of fraud and force fast woven: Domestic propaganda during the First World War. Retrieved from http://www.propagandacritic.com/articles/ ww1.drift.html

Eco, U. (1976). *A theory of semiotics.* Bloomington: Indiana University Press.

Fiske, J. (1989). *Understanding popular culture.* London, UK: Routledge.

Fiske, J. (2011). *Introduction to communication studies.* London, UK: Routledge.

Frentz, T. S., & Rushing, J. H. (1993). Integrating ideology and archetype in rhetorical criticism, part II: A case study of *Jaws. Quarterly Journal of Speech, 79,* 61–81.

Gaines, E. (2008). Media literacy and semiotics: Toward a future taxonomy of meaning. *Semiotica, 171,* 1–4, 239–249.

Hartmann, E. G. (1948). *The movement to Americanize the immigrant.* New York, NY: Columbia University Press.

Irwin, W. (1919, December). An age of lies: How the propagandist attacks the foundation of public opinion. *Sunset Magazine 43,* 84.

Jirousek, L. (2008). Mary Antin's progressive science: Eugenics, evolution and the environment. *Shofar: An Interdisciplinary Journal of Jewish Studies, 21,* 58–79.

Lasswell, H. D. (1927/1971). *Propaganda technique in World War I.* Cambridge, MA: M.I.T Press.

Lemke, J. (2009). Multimodal genres and transmedia traversals: Social semiotics and the political economy of the sign. *Semiotica, 173,* 283–297.

Levi-Strauss, C. (1978). *Myth and meaning.* New York, NY: Schocken Books.

Lippman, W. (1922). *Public opinion.* New York, NY: Free Press.

Martin Goodman, 84; Began Marvel Comics. (1982, June 11). *New York Times.* Retrieved from http://www.nytimes.com/1992/06/11/obituaries/martin-goodman-84-began-marvel -comics.html

Miller, M. C. (2004). Introduction. In E. Bernays, *Propaganda.* New York: Ig, pp. 9–33.

Peterson, T. R., & Horton, C. C. (1995). Rooted in the soil: How understanding the perspectives of landowners can enhance the management of environmental disputes. *Quarterly Journal of Speech, 81,* 139–166.

Posner, R. (2011). Post-modernism, post-structuralism, post-semiotics? Sign theory at the fin de siècle. *Semiotica, 183,* 9–30.

Scott, C. (2007). Written in red, white, and blue: A comparison of comic book propaganda from World War II and September 11. *The Journal of Popular Culture, 40,* 325–-343.

Simon, J., & Kirby, J. (2011). *Captain America No. 1* (70th anniversary ed.). New York, NY: Marvel Comics. (Original work published 1941)

Sproule, J. M. (1994). *Channels of propaganda.* Bloomington, IN: ERIC Clearinghouse.

Storer, C. (2009). "The German of caricature, the real German, the fellow we were up against": German stereotypes in John Buchan's "Greenmantle." *Journal of European Studies, 39,* 36–57.

Taylor, P. H. (1999). *British propaganda in the twentieth century: Selling democracy.* Edinburgh, UK: Edinburgh University Press.

White, Mark D. (2014). The virtues of Captain America: Modern-Day lessons on character from a World War II superhero. Malden, MA: John Wiley and Sons.

Wilt, D. (2011). Deconstructing propaganda: WWII comic book covers. Dwilt55, *YouTube.* Retrieved from http://www.youtube.com/user/DWilt55

★★ 8 ★★

Tell the Whole Truth

Feminist Exception in World War II *Wonder Woman*

Elliott Sawyer and Derek T. Buescher

In response to the evil Baroness's proclamation that being forced to take a lie detector test is against the law, Captain Steve Trevor responds to Wonder Woman's nemesis that "American law does not protect enemy spies in war-time" (Marston & Peter, 1998, p. 174). Although it appeared in 1942, Trevor's declaration actually foreshadows rationalizations of U.S. torture policies during the more recent War on Terror and the Iraq War. Indeed, his statement is akin to the infamous torture-justification memos written by then-assistant attorney general Jay S. Bybee, which stipulated that under the conditions of war, laws carry with them exceptions to the very ideals and conditions of those laws.

The troubling exchange between Trevor and the Baroness emphasizes the continuing relevance of Wonder Woman's experiences to today's world. Specifically, a careful reading of the heroine's WWII-era comic book storylines offers cultural and rhetorical critics an opportunity to reexamine the past in order to illustrate exigent events where "a state of exception is really the rule" (Chappell, 2006, p. 316). Wonder Woman, of course, continues to be a vibrant symbol of modern feminism—and for good reason. Yet overemphasizing the character's feminist imprint demonstrates how feminism and womanhood can foster a distraction and disavowal of U.S. practices in war and beyond. Hence, we concur with Chappell's contention (as, apparently, does Steve Trevor) that the state of exception is really the rule, especially under conditions of perpetual war.

This chapter critically examines the comic book introduction of Wonder Woman as a feminist ideal and as a U.S. ally persona grata. It argues that the character's feminist identity, while important, functions within the context of war as a disavowal of torture. This argument relies heavily on the work of Sturken (2011), who insists that torture "demands a moral response" (p. 424). The material that follows offers one such response, believing it necessary to confront and contest arguments of torture, and further cautioning against historical examination and cultural memory work that might simultaneously forget contemporary events and present moral obligations. Indeed, viewing Wonder Woman's feminism as distancing from the political, rather than as inherent to the political, allows for a more thoroughgoing critique of U.S. nationalism, particularly in times of war. The 1940s Wonder Woman comics function as U.S. war effort propaganda that justifies torture. Wonder Woman's inscription as a feminist icon veils both the nationalistic propaganda and use of torture inherent in the comics.

In contending that feminism can serve as proper distance" to the politics of war and, subsequently, torture, this chapter first turns to a brief description of disavowal as outlined by Sturken (2011) before a brief discussion of Wonder Woman's emergence. Later sections detail the character's tacit role in endorsing torture, how her actions are complicit in the construction of the enemy, and the enabling role of her famous, truth-telling lasso. The resulting assessment diverges in a significant way from traditional feminist readings of Wonder Woman and her actions.

Distance and Disavowal

Nearly every American comic book that was published from 1941 to 1945 had some relationship to WWII, even if it was only on the cover. Given the emphasis and force of the war, it might be easy to overlook or excuse the nationalistic basis of Wonder Woman's story. Yet given that Wonder Woman's role as protector and defender of the United States sets the foundation for her nationalism and eventual justification of torture, that relationship is too important to ignore. From one perspective, then, Wonder Woman serves as a contemporaneous distraction that invokes what Sturken (2011) referred to as *distancing*. In her essay on the "mediation of torture," she argues that the ability to disavow or deny U.S.-sanctioned practices of torture requires a structure of proper distancing that itself acknowledges the presence of torture, not too close and yet not too far. Sturken's goal in this respect "is to understand the mechanisms by which torture is both sanctioned and disavowed in American culture, [and] how it functions as a shadow to U.S. concepts of liberal democracy that must deny its existence" (Sturken, 2011, p. 424). Disavowal is enabled, she concludes, "through the distancing strategies of domestication, trivialization, kitschification, and irony" (Sturken, 2011, p. 424). Wonder Woman, in the guise of a feminist and through her feminist actions, uses just these strategies to distance the power relations of torture. That is, instead of witnessing a U.S. subject/citizen dressed in red, white, and blue torturing enemies, readers are asked to celebrate the triumphs of a woman over nefarious and racialized enemies of Nazi Germany and Japan. As Burdock (n.d.) wrote, Wonder Woman is a "model for women's participation in the military industrial complex" (p. 4) where her feminist persona serves as a foil to enable distancing of potential moral responsibility.

Because of her womanhood, Wonder Woman's use of torture is always already an exception to the normalcy of sanctions against torture. On the one hand, one could suggest that the ubiquity of her torture/lasso use merely anesthetizes audiences to the actualities of the practice. On the other hand, one can view the lasso itself as an iconic image (in this case of the lasso-yielding superhero), something decontextualized or even extra-discursive. Regardless, in Wonder Woman one finds the embodiment of American Empire, as Sturken (2011) framed it, within a "culture of defense." As a defender of the nation in times of war, Wonder Woman, like the nation, "must . . . paradoxically represent itself as *both* powerful and vulnerable" (Sturken, 2011, p. 431).

That Wonder Woman is vulnerable, both as Wonder Woman and as Diana Prince, is without question. When struggling with enemies, Wonder Woman is caught, trapped, chained, and bound on nearly every page. While she eludes such captivity, the chaining and binding (outside of the potential psychosexual reading) reinforces the very vulnerability that necessitates her defense of self and nation. Tracing the post-9/11 discourse of torture, Sturken (2011), invoking Judith Butler, argued that "an acceptance of torture as a sanctioned practice of the nation follows from this position of vulnerability and perceived need for revenge" (p. 438). Although the threat of imminent danger for Wonder Woman might be different than the ticking-time-bomb scenario of, say, Jack Bauer's *24*, the need to respond to the threat and prevent the abuse of one's vulnerability is all the same. In other words, vulnerability is intrinsic to Wonder Woman within the pages of the comic book because she is a woman, and women are, according to the cultural narrative, inherently vulnerable. Indeed, Wonder Woman (or her alter ego, Diana Prince) is continually placed in danger that threatens her as a woman. Her womanhood, what enables her femininity, is precisely what makes her vulnerable and thus, according to the narrative, legitimates and necessitates her use of violence and torture.

Prince/Wonder Woman's paradoxical position as both an enactor of justice and a vulnerable woman requiring protection and revenge thus poses two sides of the feminist/torture disjuncture. On one side, Wonder Woman is powerful and capable, and she defeats enemies. On the other, she defeats enemies who threaten her *because she is a woman.* In simpler terms, Wonder Woman falls victim to the position of young woman in distress (reaffirming the stereotypical narrative of women needing protection) *even as* she acts as a rescuer/savior of women (reinforcing the same essential idea: women need protection even if a woman, albeit a superhero, is protecting them). To borrow Sturken's (2011) phrasing, Wonder Woman suggests "a distanced relationship that offers a sense of closeness and proximity as part of its veneer" (p. 425). Readers' understanding of this heroine is enabled by her feminism even as that feminism distances them from nationalism and torture as sanctioned acts in the state of exception dramatized in Trevor's wartime admonition to the Baroness.[1]

Wonder Woman's Emergence, War, and Women

To be sure, Wonder Woman's origin story may not have appeared so politically motivated at its inception. First appearing in late 1941 and garnering her own title publication in 1942, Wonder Woman stands apart from other characters as a unique cultural icon of the U.S. comic book genre. Symbolic of both femininity and feminism, she follows in the path carved by Superman: both are outsiders who embrace fully the ideals of an America at war. Additionally, Wonder Woman's comics mimicked other series at the time, like *Captain America*, by functioning as a form of U.S. propaganda (Murray, 2012). Wonder Woman's superhero status essentially compels her to reinforce a United States at war, to battle the Axis enemies, and to use whatever means necessary to protect the nation-state.

The basic story of Wonder Woman is as follows. Diana (named after the goddess) lives on Paradise Island, which the Amazons have inhabited since Hercules tricked Diana's mother, Hippolyte, into giving up her magic girdle. Without the protection of the girdle, Hercules enslaves the Amazons with bracelets. Hippolyte prays to Aphrodite, who helps free the Amazons but forces them to continue wearing their bracelets as a reminder of their former enslavement. Aphrodite also provides them with Paradise Island, where their powers remain active as long as a man does not set foot onto the island. However, U.S. Army pilot Captain Steve Trevor crashes into the island while chasing a Nazi plane. The Amazons heal him of his wounds (without ever letting his feet touch the ground), and Diana is chosen to escort Trevor back to the United States, and thereafter to fight on the side of the Allies.

The idea behind Wonder Woman and her story came from William Moulton Marston, a Harvard-educated psychologist, who put himself into the center of the comic book growth industry by creating Wonder Woman in 1941. He convinced the comic book publisher Max Gaines to take a risk with a female superhero. As Stanley (2005) explained, "by the time [Wonder Woman] publicly debuted, she was fully grown and fully conceptualized—a modern-day Athena born from the head of a psychologist" (p. 146). Marston, along with his wife, Elizabeth, invented a systolic blood pressure test as a precursor to the polygraph machine (and to Wonder Woman's magic lasso). According to Madrid (2009), Marston's primary purpose for creating Wonder Woman was to design a hero "who would triumph using love rather than fisticuffs" (p. 34–35). Although this notion of love or strength did not always emerge in the stories, it was a revolutionary idea that challenged assumptions of conflict management and offered a feminized approach to battle.

Not surprisingly, Marston himself held a number of beliefs that were consistent with second-wave feminism. He "felt that women were superior to men, and his goal was to create a female role model to inspire young girl readers to stand up for themselves and achieve their true potential" (Madrid, 2009, p. 35). Through Wonder Woman, Marston hoped to reach reading audiences that included not only young women and girls but also war-supporting adults, "new audiences [who were] specifically constructed through representations of nation and nationalism" (Emad, 2006, p. 961). As Stanley (2005) argued, "the theme through [Marston's] work . . . [of] the need for males to submit to alluring but sexually dominant females" recasts the 1940s woman within a guise of powerful femininity (p. 146). Marston's crafting of Wonder Woman to be an authoritative woman created the groundwork that later feminists like Gloria Steinem or Trina Robbins would celebrate.

That Wonder Woman is feminist is a simple assumption for fans and critics alike: she is powerful and beautiful, knows how to function in the world, and often tries to reason with criminals rather than beating them up. Marston (1943–44) stated as much explicitly:

> Not even girls want to be girls so long as our feminine archetype lacks force, strength, and power. . . . Women's strong qualities have become despised because of their weak ones. The obvious remedy is to create a feminine character with all the strength of a Superman plus all the allure of a good and beautiful woman. (p. 42–43)

Wonder Woman was thus designed to celebrate the unique qualities of women while challenging some notions of their male counterparts.

The cultural memory of Wonder Woman's origin narrates her as a feminist icon, albeit a sometimes problematic feminist because of her visual rendering, her alter ego Diana Prince, and story arcs in which she pursues prototypical affirmation through love. Where other studies have focused on Wonder Woman's feminist possibilities, our examination focuses on how feminism functions as a foil for the centrality of U.S. nationalism defined as honor, justice, and, most essentially, truth, and also how such feminism functions as a form of disavowal or distraction from the politics of war. Since, like her predecessor Superman, Wonder Woman cannot kill her enemies, the tools by which she subdues them offer both insight into the values of WWII U.S. nationalism and relevance for contemporary audiences. Wonder Woman employs two primary strategies beyond fighting and "deflecting": the lie-detector test and the lasso of compulsion. These tools of "truth" allow Wonder Woman to maintain her feminine style while she protects the American way.

Yet there is a less positive side to the heroine's feminism. Emad (2006), citing Landay, pointed out that "war time popular culture primarily represented femininity as heroic, self-sacrificing, and good—again overwhelmingly positive connotations, but also meanings that render the separate spheres of femininity and nationalism sacrosanct" (p. 964). Emad continued to argue that "Marston constructs women's empowerment, even equal rights, out of particular narratives of nationhood . . . however, he must cloak this mythology in conventional femininity via the apparatus of 'Diana Prince' in order to protect the separation of gender and nation" (p. 964). She concludes that Wonder Woman is tied to female empowerment solely because the government pushed women to contribute to the war effort. Therefore, the heroine's source of agency is still directed by men to inspire women—in order to serve men. "The ropes and chains," Crawford (2006) explained, "are symbols of patriarchy and the drama is her ability to break the shackles of male domination they symbolize" (p. 31). However, she can only break these chains in her Wonder Woman persona. The secret Prince identity restores her femininity and continues to support the assumptions of the nation. Nevertheless, her agency exerted over enemies *within* the comic provides for a source of nationalism and desire for control reading audiences required. Wonder Woman's role as a feminist and nationalist icon thus justifies her use of torture in times of crisis and war.

Feminism as Disavowal of Torture

Wonder Woman's "feminism" is important because it serves to distract readers from the state-sanctioned violence in the guise of torture. Readers see a liberated woman as opposed to an apparatus of the state. To understand how Wonder Woman's femininity conceals while also clarifying torture as necessary, it is vital to recognize her participation in acts of torture. Of course, while it is true that Wonder Woman's use of torture is not precisely the same as the kind that emerged from Abu Ghraib or Guantanamo Bay or that President Obama acknowledged as part of the U.S. wars in Afghanistan and Iraq in the summer of 2014 (Lewis, 2014), there are obvious similarities between assumptions about and representations of contemporary torture and Wonder Woman's tactics of divining truth and incapacitating foes.

Although the lie detector is a passive machine that divines the truthfulness of its subject, the administration of the test is not necessarily (as the Baroness argues in *Wonder Woman* #1) always within the realm of law. On the other hand, the lasso has strong associations with the Wild West, with cattle or types of animal wrangling. Indeed, the novelty of Wonder Woman's primary weapon lies in its connotations of the American West and the cowboy. Once snared in the lasso, the victim is not only caught but also subject to her control. Through the lasso, she saps the will from her enemies and forces them to do her bidding. Saunders (2011) described the lasso as a form of loving and/or sexual submission to the point that the bondage featured in the comics "is a form of submission-as-liberation, a freedom-in-chains that can only come from surrender to the loving authority of divinity" (p. 64). We disagree, to an extent, with Saunders' theory, in that we contend there is no liberation inherent in what Wonder Woman inflicts upon her enemies. It is, by its very nature of interrogation and violence, a form of torture that her status as a feminist icon masks, whether at the time of publication or looking back retrospectively. In many instances, Wonder Woman being tied up or tying up others can be a highly sexual appeal to individuals regardless of gender identity, but that loses sight of the actual brutality of interrogation through the lasso. Her use of the lasso functions as a way to intimidate and harm her enemies rather than provide them with some form of sexual liberation. Both the lie-detector test and the lasso remove the agency of the captives and rob them of some of their humanity.

At first glance, many of the instances of Wonder Woman's lasso use might not appear to be torture, but we define them as such since they contain *elements* of torture. Consider, for example, the *United Nations Convention against Torture* (1984), which defines torture as:

Any act by which severe pain or suffering, whether physical or mental, is intentionally inflicted on a person for such purposes as obtaining from him or a third person, information or a confession, punishing him for an act he or a third person has committed or is suspected of having committed, or intimidating or coercing him or a third person, or for any reason based on discrimination of any kind, when such pain or suffering is inflicted by or at the instigation of or with the consent or acquiescence of a public official or other person acting in an official capacity. It does not include pain or suffering arising only from, inherent in or incidental to lawful sanctions.

While there is no need to construct an in-depth legal case against Wonder Woman, her actions, by this definition, constitute a contemporary understanding of torture. To wit, she uses her lasso to force enemies to do as she wishes, to intimidate, to physically harm, to tie up, and even to hang people from trees. In other scenes, discussed below, she repeatedly dunks opponents in water tanks and physically overpowers foes.

What could possibly justify these tactics of torture? Importantly, the manner by which Wonder Woman receives the lasso of compulsion narratively demonstrates her need for and right to such a weapon. After the heroine prays for guidance and strength, the gods Aphrodite and Athena come to her in *Sensation Comics* #6 and declare, "Having proved thyself bound by love and wisdom, we give thee power to control others! Whomsoever thy magic lasso binds must obey thee!" (Marston & Peter, 1998, p. 93). Wonder Woman, having been deemed exceptional (akin to the nation for whom she fights), is thus justified in using the power of the lasso. The full extent of the lasso's power is later explained by Wonder Woman: "With this great gift I can change human character! I can make bad men good, and weak women strong!" (Marston & Peter, 1998, p. 100). Not surprisingly, Wonder Woman uses this fearsome power against numerous enemies in her role as an Allied partisan.

Our and Wonder Woman's Enemies

Interestingly, many of the primary villains within the WWII Wonder Woman comics are women. While many of those villains are seen only once and therefore deemed expendable, it is compelling that, in a war where the literal combat was conducted primarily by men, the fictional story happens to be fought by women. These villainous women illustrate that women can be just as evil as men. Of course, in battles with her evil counterparts, Wonder Woman triumphs with skill and inherent goodness. The evil men Wonder Woman opposes are often repetitive and unmemorable, while the women are made singular and unique, as is the case with her nemesis, the Baroness Paula von Gunther. This suggests that, as a woman, Wonder Woman is better equipped to fight women and leave the men to Superman or Captain America. even the struggles of the Baroness, the primary recurring villain, are isolated to female figures, as she preys mostly on other women. The Baroness's trajectory is intriguing, because she appears in a handful of issues as an evil villain, but, suddenly, in *Wonder Woman* #3 she becomes a victim of the Nazis and changes allegiances to join with the United States and Wonder Woman.

First appearing in *Sensation Comics* #4 as a wealthy socialite under suspicion, the Baroness's unique brand of evil is her abuse of other women. In *Wonder Woman* #1 the Baroness finds herself in a standoff, and readers are led to believe she plummets to her death, affirming her allegiance to the Nazis as she yells "Heil Hit—Ohhh ..." (Marston & Peter, 1998, p. 184). Because the Baroness appears so ensconced in her unquestioning allegiance, her shift strikes as sudden but nonetheless explainable, as readers discover she was blackmailed by the Nazis to do their bidding. This new change, however, reinforces her female vulnerability and apparent lack of agency. Even her evil actions are not her own. Eventually, Paula provides Wonder Woman another female bond; however, on balance, the story of Wonder Woman is one where women fight women or undistinguished men.

When Wonder Woman does battle men, those masculine enemies are often rendered as a racial or exaggerated other, such as the brute German or snakelike Japanese. In such conflicts with men, Wonder Woman employs tactics beyond using the lasso of compulsion as merely a strategy of containment. That is, Wonder Woman's inquisition of captured enemies reinforces the status of the enemy as different and needing to be contained. Her inquisition is less about extracting vital information from the enemy and more about demonstrating her superior positionality in contrast to the now defeated enemy. Wonder Woman, as in Sturken's (2011) read of contemporary torture, engages in "a practice that marks its interestedness in the other because of their otherness, not because of information they possess" (p. 428). For example, in a scene from *Sensation Comics* #3, Wonder Woman tortures the Nazi Herr Gross, repeatedly dunking him in water by his ankle until he provides information. Wonder Woman's status as exceptional to the other and justified in her use of extraordinary measures elevates her and the nation's status in comparison to the enemy.

Wonder Woman embodies a lack of sympathy when enemy characters happen to experience pain or die, and this is predicated upon *Wonder Woman* continuing the social narrative of "*we* are civilized, *they* are barbaric" (Sardar and Van Loon, 2005, p. 13). Indeed, the images of snakelike Japanese combatants provide one primary focus of distancing for readers to trust Wonder Woman's justification while disavowing her means to achieve her goals. In WWII U.S. comic books, the Japanese were completely barbaric; they were soulless shells intent on killing as many Americans as possible, even at the risk of ending their own lives. As Wright (2001) explained, "perhaps more than any other medium, comic books proved uniquely suited to portray the Asian enemy as many Americans saw him—a sinister, ugly, subhuman creature who asked for and deserved no quarter" (p. 45). The Japanese were depicted as "ghastly yellow demons with fangs and claws or bucktoothed little monkeys with oversized spectacles" and they "appeared subhuman, inhuman, or even superhuman, but never simply human" (Wright, 2001, p. 45). In *Sensation Comics* #10, one can clearly see the common representation of the Japanese in the form of Ishti, a high-ranking Japanese officer. Ishti aims to destroy some trains and interrogates Wonder Woman after having her chained by another woman. Because Wonder Woman's powers mean she cannot be contained or bound by another woman, she escapes and captures Ishti. He is drawn with narrow eyes, yellow skin, and hands always ready to strike. His continual hissing of the letter "s" emphasizes his snakelike demeanor, and his speech blends entire sentences into one long hiss. Ishti offers *Wonder Woman* readers the necessary justification of difference and dehumanization that necessitates torture and violence as a response, in this case, to Pearl Harbor. Although the portrayal of the Japanese is troubling and often more graphic than the Germans', that does not mean the Nazis escaped unscathed.

Since Wonder Woman's introduction revolves around the Nazi attack on a U.S. airbase, Nazis are inherent to her initial character development. A Nazi in the first *Wonder Woman* story, Von Storm, illustrates Wright's (2001) typology regarding representations of Nazis: he is ruthless and large and sports a monocle. The German as enemy continued to appear in many *Wonder Woman* stories. DiPaolo (2007) characterized the depictions of Germans in *Wonder Woman* by explaining, "Marston and Peter pitted their Amazon champion against Nazis who were clearly bloodthirsty, sexually deviant pawns of Ares" (p. 155). He continued to explain that "they were also frequently portrayed as sexually repressed and would-be rapists, greeting the sight of Wonder Woman's exposed flesh with either too much moral outrage or too much lust, and failing the test of reacting to Diana's appearance in a well-adjusted manner" (p. 155–156). The apparent Nazi desire and lust for U.S. women, not merely Wonder Woman, both reinforces the Nazis as justified enemy and signifies the unique threat to female vulnerability.

The Lie-Detector Test and Lasso

Within Wonder Woman comics, it is difficult to discern where the lie-detector test ends and the magic lasso begins. Most single stories feature Diana Prince using the lie-detector test before Wonder Woman must resort to using the magic lasso. Occasionally, the lie-detector appears later in the story, but, on face, the magic lasso is an extension of the lie-detector and the hero's ability to seek the truth. This concept of truth was a particular obsession of Marston. Earlier we argued that Wonder Woman in her Diana Prince persona does not have much agency. In opposition, we present one form in which Diana breaks out of her preordained role as a secretary in the armed forces: she administers the lie-detector tests. Although more subtle than the directness of capturing someone with a lasso and interrogating them, especially since the lasso compels one to tell the truth, whereas the lie-detector test does not, the lie detector functions as a form of control. With the lie detector, the villain, or spy, is sat down, tied up, and hooked up to a machine, rather than being closely bound by the lasso.

In *Sensation Comics* #3, Diana must administer lie-detector tests to all of the girls who work on the army base in order to find a spy in their midst. Diana begins the lie-detector test on a girl named Lila, only to discover that she is hiding something. Lila's blood pressure spikes when Diana mentions a letter. As Trevor rationalizes in *Wonder Woman* #1 the lie-detector test can transgress laws if such exceptions support U.S. wartime efforts. In the case of Lila, the lie-detector test also demonstrates the U.S. desire and need for control, as the presence of the test compels Lila, and later the Baroness, to speak the truth through a machine or risk having the machine expose their lies. In *Wonder Woman* the direct relationship between the lie-detector test and the lasso of compulsion collapses the distinction between potentially legitimate uses of interrogation and excessive force in interrogation that verges on torture.

The lasso of compulsion embodies a direct approach to control and torture that sanctions violence in times of exception, for example, in Trevor's "wartime." In her second outing with the magic lasso in *Sensation Comics* #7, Wonder Woman faces the Baroness while exposing a milk-racketeering ring in which the Baroness controls the price of milk and starves the poor. After successfully dismantling the ring, Wonder Woman captures the Baroness with her lasso and forces the Baroness, while still tied up, to sign a confession. This action is a primary example of torture. In the frame where Wonder Woman forces the Baroness to sign her confession, she stands behind the Baroness and holds the lasso that requires the Baroness to sign to her guilt. As the lasso forces the Baroness to write, Wonder Woman asserts her dominance over her by appearing to tower over her, holding the lasso as a rein. Outside the boundaries of legality, the lasso and Wonder Woman's might compel the Baroness to submit.

Use of the lasso is not limited to Nazis. In *Wonder Woman* #4, Wonder Woman uses her lasso to tie up the Japanese captain Sansu Hideo. Wonder Woman first spots the captain as he and other Japanese officers drive away from her. She captures him from a moving car with the lasso while calling, "Come, Fido!" (Marston & Peter, 2000, p. 184). In the next frame, the captain is clearly made to be vulnerable as he is sprawled out on the ground and sweating through his submission to Wonder Woman. Wonder Woman faces the captain while standing and holding the lasso tightly. She excitedly proclaims that she wishes to "interview" him. In these scenes with Sansu Hideo, Wonder Woman's actions and demeanor differ from Diana Prince's use of the lie detector and illustrate the lasso's unique qualities and significance. Instead of merely sitting the captain down and binding him to a chair, Wonder Woman suspends him from a tree with the lasso of truth for the purposes of gaining information. The scene can be understood as a comedy or as irony: readers see the American enemy powerless and hanging from a branch like a piñata. The frames foreground the Japanese captain while Wonder Woman resides in the background with a firm grip on the lasso that connects her to the captain. Despite her background location, Wonder Woman remains in control as the active participant in the panels. She holds in her toned arms the lasso and effortlessly drapes the captain on the tree. Dangling in air, the captain both is no longer a threat to the United States and is racialized through his torture/lynching. Frightened, he burbles out information about a new "womania" germ that will cause American women to hate and attack men. That Wonder Woman discovers a "truth" in the Captain's plot only sanctions her use of the lasso as an instrument of torture that can defend a vulnerable nation/women. Wonder Woman affirms herself as the potential location of assault (by the womania germ) that, post hoc, necessitates her intervention and use of extraordinary measures.

Conclusion

Critics of more contemporaneous contexts may seek to understand the present in light of the past, and we do witness interesting parallels to present arguments developing a state of exception. Indeed, other critics may wish to point out, as does Sturken, that criticism's effect is found in its moral response to present public arguments. In the pages of Wonder Woman from 1941 to 1943 we witness something akin to Chappell's (2006) reading of contemporary torture practices. Drawing from Judith Butler, Chappell explains:

> The unaccountable "deeming" of persons as threats that characterizes much of the operation of the state in the war on terror is a sovereign act that brands those captives as . . . an exception to human subjectivity, which exist outside the boundaries of protection offered by law, who may be killed without need for sacrifice, without, that is, cost. (p. 319)

Although Wonder Woman never explicitly kills any of her captives subjected to either the lie detector or the lasso, they are not treated with any semblance of humanity; they are the enemy, and therefore laws no longer apply to them. The comics portray and justify Wonder Woman's torture as for the good of the nation-state in times of war, and viewing Wonder Woman as a feminist icon both then and now ignores her troubling actions.

Whether in costume or not, Wonder Woman has the power to discover truth by tacit persuasion and torture. In claiming that Wonder Woman's feminist presence serves as a justification of torture, and thereby a metonymic justification for the state of exception, we do not mean to simultaneously discount or discard her potentially progressive feminist offerings. Nor do we mean to claim that *Wonder Woman* comics' depictions of the Axis as unfavorable are unsurprising, given the context of public discourse and exigent events in which they emerged. Rather, our argument offers one reading of Wonder Woman in which we seek to trouble the acceptance of feminism in the absence of other critical inquiry and examine how feminism itself may offer readers a distancing from such critical inquiry. Moving beyond *Wonder Woman* as mere perpetuation of stereotypes, we have sought to read Wonder Woman's feminist potential as reaffirming torture as a necessary instrument in wartime. In the case of Wonder Woman's early years, her feminist empowerment demonstrates to readers the potentiality of a powerful woman. Yet those same feminist ideals, we argue, provide a "proper distance" where readers are not too far and simultaneously not too close to witnessing and tacitly endorsing torture. While we wish to celebrate Wonder Woman's feminism, we contend that it is important for cultural and rhetorical scholars to continue critical engagement with texts to understand the nuances of those texts. Wonder Woman, despite her perceived feminist persona, demonstrates that the exception offered by war to enact normally immoral practices is less the exception than the rule. WWII *Wonder Woman* comics neither tend to tell the whole truth nor represent a truly progressive stance on feminism and torture.

Notes

1. Sturken's (2011) discussion of kitsch as distancing is also prevalent in later Wonder Woman wartime comics. One way to read the heroine's adventures involving the riding of kangaroos and being turned into a butterfly is the creation of kitsch storylines, a form of trivialization of the power and violence of Wonder Woman.

References

Berger, J. (1972). *Ways of seeing.* London, UK: Penguin.

Burdock, M. (n.d.). Wonder Woman: Feminist icon or patriarchal pawn? Unpublished manuscript, available at https://www.academia.edu/24892106/Wonder_Woman_Feminist _Ico n_or_Patriarchal_Pawn.

Bybee, J. S. (2002, August 1). Memorandum for Alberto R. Gonzales, Counsel to the President. RE: Standards for conduct of interrogation under 18 U.S.C 2340-2340A. United States

Department of Justice, Office of Legal Counsel. Available at http://dspace.wrlc.org/doc /bitstream/2041/70964/00355_020801_001display.pdf

Bybee, J. S. (2002, August 1). Memorandum for John Rizzo, Acting General Counsel of the Central Intelligence Agency. Interrogation of al Qaeda operative. United States Department of Justice, Office of Legal Counsel. Available at: http://dspace.wrlc.org/doc /bitstream/2041/70967/00355_020801_004display.pdf

Chafe, W. H. (1991). *The paradox of change: American women in the 20th century.* New York, NY: Oxford University Press.

Chappell, B. (2006). Rehearsals of the sovereign: States of exception and threat governmentality. *Cultural Dynamics, 18*(3), 313–334.

Crawford, P. C. (2007). The legacy of Wonder Woman: An enlightening look at the feminist ideals that informed this American icon. *School Library Journal, 53*(3), 30–31.

DiPaolo, M. E. (2007). Wonder Woman as World War II veteran, camp feminist icon, and male sex fantasy. In T. R. Wandtke (Ed.), *The amazing transforming superhero! Essays on the revision of characters in comic books, film and television* (pp. 151–173). Jefferson, NC: McFarland.

Duncan, R., & Smith, M. J. (2009). *The power of comics: History, form and culture.* New York, NY: Continuum.

Emad, M. C. (2006). Reading Wonder Woman's body: Mythologies of gender and nation. *The Journal of Popular Culture, 39*(6), 954–984.

Hartman, S. M. (1982). *The home front and beyond: American women in the 1940s.* Boston, MA: Twayne.

Lewis, P. (2014, August 1). Obama admits CIA "tortured some folks" but stands by Brennan over spying. *The Guardian.* Retrieved from http://www.theguardian.com/world/2014 /aug/01/obama-cia-torture-some-folks-brennan-spying

Madrid, M. (2009). *The supergirls: Fashion, feminism, fantasy, and the history of comic book heroines.* Ashland, OR: Exterminating Angel.

Marston, W. M. (1943). Why 100,000,000 Americans read comics. *The American Scholar, 13*(1), 35–44.

Marston, W. M., & Peter, H. G. (1998). *Wonder Woman: Archives volume 1.* New York, NY: DC Comics.

Marston, W. M., & Peter, H. G. (2000). *Wonder Woman: Archives volume 2.* New York, NY: DC Comics.

Murray, C. (2012). Propaganda: The pleasures of persuasion in *Captain America.* In M. J. Smith & R. Duncan (Eds.), *Critical approaches to comics: Theories and methods* (pp. 129–141). London, UK: Routledge.

O'Reilly, J. D. (2005). The Wonder Woman precedent: Female (super)heroism on trial. *The Journal of American Culture, 28*(3), 273–283.

Peters, B. M. (2003). Qu(e)erying comic book culture and representations of sexuality in *Wonder Woman. CLCWeb: Comparative Literature and Culture, 5*(3), 2–9.

Robbins, T. (1996). *The great women superheroes.* Northampton, MA: Kitchen Sink.

Sardar, Z., & Van Loon, B. (2005). *Introducing: Cultural studies.* Royston, UK: Totem Books.

Saunders, B. (2011). *Do the gods wear capes?: Spirituality, fantasy, and superheroes.* New York, NY: Bloomsbury Academic.

Smith, J. S. (2001). The tyranny of the melting pot metaphor: Wonder Woman as the Americanized immigrant. In M. P. McAllister, E. H. Sewell, Jr., & I. Gordon (Eds.), *Comics & ideology* (pp. 129–150). New York, NY: Peter Lang.

Stanley, K. E. (2005). "Suffering Sappho!": Wonder Woman and the (re)invention of the feminine ideal. *HELIOS, 32*(2), 143–171.

Sturken, M. (2011). Comfort, irony, and trivialization: The mediation of torture. *International Journal of Cultural Studies*, *14*(4), 423–440.

UN General Assembly, *Convention Against Torture and Other Cruel, Inhuman or Degrading Treatment or Punishment*, December 10, 1984, United Nations, Treaty Series, vol. 1465, p. 85, available at: http://www.unhcr.org/refworld/docid/3ae6b3a94.html

Wright, B. W. (2001). *Comic book nation: The transformation of youth culture in America*. Baltimore, MD: Johns Hopkins University Press.

★★ 9 ★★

Debunking Hitler

True Comics as Counter-Propaganda

Steven E. Martin

Cultural memory in the United States typically positions WWII as "the good war," an effort that enjoyed unanimous support from the American public. As Michael Bess puts it, "rarely in history has a war seemed so just to so many" (2006, p. 110). Perhaps the most significant reason many Americans continue to think of WWII as a just war can be summed up in one name: Hitler. With an enemy as "perfidious and brutal as Adolf Hitler," there was little room for opposition to the war (Casey, 2001, p. xviii). No man has been vilified as consistently and as frequently; indeed, *Hitler* has become synonymous with *evil*. This association of WWII with Hitler has led to a one-dimensional historical understanding of the era. As is often the case, it is easy to oversimplify history, especially as it relates to wars, applying a morally superior framework to one's thinking. The conclusion appears to be obvious: of course WWII was a just war; the U.S. fought against an absolutely evil man who had equally evil intentions.

Yet as Steven Casey (2001) also demonstrates, public memory of support for the war effort has been exaggerated by many historians, novelists, film producers, and producers of popular culture more generally. The belief that WWII was at the time a "widely popular crusade" is "somewhat overdrawn" (p. xviii). In part, this belief persists because the WWII-era understanding of Hitler and Nazism was not the same as it is now. In fact, what frequently troubled President Franklin D. Roosevelt was that many Americans did not understand "the true nature of the enemy." Even after Pearl Harbor, U.S. citizens were largely ignorant "of what Nazism stood for, the danger it posed, and the brutal techniques it employed" (pp. xviii–xix).

Roosevelt and his administration were cognizant of the power of popular culture to influence public opinion. They were also well aware, however, that overt propaganda could cause a heavy backlash, as it had following WWI. The approach of the administration therefore was to encourage the entertainment industries to promote patriotism, to vilify Hitler and the Axis powers, and to boost morale. In short, the president asked nongovernmental media to follow voluntarily the governmental test for messages to the public: "Will this help win the war?" (Wright, 2001, p. 34).

As Bradford W. Wright (2001) points out, however, the comic book industry needed no encouragement to attack Hitler and Nazism (p. 35). Many of the authors, illustrators, and publishers in the comic book industry were politically progressive Jews. Well before Roosevelt made any official request for support from the media, many of these comic book writers and illustrators were already busy drawing superheroes who were literally beating up Hitler and the Nazis. In many ways, each superhero served as a metonymic stand-in for the United States. For example, months before the nation officially entered the war, the cover of the first volume of *Captain America* showed Steve Rogers (Captain America's alter ego) punching Adolf Hitler. Once the war started, such superhero comics aimed to boost morale, provide courage and hope, and imply that the United States and the Allies would be victorious.

Although superhero and fantasy comic books dominated the market during the war, nonfiction comic books also enjoyed some success. Shortly after superhero comics gained mass appeal, they were blamed for corrupting young adolescent males, contributing to juvenile crime and even encouraging homosexuality (Jones, 2004, pp. 270–271, 273). So serious were these charges that comic books eventually became a topic of the Kefauver hearings on crime in the United States (Sabin, 1993, p. 280). To counteract what he perceived as psychologically and socially damaging comic books, George J. Hecht founded *True Comics* to, in his words, "educate and stimulate them [adolescent males, in particular] by placing before them the examples of important and courageous people" (as cited in Blake, n.d., para. 9). Like many critics at the time, Hecht was not a fan of the dominant genre of superhero comics. He once told an interviewer that he "disapproved strongly of most of the comic book magazines in the late 1930s and early 1940s" (as cited in Blake, n.d., para. 9).

A glance at the tables of contents of 83 volumes of *True Comics*, which ran from 1941 to 1945,[1] reveals that the series primarily contained two types of stories: biographical and historical. Biographical stories were written about everyone from U.S. presidents and other world leaders to famous athletes, inventors, and entertainers. Historical pieces were frequently about famous military battles throughout U.S. history—including recent Allied victories—but also covered a wide range of topics not related to war, such as "Drake's Folly: The Story of the First Oil Well Ever Drilled" (1941) and "The Cotton Gin" (1941).

However, there was a third category of stories in *True Comics* that went beyond telling about a famous person or historical event. These stories made the reader aware of divisive beliefs and the rhetorical strategies used to spread them; in short, they functioned as counter-propaganda. Specifically, these comics dealt with perceived, but widely believed and well-established racial, religious, and cultural differences. Two stories in this genre were particularly prominent. The first piece, "They Got the Blame: The Use of Scapegoats in History" (Gould, 1944), exposed the scapegoating technique, while "There Are No Master Races" (1944) tackled racism.[2] Because racist doctrine and the Jew-as-scapegoat strategy were central to Nazi propaganda, analyzing these comics broadens understanding of the comic book industry's wartime counter-propaganda efforts against Hitler. In short, not only did comic books of this era convey stories in which Axis forces were defeated in battle, but some of them also critiqued the rationale that created and propelled Nazi fascism.

"They Got the Blame" (Gould, 1944) is a seven-page story, originally published in the December 1943 issue of *True Comics*, that teaches the reader about scapegoating, or the practice of shifting blame for societal ills onto a source that has no causal relationship to the problem. The comic unfolds as a series of mini-stories, each of which serves as a historical example of scapegoating, from primitive times to Hitler.

"There Are No Master Races" (which was also a seven-page story) appeared in the September–October 1944 issue of *True Comics*. As the story's title implies, it advocates racial equality in an effort to debunk Nazi propaganda. Most of the comic's narrative occurs in the form of a teacher instructing a class of youth about the science of race and the history of various past civilizations. The children ask questions, and the teacher answers them.

These two comic book stories explain not merely *that* Hitler was the enemy but *why* he was wrong. In so doing, the comics debunk Hitler's claims and subsequently counteract Nazi propaganda. In examining the stories more closely, this chapter proceeds in three major sections. First, I demonstrate the methods used in *True Comics* to explain and expose the scapegoat trick. Second, I examine how the comics debunk racist ideology. Finally, I consider the implications of *True Comics* in relation to Nazi propaganda.

Using Religion and Science to Expose the Scapegoat Trick

Religion plays a strong role in shaping beliefs and behaviors, and, of course, also played a critical role both in Hitler's propaganda against Jews and in the counter-propaganda of the United States. Religious beliefs can be divisive, but they can also unite people in common cause. *True Comics* appealed to religious beliefs to unite Judaism and Christianity even as Hitler worked to drive a wedge between them. At the same time, the comics relied upon both implicit and explicit references to scientific knowledge to show how science has, throughout the centuries, corrected false beliefs and superstitions that often were religiously grounded.

The following section analyzes how "They Got the Blame" (Gould, 1944) recounts historical examples to illustrate the faulty beliefs that led to the creation of scapegoats. The story proceeds through three phases. First, it shows that the concept of the scapegoat is grounded in the superstitious beliefs of polytheistic religions. Second, the story explains how differences in sectarian religious beliefs led to the scapegoating of Catholics. Finally, having established some historical examples, the comic draws the connections to Hitler's use of the Jews as scapegoat.

The Origins of Scapegoating

The opening sequence of "They Got the Blame" explains that the idea of scapegoats originated in India, where a tribe blamed demons for a cholera epidemic. The language of the descriptive text emphasizes the superstitious belief: "These simple people know of only one cause for their troubles . . . Evil Demons" (Gould, 1944, p. 1; ellipsis in original). To stop the epidemic, the tribe's priests "swing into action" by creating a mixture of spices and straw from the tribe's dwellings. A dark-skinned priest says "then we will burn it [the mixture of spices and straw] at the altar to appease the gods" (Gould, 1944, p. 1).

On the next page, the narration explains that the priests picked out a young water buffalo from the tribe's herd. The water buffalo, remarks one priest, "must be black as midnight and a female or the *magic* [emphasis added] will not work" (Gould, 1944, p. 2). The narration, which is situated in between the two frames being described, then tells the reader that the priests painted the water buffalo with red paint and tied a yellow bag of cloves and grain to the animal (see Figure 9.1). The narration between the frames is necessary to explain what will happen in the next frame. The drawing in this frame features the water buffalo prominently; it is drawn in close-up and occupies most of the frame.

Figure 9.1: True Comics establishes the superstitious origins of scapegoating by depicting a tribe's response to an outbreak of cholera (Gould, 1944, p. 2).

Soon, the villagers are depicted chasing the water buffalo, driving it out of the village with "shouts and the beating of drums," as the text at the top of the frame explains (Gould, 1944, p. 2). After describing and showing this bizarre "magic" ritual, the narration summarizes the event for the reader: the water buffalo is the tribe's *scapegoat*, and its members now believe that the cholera plague has been "carried away in the body of the animal" (Gould, 1944, p. 2).

Even if unintentional, the visual images used throughout this example put further distance between the familiar and the unfamiliar. This effect is due in large part to the characters' traditional attire of Indian tribes, such as the turban (head wrap) and pajamas (baggy pants with a drawstring at the waist), which would have seemed strange to most of *True Comics*'s audience. The frame that shows villagers burning something (the drawing shows smoke rising from some of the villagers' hands) and beating on drums while chasing a beast out of the village adds to the peculiar scene. Taken collectively, the visual images of these frames work with the narrative elements in creating a story that demonstrates the farcical nature of the origin of the scapegoat technique.

Following the story about the ancient tribe, the comic continues with a story about Christian persecution in the early Roman Empire. Again, polytheism is identified as the cause of scapegoating. In the first frame, a Roman nobleman is speaking out his window to a crowd below. He is telling the people that "Christians among us have brought the wrath of the gods upon us" (Gould, 1944, p. 2). In the next frame, three Roman citizens consider the words of the nobleman. A male character on the left side of the frame says, "He is right. The gods are angry because we permit the Christians to live among us! Let us drive them out!" A second character in the middle of the frame remarks: "Look! Christians! After them!" A third character's face is shown in the bottom right portion of the frame. He is silent, but the look on his face suggests that he is contemplating the words of the others (Gould, 1944, p. 2). The interaction of the characters in this frame demonstrates how people often follow their leader. Regardless of an idea's truth value, once it is stated aloud (the gods are angry *because* of Christians), the masses often follow.

The story continues in the bottom two frames of the same page. The left-hand frame depicts a scene where stones are being thrown at a group of Christians. The narration contends that "Christians were beaten, tortured, and executed" (Gould, 1944, p. 2). In the right-hand frame, a small group of Christians is shown cowering fearfully before a lion in a gladiatorial arena. With knowledge that these victims were innocent, the scene possesses the potential to elicit fear, anger, and empathy from the viewer. As the text above the gladiatorial arena scene reads, "if there was a fire, flood, drought, or famine, the Christians were blamed, made the scapegoat. Often they were thrown to the lions" (Gould, 1944, p. 2).

These four frames demonstrate how the early Romans created the concept of a scapegoat: blame a group of people for a problem (drought, fire, epidemics); suggest that the group, which is in some way distinguishable from one's own group (religious belief, skin color), has angered some higher power (gods, demons); and speak convincingly to followers, instructing them to eliminate the threat, which will allegedly solve the problem. Within a few quick frames, the action of the comic goes from accusation (the image of the leader speaking from his balcony to the masses) to execution (the image of Christian scapegoats being fed to lions), showing that those who are victimized often are treated cruelly, or even are killed, because they were blamed for societal problems.

Importantly, because the U.S. public would have been unlikely in the 1940s to believe in cholera-causing demons or Roman gods who were angered by the presence of Christians, the scapegoat is clearly innocent in these examples. As such, these stories more easily would have been understood as instances of scapegoating. The opening stories of the comic therefore provide building blocks that eventually will link these obvious examples of scapegoating to more contemporary, but less obvious, examples. A 1940s audience might have viewed animal sacrifice as a strange way to deal with illness, and feeding Christians to lions as a nonsensical way of appeasing Roman gods, but they were themselves susceptible to stereotypes that blamed Jews and certain sects of Christianity for societal problems. The comic sought to show that those situations were no different.

Catholics as Victims of Scapegoating

In "They Got the Blame" (Gould, 1944), Christians are the victims not only of the early, polytheistic Romans but also of other Christians. Sectarian divisiveness—in particular, the anti-Catholic movement—thus appears as a type of scapegoating. Afterward, Hitler himself is shown as being anti-Catholic.

This section of the comic begins with the following narration: "The persecution of minorities because they were considered 'foreign' was a short step to persecution of these same groups because of a difference in religion" (Gould, 1944, p. 4). The first frame of the section shows a young boy asking a priest if Irish Catholics are going to start a violent revolution against the U.S. government. The priest says, "No, my son," and in the next frame continues with "we Catholics are accused of many things. America is a young nation, my son, someday all the different races and religious sects here will learn to live in peace together!" (Gould, 1944, p. 4). In 1834, the next frame shows, there were riots against Catholics. The visual image of this frame shows four nuns, two of whom are protecting two young children as they flee from a burning church. The drawing portrays the nuns as protectors of children, thus visually reinforcing the message that Catholics are not violent, like the conspiracy theories would have people believe. The text tells the reader that the nuns' convent was burned to the ground. Thus, members of the anti-Catholic movement, not the Catholics themselves, are shown as violent.

In the subsequent section of the story, Hitler himself is associated with anti-Catholicism. One frame in "They Got the Blame" shows a shadowy Nazi official entering a church to declare that "in Germany you preach only the word of ADOLF HITLER!" The explanatory text remarks that "Hitler was aware that freedom of worship was dangerous to his dictatorship. He closed between 9,000 and 10,000 Catholic schools, arrested and imprisoned countless priests and ministers" ("Gould," 1943, p. 6). Although historically glossing over the real reason for this alleged anti-Catholic behavior, this part of the comic associated Hitler with the U.S. anti-Catholic movement.[3]

The stories about Christians (and, more specifically, Catholics) as scapegoats instruct the reader that Jews have not been the only victims of such beliefs. Combined, the verbal and visual messages in these passages encourage empathy for and identification with Jews, which becomes important later in "They Got the Blame" when Jews are introduced as Hitler's scapegoat.

Jews as Scapegoats

Hitler knew well that one of the most effective ways to unite many Germans (and, indeed, many people beyond Germany) against Jews was to use religious appeals. Throughout his writings and speeches, Hitler frequently remarked that he was doing the work of the "Almighty Creator." As he wrote in *Mein Kampf*, "by warding off Jews I am fighting for the Lord's work" (1932/1971, p. 65). Moreover, Hitler made the claim that Jesus was an anti-Semite who "made no secret of his attitude toward the Jewish people, and when necessary he even took to the whip to drive from the temple of the Lord this adversary of all humanity" (p. 307). Hitler also blamed the Jews for Jesus's crucifixion: "In return, Christ was nailed to the cross" (Hitler, 1971, p. 307). Clearly, he aimed to vilify the Jewish people and to associate his own agenda with Christianity. Hitler's discourse and other Nazi propaganda might not have mattered to the war efforts in the United States, except that anti-Semitism on the home front also was quite prevalent in the WWII era (Carr, 2001).

All of the examples of scapegoating in "They Got the Blame" (Gould, 1944) guide the reader toward a particular conclusion. Specifically, they progressively teach one how to detect the scapegoat trick, especially regarding the ultimate example of victimizing a particular group: Hitler's treatment of Jews. This section of "They Got the Blame" begins with a narration set-up frame, which tells readers that "while America was successfully developing the democratic ideal of freedom and equality, 3,000 miles away a new exploiter of 'scapegoatism' was rising to power." Immediately to the right of the text is a close-up drawing of Hitler's face. He is saying that "the Jews are responsible for all of Germany's ills. I will drive them out, destroy them utterly. Then you will all be prosperous and happy once again" (Gould, 1944, p. 5). In short order, this frame summarizes Hitler's basic agenda.

Hitler's big lie did not stay in Germany, however. On the final page of "They Got the Blame," the comic shows how the scapegoating technique was exported to the United States: "Hitler flooded the U.S. with Nazi propaganda. His agents tried to split America into hostile groups" (Gould, 1944, p. 7; see Figure 9.2). Following the set-up description, a visual frame at the top left of this last page shows a group of men sitting around a table. One man, his back to the viewer, says to "blame everything on the Jews! Unemployment, high prices . . . Everything! It worked in Germany and it will work here." In the background, a figure in the dark (visually reinforcing his evil intentions) replies, "Ja, these Americans

Figure 9.2: The story line suggests that shadowy groups are intent on using scapegoating propaganda to divide Americans (Gould, 1944, p. 7).

will believe anything" (Gould, 1944, p. 7). Nearby is a flag with the swastika, which indicates that Nazism is no longer restricted to Europe but is infiltrating the United States as well. A light hangs over the table, illuminating only a few of the men in the room, leaving some in the shadows. The technique of this drawing conveys a sinister feel, reinforcing the message that the Nazis had conspired to spread their anti-Semitism in the U.S.

Yet the middle section of the page expresses a sense of hope that most Americans will not be fooled by Hitler. The visual image of this frame shows a speaker who looks similar to Hitler (at the very least, he has a similar mustache, a visual allusion that persists to this day) addressing a crowd of Americans. In the background is a U.S. flag. The narration claims that most Americans "were aware of Hitler's plan to 'divide and conquer' America from within" (Gould, 1944, p. 7). Bolstering that narration is a man, arm held in the air to signify his strength, telling the speaker "you can't pull the wool over the eyes of REAL Americans. We know who's trying to get us to hate our neighbors. He's the man who pays your salary ... ADOLF HITLER" (Gould, 1944, p. 7; ellipsis in original).

All of these narrative examples provide instructions for how to detect the scapegoat trick, ultimately leading to an understanding that Hitler's treatment of Jews is yet another example in a long history of blaming innocent groups of people. In other words, the comic book story conditions the reader via the accrual of previous, easy-to-comprehend examples to view Hitler's scapegoating of Jews as no different. Blaming the Jews for Germany's problems, implies the entire line of reasoning, is as ridiculous as blaming demons for cholera or Christians for Rome's problems.

Explaining Race

Working hand-in-hand with scapegoating based on religious differences, Nazi propaganda also promulgated pseudo-scientific racism (which had its roots in religious texts as well). Hitler advanced the claim that so-called Aryans were a master race meant to rule the world by some kind of divine authority. Nazi scientists thus set out to prove this claim, ultimately arguing that darker-skinned races were inferior to lighter-skinned races because those with darker skin coloring were somehow less human. In Nazi propaganda, all non-Aryans were, in fact, called, *untermesch*, meaning *subhumans*.

"There Are No Master Races" (1944) counters this kind of Nazi rhetoric, as it teaches that race is not a meaningful delineation. First, the comic makes a quick religious argument, based on the biblical story of Adam and Eve, that all humans emerged from the same ancestors and are therefore all from the same race. Second, the determinants of skin color, nose shape, and hair type are explained by science as a result of geographic origins. Finally, the comic demonstrates that one's environment and upbringing, not one's race, influences intelligence and other personality traits.

Significantly, the very first frame of "There Are No Master Races" (1944, p. 36) *combines* appeals from religion and from science, making the claim that science confirms religious belief. This strategy piggy-backs scientific knowledge (that all *homo sapiens* are the same species because races are genetically indistinguishable), which was a long way from being accepted as true, onto existing religious belief (the Judeo-Christian creation myth), which many of the comic's readers likely accepted as truth.

This opening frame of the comic contains an Edenic image of a male character (Adam) and a female character (Eve) surrounded by various species of animals, including a deer, lamb, peacock, lion, and large bird (perhaps a crane or a heron). Adam appears to be petting the peacock, and Eve appears to be petting the lion. Most recognizable, however, is the serpent coiled around the tree of knowledge in the background. The positioning of the characters is similar to what one might expect of a family portrait, with each character and animal facing the viewer—a technique that reinforces the claim that Adam and Eve are humanity's parents. As the text above the illustration reads, "the

Bible story that Adam and Eve were the parents of the human race gains new strength from science, which shows that all human beings are related, and that no one race is superior to another" ("There Are No Master Races," 1944, p. 36). This first frame appeals to the Bible's creation myth as an assumed common reference for the conversation that is about to unfold and as a transition to the scientific findings.

Beyond the first frame, the visual and narrative method used throughout the remainder of "There Are No Master Races" (1944) is an educational motif (see Figure 9.3). The setting is a classroom. Most of the narrative unfolds as a teacher explaining to his students what science and the study of history reveal about race and human cultures. Children are taught to trust their teachers, so this narrative framework enhances the likelihood that the reader would perceive the information as accurate.

In response to Nazi propaganda of a hierarchy of races, with an Aryan race on top, *True Comics* equalizes all races. Although the comic does not go so far as to argue that there actually are no separate human races at all, it does teach that race is not a meaningful delineation. No doubt an argument that would have attempted to eliminate the very idea of different human races would have failed in the 1940s. Nonetheless, the discourse of "There Are No Master Races" (1944) was in many ways ahead of its time.

In human perception, the most obvious markers of race have always been visual: skin color, hair color and type, nose shape, and so on. Differences in skin pigmentation are readily evident and can seem to suggest an equally self-evident conclusion: that so-called races of humans are quite different. However, the comic teaches that visual differences do not logically entail any other differences.

"There Are No Master Races" (1944) teaches the reader about the reasons for these noticeable visual differences. Indeed, the scene of much of the comic's narrative is a classroom. A boy asks a teacher, "But if we are all the same, why do some people have dark skin and others have light or white skin?" The teacher responds "that is a good question, and the answer to it is a thrilling adventure story! Now, look at this map" ("There Are No Master Races," 1944, p. 37). The next four frames explain why humans have different skin pigmentations. In the first frame, a hand is pointing at a globe of the Earth. The voice, presumably belonging to the same person as the hand, explains that skin color is merely the result of chemicals in one's skin based upon how near or far one's ancestors lived to the equator. Dark-skinned people lived nearest the equator, those in the "middle" had "in-between" skin color, and those in northern regions had the lightest skin color. The boy, after hearing this information, asks "in other words, differences in skin color are not as big as we thought?" The teacher, excited

Figure 9.3: The consistent appearance of an authoritative teacher figure provides a narrative frame for the story's arguments ("There Are No Master Races," 1944, p. 36).

that his pupil understands, replies "exactly!" and then continues his lecture. "Yellow" skin tones, the teacher contends, are the result of carotene, and darker skin tones have more melanin. The teacher concludes "that's all there is to it," a remark that illustrates just how simple it all is once one possesses the correct knowledge ("There Are No Master Races," p. 1944, 37).

The final lesson specifically regarding race is that the term *Jewish* is descriptive of a religion, not a race of people. A critical component of Hitler's big lie was that Jews were in some way a race of humans. "There Are No Master Races" (1944) corrects this misunderstanding: "Jews are not a race. They have a common religion but are of many different stocks. There are Jews in virtually every country" (p. 41).

Influences on Human Intelligence and Personality Traits

Science can easily explain differences in skin color, but what about differences that are not visual? What about nonphysical attributes, like intelligence and morality? Non-Aryans, according to Nazi propaganda, do not merely look different; they are also less intelligent, less moral, and less civilized. The message of the comic in response to arguments about the inferiority of other races is that environment, not one's race, is the greatest determinant of one's intelligence and other attributes. Following the comic's explanation of skin color is a scene in which a group of approximately 10 men are sitting at desks taking a test (see Figure 9.4). This argument relies upon accepting the results of a test—a method often perceived as objective—over unfounded racial stereotypes. In the frame, a light-skinned male is thinking, "This is tough," while another light-skinned male is thinking, "A cinch!" One dark-skinned man is thinking, "I don't get it," while another is thinking "What a push-over." The description to the left of this frame reads that "intelligence has nothing to do with skin color. In World War I, tests given to U.S. soldiers of all colors showed that education, not skin color, determined their intelligence rating" ("There Are No Master Races," 1944, p. 39). Visually, the comic shows that there is no correlation between skin color and intelligence, because the thought bubbles above the heads of the men taking the test do not show a pattern. Some of the dark-skinned test-takers are struggling; others think it is easy. Some of the light-skinned characters find the exam easy; others find it difficult. This combined verbal and visual display is a simple way to counter stereotypes about race and intelligence.

The comic also tackles issues of savagery and morality, such as how prone a race of people might be to violence. The story contends that Mexican "Indians" [the indigenous inhabitants of what is now Mexico] "were continually fighting each other—until the Spaniards invaded their country" ("There Are No Master Races," 1944, p. 39). This two-frame vignette occurs as a sort of before-and-after sequence. The visual imagery of the frame on the left (the "before" frame) is chaotic, showing warriors in battle with spears and shields. Distinguishing who is fighting against whom in this image is difficult. Bodies are on the ground, apparently dead or injured. In the background are more warriors engaged in battle on the top of a protective wall, presumably surrounding a city. The narrative of the right-side frame (the "after" frame) states that "after the Spanish conquest, fighting Spaniards and belligerent Indians settled down and intermarried. Today their descendants are our peaceful good neighbors below the Rio Grande" ("There Are No Master Races," 1944, p. 39). In this frame, in stark visual contrast to the violent and chaotic "before" frame, appears a peaceful farming scene in an idyllic countryside. One farmer is hoeing the field, while another plants seeds in the distance. The lesson of this brief, two-frame historical example appears to be that although the indigenous inhabitants of Mexico were continually violent, and the Spanish were also an invasive force, all the races now live a peaceful farming lifestyle. There is, as this lesson suggests, nothing inherently violent about a particular group or race of people.

A second story similarly argues that there is no correlation between violence and race, this time in the reverse direction. In an attempt to explain Japanese aggression in the WWII era, the story contends that the Japanese were once

Figure 9.4: True Comics uses this frame to succinctly debunk any correlation between intelligence and skin color ("There Are No Master Races," 1944, p. 39).

peaceful "fishermen and farmers, poets and artists," until they first saw U.S. Navy ships ("There Are No Master Races," 1944, p. 39). The first frame shows two fishing boats sailing on the water with mountains in the background. Much like the farming scene mentioned above, this frame conveys a sense of tranquility. But soon this will change, and, in the next frame, several Japanese people are shown looking at U.S. naval vessels approaching a port. According to the story, Japan's leaders were lured by the naval power of the United States, thinking that such war vessels could make Japan more powerful. One of the characters, drawn wearing a conical hat often associated with Asian attire, is pointing at the naval ships, remarking, "Our nation should build ships of war like those of the Americans." A second Japanese character, drawn wearing a kimono and an even larger hat, says, "But our people are too peaceful for such things. We will have to teach them to think otherwise, if we wish to gain power" ("There Are No Master Races," 1944, p. 39). The third frame represents what the Japanese became by the time of WWII. "Within two generations," contends the comic, "the Japanese have been taught to be warlike to satisfy the ambitions of their military rulers." In that same frame, Japanese soldiers are shown with rifles and bayonets, charging an unseen foe. One of them is screaming "Banzai! We are the sons of heaven. KILL! KILL!" ("There Are No Master Races," 1944, p. 40). This three-frame example contends the opposite of the story about colonial Mexico, in that a once-peaceful people could be *taught* to become violent.

These two stories about the early inhabitants of Mexico and the Japanese lead the reader to the Germans and Hitler. Not unlike the Japanese, Germany's ruling class trained Germans to be aggressive and warlike. The majority of the next two full pages tells how Hitler indoctrinated Germans, especially German youth, to believe that they were both mentally and physically superior so that they could be trained as warriors who believed they were unbeatable. A text frame in the comic asserts that the German youth were taught to believe "only what Hitler wanted them to believe." As a result, they "became warlike, for they knew no other way of life" ("There Are No Master Races," 1944, p. 40).

The visual image to the right of this text frame shows a scene of marching Nazi soldiers (see Figure 9.5). In this scene, which is nearly double the size of a single frame, there are three Nazi swastika flags. Hitler, his back to the viewer, is saying to a Nazi officer, "Our plans are working well! We are raising a generation of brutal killers" ("There are No Master Races," 1944, p. 40). But training an army, contends the comic, was not enough. The Nazis also instilled a sense of racial superiority in their soldiers by making the claim that the so-called Aryan race was superior. One of Hitler's underlings questions the strategy: "Will the public be convinced?" Hitler responds, "The public will accept what we want them to believe because we have taught them to do so!" ("There Are No Master Races," 1944, p. 41). With the use of dialogue between Hitler's character and Nazi officers, the comic attempts to reveal the process necessary to brainwashing the German people into becoming an army of racist warriors. By implication, if racism and aggression can be learned, then presumably they can also be unlearned.

The historical accuracy of these particular vignettes notwithstanding, the *True Comics* stories advance the case that the nature of one's character is not inherently built into one's race. In the nature-versus-nurture debate, in other words, nurture wins; environmental influences, not one's race, are the main factors that determine one's intelligence and character. Education or, in the case of the Nazis, propaganda determines belief. Racial superiority is not innately understood. These stories explain how racism and other forms of bigotry are invented, cultivated, and perpetuated.

Conclusion and Implications

During much of WWII, Franklin D. Roosevelt and his administration were concerned not only about the often-tepid support for U.S. involvement in the war but also that the public was largely unaware of the true motives behind Hitler's aggression. Nazi propaganda was highly effective, not only in Europe but also in areas of the United States. The two stories in *True Comics* discussed

Figure 9.5: Here the story line depicts the eventual outcome of the German people's indoctrination as a result of Hitler's overpowering propaganda messages ("There Are No Master Races," 1944, p. 40).

here unveiled and taught readers to detect the strategies and faulty arguments Hitler used to spread misinformation and hatred. To achieve that goal, the comics addressed the major themes of racial, cultural, and religious differences that, not coincidentally, addressed the primary fabrications of Nazi propaganda.

The comic book form was able to provide these lessons in a unique manner, in no small part because of the role of the visual elements. As Gabilliet (2005/2010) argues, "cartooning easily made 'reality' as eye catching as fiction" (p. 27). At the same time, putting truth in comic book form made it more likely to be read and understood by youth, in particular, but also by many adults. These verbal and visual messages in combination reinforced each other. The text often set up the claim, and the visual image reinforced the argument. Showing an image of Christians cowering in front of a lion, for example, is more powerful than merely saying, "Christians were persecuted," because it bolsters the message, offering the argument in two distinct yet simultaneous forms.

The teaching lessons in "They Got the Blame" began with illustrations of far more obvious examples of scapegoating. For instance, twentieth-century U.S. citizens knew that evil demons do not cause cholera and that using ritualistic magic upon a water buffalo cannot cure an epidemic. The example makes it easy to understand scapegoating, because the drawings are, first, unfamiliar, and, second, the scapegoating victim is nonhuman and thus easy to *see* as different. The image of a water buffalo being chased out of a village demonstrates clearly how an animal that was not responsible for cholera is being made to suffer as a result of a faulty belief (that evil demons could magically be made to enter the body of an animal, thus also taking a disease with them). Thus, the progression of visual elements aids in teaching the causal links of each example of scape-goating. Once these examples were established, the comic was able to uncover more difficult-to-detect examples of scapegoating. These more contemporary examples, because they relied heavily upon widespread and largely accepted stereotypes such as racism and religious bigotry, were not as glaringly obvious as practices that blamed evil demons or angry gods for diseases and droughts.

The majority of U.S. citizens in the 1940s likely were not ready, however, to accept the argument that differences among races are nonexistent (and they certainly were not ready to consider that the entire concept of race is socially constructed). Drawing upon the fields of biology and anthropology, "There Are No Master Races" (1944) worked to discredit racist assumptions and be-liefs. For example, it tackled head-on the assumption that persons of African ancestry were somehow less intelligent. Advancing the claim that intelligence has nothing to do with skin color, the comic also *showed* the viewer concrete examples. Visual illustrations of a dark-skinned test-taker breezing through a test, and a lighter-skinned person struggling with that same test, bolstered the claim that visual racial identifiers such as skin color do not determine one's abilities. Historical lessons in the comic also taught that past civilizations were both passive and violent. Some cultures were transformed from violent to civilized (Mexico), while others reversed that process (Japan). Frames showing stark visual contrasts of tranquil-versus-violent scenes demonstrated further that there is no link between race and the degree to which one is civilized.

"They Got the Blame" (Gould, 1944) and "There Are No Master Races" (1944) thus sought to explain and expose the flaws in Hitler's rationale for a war that targeted Jews and other non-Aryans because of their alleged inferiority. At the same time, these stories were careful to *demonize* only Hitler and the Nazis; they did not *dehumanize* all Germans. Likewise, only Japanese military leaders, not all Japanese people, were portrayed as responsible for Japanese aggression. At a time when most U.S. propaganda dehumanized the Germans (often as a large gorilla with a huge club) and the Japanese en masse (as rats, bats, snakes, and octopi), these authors argued that socialization (nurture), not inherent racial traits (nature), was to blame for their aggression. In short, the comic book stories examined in this chapter demonized leaders without dehumanizing their followers.

"They Got the Blame" (Gould, 1944) and "There Are No Master Races" (1944) thus avoided a fundamental contradiction that was found in most U.S. propaganda: that Hitler was wrong, but at the same time enemies of the United States were subhuman or nonhuman. U.S. propaganda, in that regard, was indistinguishable from Hitler's, but these comic book–based stories made much more nuanced arguments that were logically consistent in debunking the foundation of *all* WWII propaganda (both sides dehumanized their enemies). After all, how could one have expected people to believe that Hitler was wrong about a master race when in the United States many still believed that people of African and Asian ancestry were inferior to Caucasians? How could one be expected to believe that Germans and Japanese were victims of indoctrination if U.S. propaganda dehumanized *all* of them?

Wars are fought as much with discourse as with weapons, and many in the comic book industry were aware of the power of propaganda. Defeating Hitler's forces only on European battlefields would not win the far more ubiquitous war against ignorance, misunderstanding, and hatred toward other races, religions, and cultures. Yet education and critical thinking, cultivated as a kind of counter-propaganda in the unconventional and supposedly unsophisticated medium of the comic book, might have created a foundation to wage and win the much lengthier war against ignorance and intolerance.

Notes

1. The comic books in the series at first appeared monthly, but then bimonthly after paper rations were implemented.

2. The comic version of the scapegoating story first appeared in *True Comics* in late 1943. The version I am citing here was republished as a separate booklet (although it was the same in content) by the CIO (Gould, 1944) and was distributed to its membership. The basic content of both story lines was not original to *True Comics*. Both were based upon other publications. "They Got the Blame" was originally a 63-page book by Kenneth M. Gould (1942). "There Are No Master Races" (1944) was based on a lengthier work by anthropologists Ruth Benedict and Gene Weltfish (1943).

3. Although it was true that Nazis did this, the implication that Hitler did it *because* the victims were Catholic is false. What the comic book does not clarify is that Hitler was not closing those churches and schools *because* they were Catholic, but rather because they opposed his leadership and Nazi fascism. Their religious beliefs and specific doctrine were inconsequential. Churches that supported Hitler were left alone. See, for example, Kershaw (2008, pp. 160, 166, 171–172).

References

Benedict, R., & Weltfish, G. (1943). *The races of mankind.* New York, NY: Public Affairs Committee.

Bess, M. (2006). *Choices under fire.* New York, NY: Knopf.

Blake, W. E. (n.d.). *A view of history:* True Comics, *1941–1945.* Retrieved from http://www.library.vcu.edu/jbc/speccoll/blake2.html

Bongco, M. (2000). *Reading comics: Language, culture, and the concept of the superhero in comic books.* New York, NY: Garland.

Carr, S. (2001). *Hollywood and anti-Semitism: A cultural history up to WWII.* New York, NY: Cambridge University Press.

Carrier, D. (2000). *The aesthetics of comics.* University Park, PA: Pennsylvania State University Press.

Casey, S. (2001). *Cautious crusade: Franklin D. Roosevelt, American public opinion, and the war against Nazi Germany.* New York, NY: Oxford University Press.

The cotton gin. (1941). In *True Comics* (pp. 48–54). (Vol. 1, no. 7). New York, NY: Parents' Magazine Press.

Drake's folly: The story of the first oil well ever drilled. (1941). In *True Comics* (pp. 37–43). (Vol. 1, no. 5). New York, NY: Parents' Magazine Press.

Eisner, W. (1985). *Comics and sequential art.* Tamarac, FL: Poorhouse.

Gabilliet, J. (2010). *Of comics and men: A cultural history of American comic books.* Jackson: University Press of Mississippi. (Original work published 2005)

Gould, K. M. (1942). *They got the blame: The story of scapegoats in history.* New York, NY: Association Press.

Gould, K. M. (1944). *They got the blame: The use of scapegoats in history.* Washington, DC: Congress of Industrial Relations.

Harvey, R. C. (1996). *The art of the comic book: An aesthetic history.* Jackson: University Press of Mississippi.

Heilbrunn, J. (2000, June). Ker-splat! *The Washington Monthly,* 46–49.

Hitler, A. (1971). *Mein Kampf* (R. Manheim, Trans.). Boston, MA: Houghton Mifflin. (Original work published 1932)

Jones, G. (2004). *Men of tomorrow: Geeks, gangsters, and the birth of the comic book.* New York, NY: Basic Books.

Kershaw, I. (2008). *Hitler, the Germans, and the Final Solution.* New Haven, CT: Yale University Press.

Sabin, R. (1993). *Adult comics: An introduction.* London, UK: Routledge.

There are no master races. (1944). In *True Comics* (pp. 36–42). (Vol. 4, no. 39). New York, NY: Parents' Magazine Press.

Wertham, F. (1954). *Seduction of the innocent.* New York, NY: Rinehart.

Witek, J. (1989). *Comic books as history.* Jackson: University Press of Mississippi.

Wright, B. W. (2001). *Comic book nation: The transformation of youth culture in America.* Baltimore, MD: Johns Hopkins University Press.

Young, J. E. (1998). The holocaust as vicarious past: Art Spiegelman's *Maus* and the afterimages of history. *Critical Inquiry, 24,* 666–699.

★★ 10 ★★

"Everyone Can Help, Young or Old, Large or Small"

Novelty Press Mobilizes Its Readers

David E. Wilt

In contrast with the superhero comic books so prevalent in cultural memories of the WWII era, Novelty Press comics portrayed the home-front effort through the eyes of a group of conventional protagonists, whose adventures more closely approximated the life of youthful, civilian comic book readers of the war years. Novelty Press had a policy of downplaying fantastic content in its comics in favor of realistic stories and juvenile, non-superhero characters with whom readers could identify and use as role models. Furthermore, as this essay will show, Novelty Press was not content to merely depict home-front life in realistic terms but actively encouraged its youthful audience to participate in the war effort, doing this by using narrative content such as covers and individual story lines, as well as editorial commentary and letters from readers themselves.

Novelty Press employed most of the standard methods of promoting the war effort—from overt propaganda on covers and in interior stories, to war-related house ads, final-panel messages, patriotic slogans printed on the bottom of each page, and a very active editorial/letters page. This synergistic combination of methods and content makes the company an interesting case study in the methodology of wartime comic book propaganda.

This chapter begins with an introduction to the Novelty Press company and its general editorial policy, examines the common themes which appeared in the company's wartime product, and then demonstrates how these themes were utilized by the publisher to promote active participation in the war effort on the part of its readership.

Novelty Press: Publisher of "Sensible" Comic Books

Novelty Press was a small comic book company owned by Curtis Publishing, which also published, among other titles, the mainstream magazine *The Saturday Evening Post*.[1] The success of Superman and Batman in 1938 and 1939 had sparked a boom in comic magazine publishing, with numerous new companies entering the market. The first Novelty Press publication was *Target Comics* #1, cover dated February 1940 (meaning it was available on newsstands in late 1939), followed by *Blue Bolt* in June. Novelty published only three comic book titles throughout the war years—*Target, Blue Bolt*, and *4Most* (which debuted with the Winter 1941 issue)—although several new titles appeared in mid-1945 as wartime paper restrictions eased.[2]

Most if not all of the material in the early Novelty Press magazines was supplied by the Funnies Inc. shop, a studio that provided ready-to-print comic book stories written and drawn by its own staff and freelancers. Novelty later began producing its own content, although some of the earlier features and their creators were retained.[3]

Novelty Press was not oriented toward superhero/fantasy subjects (as were, for example, publishers like Fawcett or DC) or action-genre comics (for instance, those published by Fiction House). Although the comic features provided by Funnies Inc. contained a considerable amount of superhero/fantasy material, by early 1942 this was being phased out and replaced with more realistic content. For example, science fiction superhero Blue Bolt was rechristened Blue Bolt the American and soon exchanged his costume for a uniform, joining the Air Corps for the duration. Costumed-hero trio Target and the Targeteers split up and enlisted in the U.S. Army, Navy and Marine Corps (retaining their costumes, however). To illustrate the changing emphasis of the Novelty Press comics, only 5 of 42 (12%) wartime *Target* covers featured costumed heroes as the primary characters, compared with 16 of the first 22 issues (73%) published in 1940–1941.

The company had, like many other publishers, already demonstrated a pro-American, antifascist attitude prior to the entry of the United States into WWII. The cover of the March 1941 issue of *Target* featured an image of Uncle Sam, the American flag, and the comic's main characters saluting, with the caption

"Your favorite characters mobilized to defend America!" (*Target*, 1941, cover)
Editorials also reiterated this stance, with statements such as "Patriotism is
now the theme of TARGET and BLUE BOLT" ("Ye Editors' Page," 1941a, inside
cover) and "The two 'isms' that TARGET wants to stand for are Americanism
and patriotism" ("Ye Editors' Page," 1941b, inside cover). The editorial policy became more pronounced after Pearl Harbor, with generic appeals for patriotism
replaced by concrete suggestions for readers to buy war bonds, participate in
scrap drives, and take part in other home-front activities.

As the publisher began to deemphasize fantasy content and openly promote American values, Novelty Press became increasingly focused on youthful
protagonists in stories with realistic settings and relatively realistic plots.[4] This
policy was at least in part prompted by reader feedback such as "I am really
fed up with all the fantastic super types of characters that comic artists seem
to think we kids like ... [we] prefer good sensible stories ..." (Pool, 1940, inside
cover). The editorial in the first issue of *4Most* stated: "Many of your letters lead
us to believe that the super-fantastic type of character is losing its popularity.
We further believe that the clean living, straight shooting American boy type ...
will never lose their popularity. We believe that they are the modern counter-
part of the foremost heroes of our great country. They represent the ideals
of liberty, honor, integrity, and manhood towards which the free people of
America are always striving" ("Ye Editors' Page," 1942a, inside cover).

Novelty's major non-superhero features included "Dick Cole, Boy Wonder,"
"The Cadet (Kit Carter)," "Edison Bell, Young Inventor," and "Speck, Spot and
Sis." All of these strips were relatively realistic, at least in comic book terms.
Almost nothing occurred in wartime "Edison Bell" or "Speck, Spot and Sis"
stories that could not feasibly happen to comic book readers of the day in real
life (Dick Cole and the Cadet tended to cross paths rather frequently with Axis
agents and non-political criminals, but there were otherwise very few overtly
fantastic elements in these series during the war years, and many stories dealt
with rather mundane events such as school athletic contests).

Not coincidentally, these four series also account for most of the home-front
messages in the company's magazines. The three Novelty Press titles contained
other regular features during the war years—the aforementioned "Blue Bolt the
American" and "Target and the Targeteers," plus "Old Cap Hawkins," "Bullseye
Bill," "Krisko & Jasper," "Fearless Fellers," and "The Chameleon," to name a few—
some with occasional home-front references,[5] others war-oriented but chiefly
dealing with actual armed conflict or battles against spies and saboteurs, and
others containing few if any war references.[6]

Reader acceptance of the realism of the Novelty Press stories and characters
was important. Based on published letters in the comics themselves, readers

apparently enjoyed having an alternative to fantastic comic books.[7] Young comic buyers might fantasize about catching Nazi spies, fighting Japanese saboteurs, or battling monsters, but they could actually emulate the home-front activities of adolescent comics characters in familiar, realistic settings. Even before the war, readers had commented on the suitability of Novelty Press characters as role models: "I like Dick Cole because he is a real American boy who could serve as a pattern for any boy" (Lance, 1941, inside cover).

Indeed, some readers openly rebelled against fantasy content, writing, "I'm glad you don't have any superhuman marvels in your book" (Otwell, 1945, inside cover). Even the relatively staid adventures of a character such as Edison Bell (who in prewar *Blue Bolt* traveled to exotic lands and met headhunters, Axis spies, etc., before settling down to a small-town existence during the war years) sometimes drew criticism: one reader wrote, "It is very seldom, if at all, that American youth ever meets up with . . . Nazi spies and saboteurs . . ." (Boehi, 1944, inside cover). The editors replied: "You're right, Ronald. Eddie Bell does get in more adventures than the average fellow would ever meet . . . Is that bad? We invite other readers to comment on whether Eddie Bell is 'overdone'" ("Blue Bolt Flashes," 1944, inside cover).

The Edison Bell stories, which one reader defined as "constructive amuse-ment," even contain "how to" diagrams so the simple inventions created by the protagonist in the stories could be replicated by readers (Thompson, 1941, inside cover). Many of these gadgets are home-front-oriented, with a particular emphasis on materials conservation, such as the "Victory Christmas Tree" (Gill & DeLay, 1943b, p. 42) and a "Victory Sled" made from scrap wood ("Edison Bell," 1945a, p. 21).

Home-Front Propaganda in Novelty Press Comics

The stories and editorials in Novelty Press convey a unified message—the im-portance of participation in home-front activities as a contribution to the war effort—in different ways. The fictional stories highlighting the actions of juve-nile protagonists and the direct, even didactic editorial messages are not only complementary but also share certain themes and motifs intended to convince readers of the value of the services young people could provide to the war ef-fort. These common themes include membership in a group: whether a specific, fictional wartime organization such as the Junior Air Raid Wardens, the Liberty Club, or the Victory Boys, or a subset of a larger group such as students in a school, residents of a town, or simply a clique of friends, joint participation in home-front activities is depicted as a bonding activity. Outsiders are granted access to the group if their motives are pure: everyone has a role to play in the war effort, regardless of age or sex. Membership in the home-front activity group is often presented as a substitute for military service or employment in a war industry, for protagonists that are too young for such work.

The Novelty Press editorials strongly imply that their readers are members of a special group, united both in their status as loyal fans of these comic magazines and as dedicated Americans contributing to the war effort. The stories featuring youthful protagonists also emphasize the shared-activity nature of their home-front participation, depicting both formal and informal groups carrying out war-oriented tasks.

A second common theme is approbation. Young people who participate in home-front activities receive praise for their efforts from their peers, from adults (including their parents) and from authority figures (such as government officials and members of the military). The desire of young people to be respected and admired for their actions cannot be understated, and nearly every story with juvenile protagonists also features adults expressing their approval. Similarly, the Novelty Press editorials praise and encourage their readers at all times, stressing the importance of their contributions on the home front and how much these efforts are appreciated by not only the editors but also the fighting men, the United States government, and America in general.

Finally, personal pleasure and material rewards are depicted. Home-front activities are shown to be work—at times arduous—but are also fun and rewarding. For example, War bonds and stamps are sold at social events such as parties, carnivals, plays, and athletic events. Even door-to-door sales provide opportunities to meet interesting people. Scrap drives, when carried out in the company of one's friends, are pleasurable activities and can be converted into friendly competitions.

Material rewards are also forthcoming, although in most cases these are not immediately redeemed for luxury items—a frequent motif is the depiction of juvenile characters receiving a monetary reward for some action and then immediately announcing their intention to invest it in war bonds and stamps; in some cases, the reward *is* a War bond. The postwar fun to be had with the fruits of wartime Bonds purchases is referred to in a number of stories. In *Target's* "Speck, Spot and Sis," Sis at one point receives a cash reward for rescuing a lost dog. In the final panel, she stands between two different storefronts, one labeled "War Bond HQ" and the other bearing a sign reading "Sale on New Bicycles." The caption reads: "Of course Sis will buy War Bonds and Stamps with the reward money now, and a new bike after the war with the money saved in bonds" ("Speck, Spot and Sis," 1945, p. 14). Referring to a $100 war bond prize they hope to win, Jerry jokingly tells his friend Edison Bell, "In ten years we'll be rich" ("Edison Bell," 1945c, p. 17).

The "Sergeant Spook" series dealt with the ghost of a policeman, and young Jerry, his (live) sidekick. In the July 1944 *Blue Bolt*, Jerry, "impressed with the urgent need to collect waste paper for the war effort," accumulates the most paper (aided by Sgt. Spook and his ghostly friends) and wins a cross-country trip as a prize. "Gosh—" he tells the awards committee, composed of adults, "I didn't collect paper 'cause there was a prize—I just did it for the soldiers! I know how important it is . . ." ("Sergeant Spook," 1944a, p. 39) Thus, Jerry earns both the approbation of adults *and* a material prize, simply for doing his patriotic duty. Similar awards ceremonies or scenes of informal congratulations appear in many home-front stories, reinforcing the concept that participation in home-front activities is not merely providing valuable support of broader war goals but also personally beneficial.

Youthful Protagonists in Novelty Press Series

In this section, the home-front propaganda in four major Novelty Press comic series is examined, demonstrating how the three major themes described above are utilized, and how the various characters serve as role models for young readers.

Dick Cole, Wonder Boy

Dick Cole, Wonder Boy was one of the most popular and enduring characters to appear in Novelty Press comic magazines. In addition to long runs in *Blue Bolt* and *4Most*, Cole was given his own title in the postwar period, and his adventures were even chronicled in a dramatic radio series in the 1940s. Cole is a cadet at the fictitious Farr Military Academy (which seems to be a college-level institution), allowing him to participate in both teenage and adult activities.[8] After a period of rather outré prewar adventures—the Dick Cole story in the Winter 1942 *4Most* features a rampaging dinosaur controlled by an insane cadet (Davis, 1942)—the majority of the remaining Dick Cole tales revolved around life and activities at Farr (or summer vacation excursions), including athletics and academics, although the school does seem to attract more than its share of gangsters and foreign agents whose nefarious schemes must be foiled by Dick and his pals.

A fair number of Dick Cole stories contain references to the war, but only a handful are directly home-front-oriented. In one *Blue Bolt* story, Dick and his pals volunteer to work on farms during their summer vacation (Wilcox, 1944b); in another, the cadets attend a Halloween party with war bonds as prizes (Wilcox, 1944a); in still another, Dick and his friends break up a black-market gang, and decide to use the reward money to pay for a poor girl's operation, and "the money that is left is going into War Bonds" (Wilcox, 1945, p. 10). As can be seen, the themes of group participation, adult approbation, and home-front work as fun and rewarding are all present here.

For the most part, however, Dick—between adventures on the grid-iron and military training exercises—was actively thrashing Axis agents, saboteurs, and gangsters and thus had little time for selling bonds or collecting scrap. Dick Cole's quasi-adult status, on the cusp between a full-time student and a responsible adult, illustrates the dichotomy in Novelty Press magazines between comics with adult protagonists, who worked or fought, and the series starring juvenile protagonists, who made their contribution to the war effort on the home front.

The Cadet

Although also a cadet at a military school (the fictitious Daunton Academy this time), Kit Carter, star of "The Cadet" series, was noticeably younger in appearance and demeanor than Dick Cole.[9] As with the Cole series, many of the stories centered around cadet life and did not address the war at all. Still, almost exactly half of the wartime Kit Carter stories in *Target* and *4Most* comics were war-relevant in some way; about two-thirds of these involved encounters with saboteurs, U-boats, and Axis spies.

However, the relative youthfulness of Carter, his sidekick Dan Merry, and the other Daunton cadets allowed them to be involved with home-front activities to a greater extent than Dick Cole and thus made them even better surrogates for young readers of the comic. These stories balance realism and plausibility with adventure and drama.

For example, in the July/August 1943 *Target*, the cadets train war dogs for the military (the final panel of the story gives an address readers could write to and inquire about the program, but were warned, "DO NOT send your dog!") ("Kit Carter," 1943b, pp. 1–12) In a subsequent story, Kit and his pals volunteer to work on farms during their vacation (Novelty Press editorials urged their young readers to participate in this activity in real life, and a number of stories depict such volunteer farm work), are hazed by local boys, then save the community when a flood threatens to destroy the local dam ("Kit Carter," 1943c, pp. 1–10). Part-time jobs in a war factory occupy the cadets' after-school time in another episode: paid the princely sum of 90 cents per hour, they vow, "Mine goes into War Bonds!" ("Kit Carter," 1945a, pp. 1–9). Earlier, in the Summer 1942 issue of *4Most*, Kit wins $5,000 in war bonds at a sports carnival and donates it to a man whose wife needs an operation (shades of Dick Cole)("Kit Carter," 1942).

Unlike the staid, slightly older Dick Cole, Kit Carter was not above personally selling war bonds, participating in scrap drives, and engaging in youth-
oriented recreational activities. For example, a desire to raise money for the
USO sparks a case of "let's put on a . . . show" among the Daunton cadets ("Kit
Carter," 1943a, p. 49). In the June 1944 *Target*, the Daunton Academy is $100,000
short of their $1 million Victory War Loan bond drive goal; fortunately, Kit and
Dan rescue a wealthy manufacturer from Axis agents posing as hoboes, and the
rich man puts them over the million-dollar mark with his purchase of bonds
("Kit Carter," 1944). In a later issue, a rival military academy has its athletic
budget cut: to earn money for needed uniforms and equipment, the school and
Daunton hold a scrap paper and waste fat drive (unfortunately, the broker who
purchases their salvaged material is actually an Axis agent who intends to destroy it rather than turn it over to Uncle Sam) ("Kit Carter," 1945b).[10]

Although Kit Carter is depicted as closer in age than Dick Cole to the
presumed average Novelty Press reader, his stories are still somewhat skewed
toward adventure and action. More realistic in their exploration of the home-
front milieu were the series "Edison Bell" and "Speck, Spot and Sis," comics with
adolescent protagonists set in small-town environments.

Edison Bell, Young Inventor

Edison Bell (whose name is a conflation of real-life inventors Thomas Edison
and Alexander Graham Bell) seems to have been originally conceived in the
mode of the fictional teen scientist Tom Swift. His early stories feature elaborate
inventions (he even had a sentient robot sidekick named Frankie Stein) and
fantastic adventures. In the immediate pre-WWII period, an extended series
appears in which Bell and his friends go pearl-diving in the South Seas, are ship-
wrecked, battle headhunters, and are rescued by a tramp steamer, only to discover the crew is made up of Axis agents. However, once the war began, Eddie
became a normal, small-town adolescent who just happens to be resourceful
and inventive. Axis saboteurs and spies and various American criminals such as
gas bootleggers and ration-stamp counterfeiters make occasional appearances,
but the Bell stories contain much more realistic—and thus exemplary—home-
front content than either the "Dick Cole" or "The Cadet" series.

Eddie Bell's home-front activities actually predated Pearl Harbor. In the
Winter 1942 *4Most*, Eddie and his friends become "Junior Air Raid Wardens"
and are also shown collecting used magazines to send to "draftees in camp"
(Gill and DeLay, 1942, p. 43). This story's invention blueprint shows readers how
to make their own "Listening Post" (p. 48) and in the Spring 1942 *4Most*, it is
reported that after Pearl Harbor (which occurred "two or three weeks" after

the previous issue went on sale), Novelty Press received numerous requests for additional copies of the comic from readers who wanted to build Bell's invention for themselves ("Ye Editors' Page," 1942b, inside cover).

The Edison Bell story in the Summer 1943 4Most was "suggested in a letter from the United States Treasury Department," according to writer Ray Gill in the final panel (Gill, 1943, p. 35). "The grown ups have their hands full with war work, so the Junior Air-Raid Wardens decide to help." Eddie tells his pals, "The more help we give them, the more time they'll have for the Red Cross and other agencies," and he initiates a program he calls "We'll Do That Chore to Win the War" (Gill, 1943, p. 25). The local children run errands, fix appliances, and do various chores, all at no charge. This brings Eddie into conflict with young bully Brock, who sees his similar, for-profit business threatened: "Be as patriotic as you want to—but I'm still warnin' ya to stay away from *our* customers, see?" "I'm not sure we can do that," Eddie retorts. "Besides, do you want it known you're *cashing in* on the war effort?" (Gill, 1943, p. 28). Brock and his pal Stinkie attempt to sabotage the Junior Air-Raid Wardens' effort but are caught by the police and sentenced to work with Eddie "for the duration." When his friends complain, Eddie tells them: "We are at war! There's no time for petty feelings. Kids can't act their ages because they have men's jobs to do—and that means each one of us who's man enough!" (Gill, 1943, p. 35). Eddie is congratulated by police captain O'Neil, who brings a message from the mayor: "Your work this past week has saved almost a thousand dollars, and all of it will go into War Bonds and Stamps!" Eddie, glum because he hasn't personally bought any bonds lately, receives a $100 war bond from the town authorities as a reward for his patriotic work: "Individual effort of any kind is rewarded, Eddie" (Gill, 1943, p. 35).

This story contains the themes that appear frequently in the Novelty Press wartime comic stories: emphasis on the positive value of membership in a group (with outcasts Brock and Stinkie joining at the conclusion), a depiction of young people receiving the approbation of adults for their war work (in this case a police official and the mayor, presumably reflecting the sentiments of the whole town), and the characterization of home-front activities as rewarding, both morally and materially. Eddie, his best friend, Jerry, and the other Junior Air-Raid Wardens don't shirk their responsibility in wartime—and although they are sacrificing their free time, the work they do is not depicted as onerous. Quite the contrary, a diagram showing how to make a bicycle trailer states, "Delivering Groceries Can Be Fun!" (Gill, 1943, p. 28). This strip is even more intellectually and emotionally accessible to young readers because it has no fantastic or especially outrageous content, taking place in a small town with nary an Axis saboteur (or even a gangster) in sight.[11]

The Edison Bell story in the Spring 1945 issue of *4Most* involves a Victory Garden contest, with Eddie and Jerry pitted against Butch Brady and his gang, who not only cheat and attempt to sabotage Eddie's garden but also have vowed to prematurely cash in the $100 war bond prize if they win. At the end of the story, Eddie and Jerry defeat Butch's gang in a push-mobile "tank" battle and compel Butch to compete fairly in the Victory Garden effort ("Edison Bell," 1945c). This story was accompanied by five different how-to diagrams, four of them related to Victory Gardens, plus a full-page blueprint for making a push-mobile "tank" ("Edison Bell," 1945c, p. 26). One of the tips advises readers how to plan their garden before planting and provides the address of the U.S. Department of Agriculture, as well as the titles of helpful pamphlets that could be requested ("Edison Bell," 1945c, p. 18). Stories such as this make it clear that Novelty Press was attempting to motivate its readers to participate in the war effort in ways beyond simple patriotic platitudes or slogans.

Brock and Stinkie return in the November 1944 *Blue Bolt*, hijacking deliveries by Eddie's new home-front service (replacing deliverymen who're in the service or working in war factories, and using bicycles and wagons rather than gas-guzzling trucks). The recidivist bad boys are defeated, of course, and Eddie reminds his pals (and the readers, in a final-panel message): "We're helping on the home front by relieving shortages, and *anything* that helps, no matter how small it seems, goes a *long way* toward winning the war!" ("Edison Bell," 1944b, p. 25).

Although a number of other Edison Bell stories deal with the popular themes of war stamps/bonds and scrap drives, several stories address different home-front topics. In a late 1943 *Blue Bolt*, Eddie and Jerry volunteer to mind little Roger Brown, whose mother is employed in a war plant. Worn out trying to amuse the boy and keep him out of trouble, Eddie and Jerry take the advice of their friend Pat, who suggests the creation of a playground for children of war workers, with the older children as overseers.[12] Brock and Stinkie scoff as usual, but Eddie has the last word: "There isn't a 'sissy' job connected with the war effort. The least important thing will help us to win!" (Gill & DeLay, 1943a, p. 23).

One of the last war-oriented Edison Bell stories, in the May 1945 *Blue Bolt*, deals with wartime economics.[13] Eddie's father receives a folder from the Office of War Information on the dangers of inflation and prepares a speech for the Chamber of Commerce on the topic, while Eddie writes an English-class composition on the same subject. The two documents get mixed up, and although Eddie's paper is a success as a speech, his father's original speech gets "the lowest mark in the [English] class!" ("Edison Bell," 1945b, p. 20). The project blueprint of the issue, "in cooperation with our government's anti-inflation campaign," is labeled "Don't Buy It—Make It Yourself!" and shows some simple household items (such as lamps and trash cans) readers could construct ("Edison Bell," 1945b, p. 21). Earlier, in the April 1943 *Blue Bolt*, a similar suggestion was made in the Edison Bell story: "Glamour Gadgets for Glamour Gals—Let's consider that you'll be helping the war effort by freeing machines for munitions that ordinarily might be making these [devices]!" ("Edison Bell," 1943, p. 26).

Even stories which were not overtly war-oriented often had a subtext, as in the Edison Bell story in *Blue Bolt* issue dated September 1944. Eddie is excited because he's going to purchase his first pair of long pants (as opposed to the knee-length knickers or "plus-fours" worn at the time by younger boys). The war is not specifically mentioned in the strip, but the project page illustrates Eddie's highly organized clothes closet and reminds readers, "To cooperate for Victory on the home front, keep your clothing in applepie order. Remember: 'Use it up, Wear it out, Make it do—or do without!'" (a standard wartime conservation refrain) ("Edison Bell," 1944a, p. 31).

The Edison Bell stories are perhaps the most effective examples of the Novelty Press style of comic book home-front propaganda aimed at young readers: they are a combination of realistic stories and art, attainable goals, explicit "how-to" tips, and a clear (if sometimes didactic) explanation of the reasons for buying war bonds, salvaging scrap, and so on. The series validates the importance of the participation of young people in bond sales, scrap drives, and other home-front activities and demonstrates the multiple rewards that such participation brings. Finally, the Bell stories show readers that home-front war work can actually be fun and entertaining, as well as patriotic.

Speck, Spot and Sis

"Speck, Spot, and Sis" began in the July 1941 issue of *Target* and focused on a young boy and his family (Pa, Ma, snobby older sister, tagalong younger sister Sis, plus Spot the terrier) who live in the small town of Smartsburg. Though drawn in a slightly old-fashioned, cartoony style by Jack Alonzo Vincent Warren (who signed his work with various permutations of his real name), "Speck, Spot and Sis" was not a gag strip but contained rather mild, homespun humor, tinged at times with pathos (one early story arc deals with Speck's unemployed father—"The Depression has about whipped Pa. He has lost his business and can't find work") (Vincent, 1941, p. 42).

The first major "Speck, Spot and Sis" home-front story appeared in the July 1942 *Target* (Vincent, 1942c).[14] The theme of membership in a group appears here, as it does in many Novelty Press wartime stories. "Speck, like all other

American boys, is doing his bit in the *all out* effort to bring this terrible war to an end. He has his gang, and many other guys, organized into a company" (Vincent, 1942c, p. 27). Speck's Pa and his business partner, both WWI veterans, purchase uniforms for the lads and agree to drill the "Victory Boys," but the strip is careful to point out that the boys aren't merely playing soldier—they sell "Victory stamps" and collect scrap iron and waste paper. Stoney the bully at first mocks the boys and gets a black eye for his troubles, but later joins up: "Gather'n this old iron an' paper is the first hard work I ever done—an' I like it!" (Vincent, 1942c, p. 30). In the final panel, Speck addresses the comic book reader directly, to solidify the message delivered by the preceding story: "Listen, Kids! We don't want this war to go on until we're grown up. So it's up to us, same as it's up to th' grown-ups—to do everything we can do to help." A text box adds: "You're right, Speck! We all, old and young, can do lots of things to help win the war" (Vincent, 1942c, p. 30).

The next four consecutive "Speck, Spot and Sis" stories in 1942 all deal with home-front issues: Speck and the Victory Boys (often referred to as VIOT for "Victory Is Our Target," the group's slogan, which also appeared on some of *Target*'s later covers) sell war bonds and stamps, collect scrap, take Red Cross first-aid courses, etc. In the October 1942 *Target*, the splash panel shows Speck and his pals as they "form a flying wedge and <u>sell</u> War Saving Stamps!" The panel also includes a reproduction of the Minute Man "For Victory . . ." war bonds symbol; references to saving scrap metal, toothpaste tubes ("almost pure tin"), and old newspapers; and a reminder to donate to the Red Cross (Warren, 1942, p. 21). When a big-city reporter senses the mobilization of the youth of Smartsburg is news, he asks Speck to "Give [with the information]," but Speck replies, "I've nothing to give except my time and the money I earn" (Warren, 1942, p. 21). The story concludes with a Victory Day Parade featuring four generations of Speck's family in uniform: his great-grandfather (Civil War), grandfather (Spanish-American War), father (WWI), and older brother (WWII). Everyone in town attends the parade "except the factory workers. The factory goes on *day* and *night*. The folks of Smartsburg are *all out for Victory!*" (Warren, 1942, p. 24).

The series continued to focus on home-front activities throughout 1943. Even the non-war stories in several issues justify their non-relevance: Speck is sent to his grandparents' farm because he needs a rest from his Victory Boys activities, and in another issue "Speck has some time to devote to just boy work," because the home-front organization he founded is operating so smoothly (Vincent, 1943a, p. 13).

In the March 1943 *Target*, Betty, a new girl in town, forms the girls' Junior Auxiliary Corps (JACs) and vows to sell more War Savings Stamps than the all-male VIOT. Speck is humiliated by this but is conflicted, because he has a crush on Betty. Meanwhile, Speck's Sis joins the JACs and sells war stamps by blackmailing and scaring people with a (fake) rat, a rare *negative* example of home-front activities (Vincent, 1943b).[15] By the following issue, however, the VIOT and JACs have agreed to cooperate, and—after a fourth-wall-breaking visit to the comic strip's artist "Mr. Vincent"—urge the boys and girls of American to form their own VIOT and JAC clubs. The artist asks readers to send in designs for VIOT/JAC insignia, and Sis reminds everyone "It's a lotta fun" to get out and sell War Saving Stamps (Vincent, 1943c, p. 53).

In the May 1943 *Target*, we learn that Speck's "Dad is an air warden, Mother is a Red Cross worker, big brother is in the Marines. Speck is Captain of the 'Victory Boys.' Little Sis is a J.A.C. And Big Sis . . ." has changed her frivolous, self-centered prewar attitude and has become a WAAC (Vincent, 1943d, p. 49). Throughout the rest of 1943, the home-front stories become even more complex, dealing with Victory Gardens, neglected children of war workers, local bully Butch (not the same Butch who bothered Edison Bell, but a name-sake who shares his bullying proclivities), who thinks working on a Victory Garden is for "sissies"—a story arc that shockingly concludes with Speck being shot and wounded by another boy—and even a visit to Speck's grandparents' farm to help bring in the wheat harvest.

However, in 1944 and 1945 the majority of the "Speck, Spot and Sis" stories published in *Target* were only peripherally war-oriented, if at all. This may be attributed in part to the unexplained departure of series creator Jack Warren from the strip; he was temporarily replaced by Milt Hammer, whose art emulated Warren's style fairly effectively, but whose stories concentrated more on humor and less on character and story development. It's also possible that an editorial policy change mandating less war content had been implemented by Novelty Press—as noted above, Robert D. Wheeler became editor and general manager in the spring of 1944[16]—or that the topic of the VIOT group's involvement in home-front activities was simply viewed as played out. There were still some topical references in the series and even full stories dealing with scrap drives and war stamps well into 1945, but the fervor and focus of the home-front activity depicted in the series from mid-1942 through the end of 1943 was definitely missing.

The "Speck, Spot and Sis" stories provide a positive and realistic role model for readers: Speck is a normal, mischievous, small-town boy who is honestly enthusiastic about participating in the war effort. The stories forgo almost all action or adventure content—although criminals appear several times and one story deals with saboteurs, such plots were rare—in favor of mild, homespun humor and earnest propaganda about the need to go "all out" for the war effort.

Conclusions

Novelty Press followed a deliberate middle path between genres and audiences, eschewing the fantastic, the superhero genre, and even the overtly juvenile funny-animal genre, concentrating instead on non-super, civilian protagonists (often adolescents) in largely realistic stories and settings. This policy was not instituted solely because of WWII, but—whether by design or coincidence—characters and stories of this type provided an ideal setting for positive home-front messages aimed at young readers. Reinforcing the themes of the stories with regular commentary on the editorial/letters pages of the Novelty Press titles, the publisher urged active participation in home-front activities by its audience.

Little ideological discourse appears in the Novelty Press comics aimed at young audiences: overt discussion of making the world safe for democracy and freeing the oppressed people of the world, even description of the evils of fascism, is conspicuously absent. Although a general appeal to patriotism is implicit in the stories and editorials, the three main selling points of juvenile participation in home-front activities focus on the benefits of group membership; the approval of others, especially adults; and the representation of war work as important but also fun and rewarding.

The stated goal of these home-front activities was simply to win the war—which meant defeating the Axis, to be sure, but without many more details than that. The war had taken away fathers, brothers, and friends and was disrupting daily life for all Americans; and victory would solve those problems. And victory could be only achieved, the Novelty Press magazines repeatedly stressed via their stories and editorials, if *everyone*—and most especially the youthful readers of their comics—did their part, on the war front and on the home front.

Notes

1. Although Curtis Publishing was based in Philadelphia, the Novelty Press editorial offices were located in New York City. Novelty Press went out of business in 1949, selling some of its titles to Star Publications.

2. Out of a total of 101 wartime issues (dated 1942–1945) of these three key titles, only 6 were not available to read; thus, approximately 94% of the Novelty comics published during the war were accessible for this study.

3. The comics were copyrighted by Funnies Inc. until the summer of 1942; after this point, Novelty Press or The Novelty Press Division of The Premium Service Co. Inc was listed as the copyright holder. The original editor of *Target* and *Blue Bolt* was David Adams, replaced in the early 1942 by Stanley H. Beaman. Beaman edited all three of Novelty's wartime comic titles until the summer 1944 issues, when Robert D. Wheeler became editor and general

manager, with Jane Spaulding Nye receiving credit as associate editor (Nye would be promoted to managing editor in late 1945).

4. Juvenile protagonists appeared in comics from many other publishers—*Boy Comics* from Lev Gleason's Comic House company almost exclusively featured stories starring adolescent boys, for example—but many of these series were relatively unrealistic superhero-, action-, or fantastic-genre product.

5. The Fearless Fellers—the group consisted of Chuck, their leader; Butch, a tomboy (the other members don't discover she's a girl until much later in the series); fat kid Pudge; and black youth Inky—also had relatively realistic adventures, as would be expected for a Novelty Press series. The Fellers participate in scrap drives, a war bond carnival, and so on. In the January 1944 *Blue Bolt*, they find a stash of Confederate money, sell it to an antiquarian, and ask for payment in War Savings Stamps, a frequent motif in wartime comics (Keifer & Gill, 1944).

6. In the March 1943 issue of *Target*, the editors wrote, "We are going to cut down on some of the war and spy stories in TARGET as a few of you readers have complained that there are too many" ("Ye Editors' Page," 1943, inside cover). The results of this announced policy change were hardly noticeable, however—in fact, some continuing strips (the western "Bullseye Bill" and the crime-action feature "The Chameleon") changed shortly thereafter to become *more* war-oriented, and new war-relevant series ("Stories of the United Nations" and "18 Men and a Boat") were added to the lineup. It was not until 1944 that the number of stories focused on the war dropped precipitously.

7. In the *Blue Bolt* dated August 1945, one reader writes: "I like BLUE BOLT COMICS very much because it has none of those supermen in it . . . I do not like 'Sgt. Spook' because nothing like that can happen" (Sphar, 1945, inside cover). It is possible the editors gave preference to printing letters that supported the comic's "realistic content" policy, although a number of letters critical of various aspects of the magazines did appear.

8. Dick Cole's origin story is somewhat reminiscent of pulp magazine hero Doc Savage: an orphan, Cole is raised scientifically by a professor to be a "perfect specimen of manhood." He becomes highly intelligent and athletically endowed, graduates from high school at age 12, and spends five years traveling around the world, honing his various skills, before enrolling in the Farr Military Academy (Davis, 1940). Cole's almost superhuman abilities were toned down in later years (and the "Wonder Boy" subtitle was mostly dropped), although he remained Farr's best student and athlete.

9. In The Cadet's debut (in *Target*, June 1941), he is introduced as an orphan, the son of a World War I hero (Gates, 1941). Within a few issues, a new artist took over the strip, and the rather mature original Kit Carter became much younger and more boyish in appearance and behavior. While Dick Cole is described as a high school graduate, and Farr Military Academy is thus a post–high school institution, Kit's Daunton Academy is clearly for students of high school age and younger.

10. The latter story is a rare example of scrap/salvage money being used for something other than the purchase of war bonds and contrasts strongly with the "Edison Bell" story in the Spring 1945 *4Most*. In that issue bad boy Butch predicts *his* gang will win the "Best Victory Garden" contest and says he'll immediately cash in the $100 war bond prize to buy new football uniforms. Hearing that unpatriotic statement, Eddie punches Butch in the jaw! ("Edison Bell," 1945c, p. 17).

11. "Edison Bell"—whose hero, with his errant forelock of blonde hair, somewhat resembles Hergé's Tintin—was drawn by Harold DeLay in a much more realistic style than

either "Dick Cole" or "The Cadet." On the other hand, "Speck, Spot and Sis" was illustrated by Alonzo Vincent aka "Jack A. Warren" and later by Milt Hammer, both proponents of a more "cartoony" art style, yet still contained a significant amount of home-front propaganda.

12. "Speck, Spot and Sis" addressed the issue of the neglected children of war workers in the June 1943 *Target*—the Junior Auxiliary Corps girls open a day nursery, because "mothers can't be working in defense industries and watch their children at the same time—--so we must do the latter!" (Vincent, 1943e, p. 28). The "Sergeant Spook" story in the July 1944 *Blue Bolt* also dealt with this topic. Spook's young sidekick, Jerry, sees two unattended children playing with matches. Their father is in the service, and "mother's at the war plant—she's building planes and stuff." The distracted Mrs. Maloney is not only neglecting her children but isn't buying enough war bonds, and she wastes valuable scrap (such as tin cans and waste fats). Jerry and Sgt. Spook pitch in to educate her and her children, helping out with child care and household chores as well ("Sergeant Spook," 1944b, p. 39).

13. War bonds and stamps provided vital financing for the war effort, but were also valuable in siphoning off "excess" money from the economy, money which might have been spent on scarce luxury items or otherwise squandered in a manner which might have contributed to inflation.

14. As early as the "Speck, Spot and Sis" story in the January 1942 issue of *Target*, the issue of buying bonds was raised (the family comes into some money from various sources, and Speck says, "I suggest we buy *Government Stamps* . . . with our other money, [and] let's give to the USO. Maybe Brother, who is in the Army, will benefit by it") (Vincent, 1942a, p. 30). In the April 1942 *Target*, Speck's older sister is now allegedly working for "war relief," which seems to consist largely of flirting with servicemen on leave, and Speck says "Dames and war is upsettin' th' world, I betcha!" (Vincent, 1942b, p. 31).

15. The "Little Wise Guys" in Comic House's *Boy Comics* perhaps gave readers some mixed messages as well. In *Boy Comics* from June 1942, the gang pesters the "local defense authorities" until they're given $100 in War Stamps to sell. Evicting a newsstand proprietor from his post, the boys set up a "Slap the Jap" game and earn $99.75. Approaching a foppish young man and his date on the street, they offer him the final stamp but are turned down. Angered, the Little Wise Guys beat up the man and (presumably) take his money in exchange for the stamp! ("Little Wise Guys," 1942a). Their behavior in the next issue was even less admirable: the local citizens feel too safe from enemy invasion and thus refuse to purchase war bonds and stamps from the gang. The boys create a fake air raid to panic the population and then reap the benefits by selling the frightened people war bonds ("Little Wise Guys," 1942b).

Perhaps to avoid confusion with a different set of Little Wise Guys in *Daredevil* comics, *Boy* dropped the strip and replaced it with "Little Dynamite," a derby-hatted New York boy. In the February 1943 *Boy Comics*, Little Dynamite and his pals are collecting scrap metal. When a bartender says, "Why don't you kids grow up and stop wastin' yer time collectin' scrap?" Little Dynamite beats him up and takes the saloon's brass rail for the scrap drive: "Anyone as unpatriotic as him deserved what he got" (Wood, 1943, pp. 26–27).

Such depictions of anti-social behavior in the service of the war effort were relatively rare, probably because the media did not want to, even inadvertently, encourage such actions.

16. Wheeler's name first appeared as editor and general manager in Novelty Press comic magazines dated summer 1944, but comics were generally available on newsstands about two months prior to the cover date.

References

Blue Bolt flashes. (1944). In *Blue Bolt* (inside cover). (Vol. 4, no. 12). Philadelphia, PA: Novelty Press.

Boehi, R. (1944). Blue Bolt flashes. In *Blue Bolt* (inside cover). (Vol. 4, no. 12). Philadelphia, PA: Novelty Press.

Davis, B. (1940). Dick Cole, wonder boy. In *Blue Bolt* (pp. 9–14). (Vol. 1, no. 1). Philadelphia, PA: Novelty Press.

Davis, B. (1942). Dick Cole, wonder boy. In *4Most* (pp. 1–30). (Vol. 1, no. 1). Philadelphia, PA: Novelty Press.

Edison Bell. (1943). In *Blue Bolt* (pp. 21–26). (Vol. 3, no. 11). Philadelphia, PA: Novelty Press.

Edison Bell. (1944a). In *Blue Bolt* (pp. 25–31). (Volume 5, no. 1). Philadelphia, PA: Novelty Press.

Edison Bell. (1944b). In *Blue Bolt* (pp. 21–26). (Volume 5, no. 2). Philadelphia, PA: Novelty Press.

Edison Bell. (1945a). In *Blue Bolt* (pp. 15–21). (Volume 5, no. 5). Philadelphia, PA: Novelty Press.

Edison Bell. (1945b). In *Blue Bolt* (pp. 15–21). Volume 5, no. 8). Philadelphia, PA: Novelty Press.

Edison Bell. (1945c. In *4Most* (pp. 17–26). (Volume 4, no. 2). Philadelphia, PA: Novelty Press.

Gates, A. (1941). The Cadet. In *Target* (pp. 36-43). (Volume 2, no. 4). Philadelphia, PA: Novelty Press.

Gill, R. (1943). Edison Bell. In *4Most* (pp. 25-35). (Volume 2, no. 3). Philadelphia, PA: Novelty Press.

Gill, R., & DeLay, H. (1942). Edison Bell. In *4Most* (pp. 43-48). (Volume 1, no. 1). Philadelphia, PA: Novelty Press.

Gill, R., & DeLay, H. (1943a). Edison Bell. In *Blue Bolt* (pp. 18-23). (Volume 4, no. 3). Philadelphia, PA: Novelty Press.

Gill, R., & DeLay, H. (1943b). Edison Bell. In *Blue Bolt* (pp. 36-42). (Volume 4, no. 5). Philadelphia, PA: Novelty Press.

Keifer, H. C., & Gill, R. (1944). Fearless fellers. In *Blue Bolt* (pp. 32–36). (Volume 4, no. 6). Philadelphia, PA: Novelty Press.

Kit Carter. (1942). In *4Most* (pp. 49-64). (Volume 1, no. 3). Philadelphia, PA: Novelty Press.

Kit Carter. (1943a). In *4Most* (pp. 49-64). (Volume 2, no. 2). Philadelphia, PA: Novelty Press.

Kit Carter. (1943b). In *Target* (pp. 1-12). (Volume 4, no. 5). Philadelphia, PA: Novelty Press.

Kit Carter. (1943c). In *Target* (pp. 1-10). (Volume 4, no. 7). Philadelphia, PA: Novelty Press.

Kit Carter. (1944). In *Target* (pp. 1-9). (Volume 5, no. 2). Philadelphia, PA: Novelty Press.

Kit Carter. (1945a). In *Target* (pp. 1-9). (Volume 5, no. 7). Philadelphia, PA: Novelty Press.

Kit Carter. (1945b). In *Target* (pp. 1-9). (Volume 6, no. 2). Philadelphia, PA: Novelty Press.

Lance, V. (1941). Ye editors' page. In *Blue Bolt* (inside cover). (Volume 2, no. 2). Philadelphia, PA: Novelty Press.

Little wise guys. (1942a). In *Boy Comics* (pp. 42-43). (Volume 1, no. 4). New York: Comic House.

Little wise guys. (1942b). In *Boy Comics* (pp. 55-57). (Volume 1, no. 5). New York: Comic House.

Otwell, A. (1945). Target hits and misses. In *Target* (inside cover). (Volume 5, no. 7). Philadelphia, PA: Novelty Press.

Pool, C. (1940). Ye editor's page. In *Target* (inside cover). (Vol. 1, no. 11). Philadelphia, PA: Novelty Press.

Sergeant Spook. (1944a). In *Blue Bolt* (pp. 39-45). (Volume 4, no. 11). Philadelphia, PA: Novelty Press.

Sergeant Spook. (1944b). In *Blue Bolt* (pp. 39-45). (Volume 4, no. 12). Philadelphia, PA: Novelty Press.

Speck, Spot and Sis. (1945). In *Target* (pp. 10-14). (Volume 6, no. 6). Philadelphia, PA: Novelty Press.

Sphar, C. (1945). Blue Bolt flashes. In *Blue Bolt* (inside cover). (Volume 6, no. 2). Philadelphia, PA: Novelty Press.

Target. (1941). (Volume 2, no. 1). Philadelphia, PA: Novelty Press.

Thompson, T. (1941). Ye editors' page. In *Blue Bolt* (inside cover). (Volume 2, no. 2). Philadelphia, PA: Novelty Press.

Vincent. [Warren, J. A. V.]. (1941). Speck, Spot and Sis. In *Target* (pp. 42-44). (Volume 2, no. 7). Philadelphia, PA: Novelty Press.

Vincent. [Warren, J. A. V.]. (1942a). Speck, Spot and Sis. In *Target* (pp. 28-31). (Volume 2, no. 11). Philadelphia, PA: Novelty Press.

Vincent. [Warren, J. A. V.]. (1942b). Speck, Spot and Sis. In *Target* (pp. 28-31). (Volume 3, no. 2). Philadelphia, PA: Novelty Press.

Vincent. [Warren, J. A. V.]. (1942c). Speck, Spot and Sis. In *Target* (pp. 27-30). (Volume 3, no. 5). Philadelphia, PA: Novelty Press.

Vincent. [Warren, J. A. V.]. (1943a). Speck, Spot and Sis. In *Target* (pp. 13-17). (Volume 3, no. 11). Philadelphia, PA: Novelty Press.

Vincent. [Warren, J. A. V.]. (1943b). Speck, Spot and Sis. In *Target* (pp. 49-53). (Volume 4, no. 1). Philadelphia, PA: Novelty Press.

Vincent. [Warren, J. A. V.]. (1943c). Speck, Spot and Sis. In *Target* (pp. 49-53). (Volume 4, no. 2). Philadelphia, PA: Novelty Press.

Vincent. [Warren, J. A. V.]. (1943d). Speck, Spot and Sis. In *Target* (pp. 49-53). (Volume 4, no. 3). Philadelphia, PA: Novelty Press.

Vincent. [Warren, J. A. V.]. (1943e). Speck, Spot and Sis. In *Target* (pp. 27-31). (Volume 4, no. 4). Philadelphia, PA: Novelty Press.

Warren, J. A. (1942). Speck, Spot and Sis. In *Target* (pp. 21-24). (Volume 3, no. 8). Philadelphia, PA: Novelty Press.

Wilcox, J. (1944a). Dick Cole. In *Blue Bolt* (pp. 1-10). (Volume 5, no. 3). Philadelphia, PA: Novelty Press.

Wilcox, J. (1944b). Dick Cole, Wonder Boy. In *Blue Bolt* (pp. 1-10). (Volume 4, no. 12). Philadelphia, PA: Novelty Press.

Wilcox, J. (1945). Dick Cole. In *Blue Bolt* (pp. 1-10). (Volume 5, no. 5). Philadelphia, PA: Novelty Press.

Wood, B. (1943). Little Dynamite. In *Boy Comics* (pp. 22-28). (Volume 1, no. 8). New York, NY: Comic House.

Ye editors' page. (1941a). In *Blue Bolt* (inside cover). (Vol. 1, no. 11). Philadelphia, PA: Novelty Press.

Ye editors' page. (1941b). In *Target* (inside cover). (Vol. 2, no. 4). Philadelphia, PA: Novelty Press.

Ye editors' page. (1942a). In *4Most* (inside cover). (Volume 1, no. 1). Philadelphia, PA: Novelty Press.

Ye editors' page. (1942b). In *4Most* (inside cover). (Volume 1, no. 2). Philadelphia, PA: Novelty Press.

Ye editors' page. (1943). In *Target* (inside cover). (Volume 4, no. 1). Philadelphia, PA: Novelty Press.

★★ 11 ★★

War Victory Adventures

Figurative Cognition and Domestic Propaganda in World War II Comic Books

James J. Kimble

The major comic book houses of the Golden Age found World War II to be a golden opportunity. National Periodicals (later known as DC Comics) shot to prominence by featuring heroic Allied partisans such as Superman, Wonder Woman, Batman, and Flash.[1] One of National's primary rivals, Timely Periodicals (later to become Marvel Comics), countered with a formidable cast of superheroes that included Captain America, Human Torch, and Sub-Mariner. Dozens of other publishers joined in the home-front fun during the war, all in support of a vast campaign of comic book propaganda that showcased a horde of superheroes doing everything possible to vanquish the Axis powers (Murray, 2011; Scott, 2007).

It is hard to believe in retrospect, but one of the most ardent book houses to join this colorful propaganda campaign was Family Comics (later to become Harvey Comics). Founded by Alfred Harvey in 1940, the organization is famous nowadays for its nonviolent, child-friendly fare, including characters such as Richie Rich, Wendy the Good Little Witch, Little Dot, and Casper the Friendly Ghost (Jackson & Arnold, 2007). One can hardly picture such characters taking up arms against the Axis powers, as so many comic book figures did in the 1940s. Yet their Family Comics predecessors did become quite involved in the war effort, as when the organization's Captain Freedom, Black Cat, Green Hornet, and Spirit of '76 fought against injustice in general and Nazi spies in particular (Arnold, 2006).

One of Family Comics' wartime series invites detailed scrutiny, since it began in an unprecedented cooperative agreement with the U.S. Treasury (1942). Dubbed *War Victory Comics*, issue number one in the series emerged in the summer of 1942. The entire booklet was an exercise not only in convincing young readers to purchase war stamps and war bonds, but in showing them ingenious ways to finagle those purchases. Given its direct sponsorship by the government, this issue amounted to an official propaganda message, and an imaginative one at that (Kimble & Goodnow, 2009). But although the Treasury was so pleased with the issue's results that it ordered a second printing, the booklet was destined to become a historical footnote. By early 1943 the government was already turning away from the direct sponsorship of comics and comic books, leaving the cartoon war to be fought by the publishers themselves—and leaving subsequent issues of *War Victory Comics* in limbo (Barkin, 1984).

Family Comics evidently saw potential in the fledgling series, even if it was only because the organization hated to lose the large reading audience attracted by the initial publication. Thus, issue #2—now transformed into *War Victory Adventures* (1943a)—appeared in August 1943, with #3 (1943b) appearing at the end of that year. Both issues featured dramatic and lurid perspectives on the war, with story lines about battlefronts, resourceful civilians at home, treacherous fifth columnists, Nazi U-boats, dauntless undercover operatives, and brave allies at war. To be sure, one cannot consider the continued series to be official government propaganda, since the Treasury was no longer involved in its production. Despite its now-unofficial status, however, the series retained a clear propaganda mission, as it offered young readers a distinctly U.S.-centric view of the war even as it depicted the inevitability of an Allied victory on every front.

War Victory Adventures' multifaceted propaganda story lines concerning the war are particularly intriguing from the perspective of cognitive linguistics. Brian Diemert contends that historical narratives tend to transform "individuals, people, classes, and nations into 'characters,' sometimes caricatures, in a piece of historical theatre." In wartime, he continues, such mythical characters "function within the morphology of the discourse as actors (the belligerents), helpers (the allies), and blocking figures (the axis)" (2005, pp. 24–25). George Lakoff offers a similar perspective, suggesting that war narratives construct antagonistic character roles through the process of "metaphorical definition" (2001, p. 23). In this view, a culture's wartime stories inevitably urge members of the culture to experience "one kind of thing in terms of another" (Lakoff &

Johnson, 1980, p. 5) by portraying nation-states in the conflict as metaphorically possessing the traits of a hero, an enemy, a victim, or an ally.

This figurative process allows participants and observers to understand the impossible complexities of modern warfare in simpler terms. No one can fully grasp the countless details, motivations, events, and consequences of international conflict, let alone those involved in a world war. To explain or describe a conflict, then, propagandists and media sources rely on a dramatic shorthand in which countries become embodied actors who personally square off on the battlefield and whose personalities and traits represent the best or the worst in humanity. Of course, nations do not have personalities, and they do not literally stab, strike, or parry with other nations on a field of battle. Yet figurative language allows humans to understand war cognitively this personi-fied way, even though the fact that this understanding is inexact remains ob-scured. At the same time, the figurative encoding of warfare provides a vital tool for propagandists, who can use it to characterize the actions and intentions of nations at war in strategic ways.

Comic books were a potent vehicle for constituting these sorts of figurative characterizations during World War II. One reason for this potency is that the booklets were widely read on the home front, and not just by children (Waugh, 1947). Another reason was that comic books generally lacked the stigma of official propaganda, enabling them to approach readers who might otherwise have been wary of the booklets' depictions (Murray, 2011). A final reason is that the intimate interaction between the visual and the verbal in such artifacts— what Scott McCloud refers to as the mingling of *"partners* in a dance" (1994, p. 156)—allowed readers "quick entry into another space, one that . . . [was] private, fantasy-driven, and lodged within a psycho-emotional and subliminal state" (Legrady, 2000, p. 79).[2] In such a state, readers were wholly open to the metaphoric characterizations and narrative story lines that emanated from the comic book industry's numerous wartime publications.

My objective in this chapter is to draw upon the insights of cognitive linguistics and the developing tradition of comic books scholarship in order to explore the rhetorical means by which the *War Victory Adventures* series, in particular, constituted the varied characters in its imagined war. I contend that the series serves as an excellent case study of the intertwining of meta-phoric and narrative cognition in order to posit distinctive national character roles in the unfolding drama of World War II. In doing so the comic books tacitly crafted an epic struggle between good and evil, one that gave readers no choice but to sympathize with the Allied war effort. The following sections of the chapter support this perspective by exploring how the series depicted: 1) the United States and its people as transformed, if plucky, heroes; 2) the

Axis powers as contemptible, if dangerous, villains; and 3) allies and occupied nations as praiseworthy supporting players in the drama. In a concluding section, the chapter returns to the symbiotic nature of narratives and metaphors in wartime propaganda, suggesting that comic books were the perfect venue for using such figurative devices to establish and reinforce for millions of home-front civilians a mythic understanding of the war and its eventual outcome.

The Accidental Heroes: Where Courage Met Pluck

The United States did not enter World War II with the same sense of invincibility that it would possess nearly four years later on V-J Day. On the eve of Pearl Harbor, much of the country was still in recovery from the greatest economic depression in national history. While President Franklin D. Roosevelt had won a third term promising that no U.S. boys would be sent to fight in a foreign war, the public itself was bitterly divided between determined interventionists and passionate isolationists. And although the defense program had ramped up significantly throughout 1940 and early 1941, the military was hardly prepared for a global war. Indeed, as Christina Jarvis (2004) points out, even media depictions of the American male body—which would typically become virile and muscular during the conflict—remained visibly weakened and occasionally emaciated in the prewar years.

On one level, then, *War Victory Adventures* represented a radical shift in national self-perception. Its story lines featured numerous roles for Americans, ranging from military servicemen to factory workers to diplomats. There was room for nearly every citizen, regardless of role or gender, to play a heroic part.[3] Each individual contribution in some way added to the construction of the larger, nationwide role of a reluctant-but-heroic United States, a metaphoric figure who personified bravery and resourcefulness in the face of undeniable evil. By portraying various Americans in action on the battlefronts and the home front, in other words, the series constituted a compelling and persuasive portrait of the United States itself as a personified participant in the war's dramatic action.

The key to the series' depiction of its U.S. characters revolved around the notion of *transformation*. In accordance with the comic books' fantastical logic, humble youngsters could become formidable forces on the battlefield, while lovable goofs and ordinary civilians could bravely blunder their way into capturing enemy spies. The crisis of wartime was responsible for precipitating such transformations, effectively turning benign American virtues into extraordinary feats and deadly fighting skills. The resulting characters were one part classic everyman (or everywoman) and one part heroic overachiever—figures well suited to inspiring both the imagination and the behavior of young readers.

The series began this transformative work in the very first story of issue #2. Chickie Ricks is, at first glance, a most unlikely hero—let alone a U.S. Marine aviator (Epp, 1943b). The shy 17-year-old volunteer first appears at home, shaving in the bathroom mirror. His younger brother watches adoringly, even as his mother wonders why Chickie is shaving, since he lacks "enough fuzz to cover a peach!" (Epp, 1943b, p. 2). Downstairs, a group of friends, including a lovestruck Betsy, wait to give Chickie a rousing send-off to boot camp. The protagonist's introverted, hesitant nature is evident in his interactions with Betsy, as well as in his final farewell to friends and family as his train pulls away: "G—g'bye—gosh—!" (Epp, 1943b, p. 4).

Predictably, Chickie's first act upon arrival at boot camp is to wander off, then absentmindedly bump into a fierce drill instructor, Shanghai Joe. Yet a few minutes later, it becomes clear that while the raw recruit might be a bumbling kid, he is also a fierce patriot. After he stumbles into Cloe, the young daughter of the camp's commanding officer, they hear the distant sound of "Taps." Immediately, they stand up for the lowering of the flag. Chickie, hat in hand, says "G—gosh—it sure is the purtiest flag in the world! I—it makes ya proud (gulp) to be an American!" Impressed with his heartfelt sentiments, Cloe intones "Hmm!—you'll do! . . . Yes sir, we'll make a real leatherneck out of ya!" (Epp, 1943b, p. 5).

Thereafter follows an intense basic training sequence, with Chickie and his fellow trainees running, climbing, and jumping "from dawn to dark—go!—go!" (Epp, 1943b, p. 5). Soon, Chickie has a noticeable swagger, though he remains shy in front of women. His new toughness appears to give him courage and strength in difficult situations. At one point, for instance, his commanding officer is kidnapped by two Nazi spies. Chickie vaults through a skylight and attacks them, interrupting their torture session. "I saw this in a comic book onct [sic]," he exclaims as he leaps, "maybe it'll work!" (Epp, 1943b, p. 8). In a follow-up story line, Chickie has become a Naval Air Corps cadet, and he dauntlessly leads a squadron of lost pilots through heavy fog to a safe landing (Epp, 1943a). Although he has retained his aw-shucks manner and fierce patriotism, it seems, he has gradually transformed into a confident soldier, one who will make a difference on the front lines for the United States.

A slightly different transformation is evident in the adventures of Deanna Dartmouth, a wealthy American heiress ("Rendezvous with Revenge," 1943). When readers meet Deanna, she is coolly sitting in a Marseille café, watching the locals flee from the invading German army. An American reporter, Paul Delton, attempts to rescue her. However, he soon finds that she is in no danger, because she is engaged to Count Boroux, a noted Nazi sympathizer. The reporter *is* in danger from the invading force, however. He is quickly arrested and dragged to an interview with the Gestapo—but not before he accuses Deanna of being a Nazi sympathizer herself.

Later, the action shifts to the count's swanky celebration party, to which Adolf Hitler himself has been invited. Paul has escaped the Gestapo and watches through a window as both the count and Deanna toast Hitler by exclaiming, "To the new order!" ("Rendezvous with Revenge," 1943, p. 17). Yet when Deanna subsequently invites herself to the Führer's bedroom, she suddenly pulls a pistol from her purse and shoots him. As she and Paul escape the party, she explains her gradual change of heart. She had initially "been thrilled at the thought of being a countess. But when I saw what was happening to the people of Europe, well[,] I got wise to myself" ("Rendezvous with Revenge," 1943, p. 20). She had transformed, in other words, from a would-be sympathizer into a de facto American agent. After coming to her senses, she concludes, "I realized who the enemy was and I went after him!" ("Rendezvous with Revenge," 1943, p. 20).

U.S. characters, to include soldiers and civilians of all sorts, underwent such transformations nearly everywhere in the series. Whether a specific story line involved better fighters, more patriotic citizens, or even super-efficient medics, the underlying message was clear: it was possible and perhaps inevitable that the wartime emergency would turn even the most unlikely citizen into a formidable force in the struggle against evil. Christopher Murray suggests that superhero comic books of this era presented home-front readers with icons "of empowerment through transformation" when they depicted the change "from an ordinary person to a superpowered being" (2011, p. 8). But the transformations among Americans in *War Victory Adventures* quite often did not involve superheroes; rather, the central lesson appeared to be that *anybody* could transform into a productive participant on behalf of the war effort.[4] Considered in the aggregate, this massive series of transformations could only invoke images of a very different United States on the world stage than the impoverished persona of the Depression years. Indeed, in the fantastical war of the popular imagination, this transformed United States was itself a courageous and resourceful figure—doubtless useful characteristics in a deadly fight against the personified archenemies of the Axis.

Awkward Evil: Germany and Japan as Contemptible Enemies

The vast majority of citizens on the U.S. home front never saw an Axis soldier or spy in the flesh. Accordingly, their conception of the enemy's appearance and nature had to be constructed. It should be no surprise to find, then, that propaganda accounts of the Axis enemy were a recurring theme through-out much of the war. Newsreels and Hollywood features portrayed enemy advances and atrocities even as they profiled Axis leaders in an unflattering light (Doherty, 1993, p. 132). Newspaper and magazine articles condemned the enemy as brutal and malignant (e.g., Dulles, 1942). And countless posters featured hulking silhouettes and leering storm troopers menacing vulnerable women and children (e.g., Grohe, 1942/1976; Koehler & Ancona, 1942/1980). If the home front needed suitable villains in order to justify its wartime urgency, ample propaganda was clearly available to provide them.

War Victory Adventures, for its part, presented readers with numerous depictions of the Axis enemy. While the series ignored Italy altogether (a choice not inconsistent with a great deal of the home front's propaganda imagery), it had plenty of room to offer unflattering portraits of the Japanese and German opponents. These portrayals took the form of individual glimpses at the appearance and character of various enemy leaders, soldiers, sympathizers, and spies. Each portrayal, in turn, helped foster the comic books' fantastical composites of those two enemy nations and their nefarious role in the war's dramatic story line.

The series' depictions of the enemy were organized as a relentless campaign of *derision*. The comic book format itself, of course, inexorably encouraged a stereotyped, cartoonish approach to its enmification. The outcome was a series of colorful caricatures and over-the-top portraits of awkward evil, all with an underlying tone of contempt. The resulting enemies were often menacing, to be sure. Yet the comic book writers and artists made certain that the depictions of these enemies never came across as infallible or omnipotent. Indeed, for the series' young readers, it must have been a comfort to feel that the Axis powers had flaws that were both comical and practical.

Family Comics wasted no time in featuring the derisive enemy in *War Victory Adventures*. Both comic book covers presented action-packed scenes in which the enemy's shortcomings were quite apparent. Issue #2, for example, depicted a battle involving an assault by U.S. Marines on entrenched Japanese troops (*War Victory Adventures*, 1943a, cover; see Figure 11.1). Here the Anglo Yanks face off against a thoroughly dehumanized enemy, one with greenish-yellow skin, simian features, claws, and (in one case) batlike ears. The enemy in the image is thus undeniably bestial, even evil. It is also remarkably inferior to the Americans. The Marines in the image visibly surpass the Japanese figures in prowess, equipment, and numbers (witness the reinforcements arriving by ship below). Perhaps more importantly, the Americans show no fear in com-bat, while the two central Japanese figures display anguish and even cowardice. The small explosive soaring toward the charging Marine does introduce some

Figure 11.1: Family Comics portrays the Japanese enemy
(War Victory Adventures.1943a, detail from cover).

uncertainty into the picture. Still, there can be no doubt that the American forces in this scene will prevail against their very dangerous but ultimately flawed
and unworthy opponent.

The cover of issue #3, meanwhile, amounted to a Family Comics character study of the Germany enemy (*War Victory Adventures*, 1943b; see Figure
11.2). In this drawing, Captain Cross bursts through a wall in order to rescue a
captured four-star general. Facing the superhero are two brutish German soldiers, while a third frantically calls for help. Interestingly, the layout and feel
of the tableau are strikingly similar to the cover of issue #2. Of course, there
are some differences: the American attacker is alone, the wounded general is a
fresh element, and the three Germans are not inhuman.[5] Much as in the other
scene, however, these enemy figures are somewhat inept as fighters, and they
are decidedly on the defensive. Indeed, the general's smug expression foreshadows the outcome of the scene: Captain Cross will knock these hapless, thuglike
Nazis out cold, prevailing despite being outnumbered three-to-one. As before,
an American victory against an incompetent foe seems all but guaranteed.

Figure 11.2: Captain Cross attacks the German enemy (War Victory Adventures., 1943b, detail from cover).

To be sure, the story lines in the series did occasionally remind readers not to take such Axis enemies too lightly. In "Masquerade for Prey" (Cazeneuve, 1943a), for instance, the crew of a Nazi ship consistently uses subterfuge to sink Allied vessels and to avoid capture. In "Attack of the Lone Avenger!" (1943), the protagonist declares that Japanese soldiers are "a bunch of die-hards, if I ever met any" (p. 35). "The Death Mask Mystery" (1943) features Nazi spies who are ruthless—they even go so far as to kill a U.S. naval attaché for military secrets. Finally, in the science fiction-themed "Terror Rides the Waves" (Cazeneuve, 1943b), a fleet of U-boat personnel takes over an underwater city through intimidation and violence—a clear reference to the real-world takeover of numerous cities in occupied Europe. The Axis powers, the comic books frequently stressed, were thus crafty and malevolent; defeating them in the war would prove to be a tremendous challenge.

Interestingly, the series occasionally emphasized the nefarious nature of the enemy by featuring *reverse* transformations. Whereas U.S. protagonists typically underwent a positive transformation, as discussed above, others in the booklet's story lines occasionally transformed from seemingly positive characters into evil ones, thereby warning readers of the enemy's perfidy. In "Grimm, Ghost Spotter," for example, a beautiful German countess turns out to be a zombie intent on killing the protagonist (Weaver, 1943). Elsewhere, in "Peril on the Pampas" (1943), an Argentinian rancher seems, at first, to be a victim of Axis saboteurs who are poisoning cattle meant for Allied soldiers. By the story's end, however, he is unmasked as the local Axis spymaster, and he pays the price for his subterfuge. Through these sorts of startling turnabouts, the comic books were able to emphasize in another way that readers should not take the enemy lightly, despite the obvious weaknesses.

Still, *War Victory Adventures* consistently returned to its derisive style of enmification. German spies and fighting men alike universally utter mangled and even humorous English, as when a U-boat captain congratulates a crew member for sneaking up on an American fighter: "Goot vork, Emil—now bring dot swine below!!" ("Uncle Cal Combats Axis," 1943, p. 46). In comparison, Japanese soldiers in the series lack even rudimentary English skills, as the story lines limit them to impenetrable kanji symbols. This awkward note extends to the enemy's behavior, too. Axis partisans, it becomes clear, not only lack social graces but are also prone to Charlie Chaplin–like pratfalls. The Gestapo agents who haul away Paul Delton in "Rendezvous with Revenge" (1943), for example, can barely get out of each other's way as the reporter escapes. Himmler himself witnesses the farce, screaming, "Vot's der matter with you idiots?" while the struggling Nazi goons desperately yell "Shtop! Shtop!" down the hallway ("Rendezvous with Revenge," 1943, p. 15). Even more telling was the series' use of traditional tropes of comic book violence against the enemy. Almost invariably, American soldiers and even civilians in the story lines were able to knock down, knock out, or kill Axis characters at will.[6] To add insult to injury, *War Victory Adventures'* artists often lingered with evident relish on the falling or unconscious enemy figures. Such imagery reinforced the apparent strengths of Allied characters while it simultaneously underlined the vulnerability and awkward nature of the Axis enemy for readers.

Despite their obviously evil nature and ruthless ways, then, the cartoon enemies in the Family Comics series ultimately emerged as contemptible and fallible. Cord Scott contends that World War II comic books tended to portray the Axis villains as "cunning, psychopathic, and malicious" (2007, p. 334). *War Victory Adventures* made those points, of course, but the series seemed to be even more concerned with emphasizing a thoroughly derisive tone that belittled and ridiculed the Axis powers even as it allowed that defeating them would be quite a challenge. For those on the home front who envisioned the enemy nations as personified states in a metaphoric struggle, such visceral propaganda messages could only reinforce the belief that the Axis opponents were bound to lose if the heroic U.S. and its allies rose to the occasion.

Rounding out the Cast: Victims and Allies at War

At first glance, a standard war narrative might seem to have only two relevant roles: us versus them. In narrative terms, these roles become the protagonist and the antagonist, or just the hero and the villain. Scholars who write in the area of cognitive linguistics (e.g., Diemert, 2005; Lakoff, 2001), however, suggest that two additional roles are typically part of the drama. The *victims* are those players whom the villain has assaulted, or figuratively raped.[7] The heroic nation sees itself as coming to the rescue of (or avenging) that victim. In the course of doing so, the protagonist often enlists helpers, or *allies*. These personified states might well diverge from the hero in a variety of ways. Yet a shared interest in redressing the victims' plight at the expense of the villain pushes heroes and allies together, forcing them to seek common ground.

By the time *War Victory Adventures* #2 (1943a) was published, these roles were well established in home-front propaganda narratives. Nations that had succumbed to Japanese incursions or to the German blitzkrieg featured prominently in such appeals, as in Ben Shahn's well-known 1942 poster informing viewers, "We French workers warn you ... defeat means slavery, starvation, death" (reprinted in Pohl, 1993, p. 71). Other messages touted U.S. allies, particularly the United Kingdom and the Soviet Union (the other two members of the so-called Big Three). As before, these sorts of messages gave civilians an opportunity to conceptualize both victims and allies as personified states who were playing memorable roles in the drama of the war—if only in support of the leading players in that drama.

The common theme uniting the comic book series' portrayal of victims and allies was an emphasis on *veneration*. The stirring message for readers was that these nations were praiseworthy for their stalwart nature in the face of overwhelming adversity. Victims in the stories came across as particularly valiant, given their status; the series even seemed to downplay the rescue trope that one might expect in such tales. It was abundantly clear, at least in the view of Family Comics, that both victims and allies in the narrative were resisting the Axis powers in every way possible. Consequently, the series took the time and space to feature inspirational portraits of those characters as a way of praising their vital role in the drama.

The primary victim featured in issue #2 was Norway. German forces had invaded in 1940, afterward controlling daily life in Norway with an occupying force of some 300,000 troops. Despite the occupation, however, the Norwegian government continued to operate in exile, while numerous soldiers and civilians who were able to escape the Nazis served the Allied cause. In the "Masquerade for Prey" story line (Cazeneuve, 1943a)—apparently based on real-life events—first officer David Knudsen and a crew of "grimly determined" (p. 21) Norwegian sailors demonstrated that although their homeland was playing the part of a victim in the war's narrative, its partisans retained a fighting spirit as well as good humor in very trying circumstances. In the story the Norwegians' ship is initially bombed by a German plane in the middle of the Atlantic Ocean. "Well, it could be worse!" ("Masquerade for Prey," 1943a, p. 22) exclaims one sailor, as the crew gamely fights the resulting fire. Not much later, however, a German ship disguising its allegiance by using an Allied flag shells them (as the Nazi captain gloats, "Ja! Ve fooled der dumkopfs completely!" ["Masquerade for Prey," 1943a, p. 24]). Their ship sinking, the Norwegians are forced to use lifeboats to rescue drowning crew members. At length, the surviving sailors find themselves prisoner in the attacking ship's hold. Their good spirits in captivity serve them well, however, as they eventually are able to outsmart their German captors. When the Nazi ship tries to fool a passing Allied convoy by deceitfully flying a Norwegian flag, the real Norwegians wave a white shirt from their porthole to alert the Allies to the masquerade. As Knudsen and his compatriots safely watch the Nazi ship sink a while later, one offers this sardonic comment: "Now ain't that just too bad!" ("Masquerade for Prey," 1943a, p. 26). The sarcastic pity in this statement makes for a fitting final word from a brave and praiseworthy victim who never gave up the fight against his oppressors.

Later in the year, issue #3 (*War Victory Adventures*, 1943b) also provided a detailed glimpse at the venerable characteristics of a narrative victim—but this time the tale took the form of a science-fiction allegory. In "Terror Rides the Waves" (Cazeneuve, 1943b), an underwater city—thriving inside a glass dome— serves capably as a symbol of the many real-world European cities that were still suffering under German occupation. As the story opens, a damaged Nazi U-boat has sunk to the bottom of the ocean. The situation looks hopeless, but the crew is unexpectedly rescued by several people in strange diving suits, who escort them to a submerged, Atlantis-like civilization. Of course, the Germans do not waste time by being grateful for the rescue. Instead, they immediately assault the city's leaders and make plans to use the location as a secret U-boat base.

While the Nazis follow their stereotypically nefarious nature, the city's residents swiftly earn sympathy as victims. They are initially nonviolent and even a bit naive, having misunderstood the evil nature of their new guests. At length, though, they recognize their danger and begin to fight back. "These men kill human beings!" exclaims one outraged resident. "I will kill them!" (Cazeneuve, 1943b, p. 15). In short order, the city has cut off the Nazis' oxygen source and allowed them to suffocate or drown. In a telling scene at the end of the tale, the citizens destroy all of the Germans' guns and equipment, since they "are instruments of evil," belonging to those who "excell [*sic*] only at killing human beings!" (Cazeneuve, 1943b, p. 16). As with the Norwegian sailors, here is a praiseworthy victim who has resisted the Axis onslaught and eliminated the evil threat, thereby restoring a sense of peace.

Meanwhile, the allies in *War Victory Adventures* stories also benefit from consistent veneration. British characters, for instance, are uniformly friendly and supportive in their interactions with Americans—just as the average home-front reader would likely have envisioned them (see Figure 11.3). At times the British do become the target of cultural stereotypes, as when the cartoonists have royal officers wearing pith helmets, using stylish cigarette holders, and uttering phrases like "righto" and "'ol chappie" ("Desert Dynamite," 1943, p. 48). But these portrayals generally come across as good-natured fun and lack the visceral nature of the Japanese and German depictions in the series. The British, it is evident, deserve praise for their consistently supportive nature on behalf of the war effort.

Surprisingly, the most prominent ally to appear in the series was the Soviet Union. Only a few years earlier, of course, the Soviets had not been U.S. allies at all (and in fact had signed an infamous treaty with Nazi Germany). Some comic books from that earlier period even referred to the Soviets as "Mosconians," adopting virtually the same unflattering imagery that was already being used to depict evil German characters (Scott, 2007, p. 327). By 1943, however, the USSR was most certainly not in league with Hitler any longer, and so a recurring point in home-front propaganda focused on reconstructing the Soviets as faithful and stalwart allies (Chafe, 2003, p. 5).

The story "Blitzkrieg Boomerang!" (1943) developed this reconstructive theme in detail. In it a peasant introduces her young son to Comrades Pavlikov and Olga Sotenko, relating how they saved Stalingrad from a series of secret Nazi rockets.[8] At first, the peasant recalls, the Soviet army is mystified at the nature of the German attacks on Stalingrad: bombs are exploding in the city, but no planes are visible. Lieutenants Pavlikov and Sotenko volunteer to parachute behind German lines to investigate, pretending to be a married couple to allay suspicion. Their general is quite impressed with this plan, telling them (note the flawless English) that "Russia will never fail with men and women like you" ("Blitzkrieg Boomerang!," p. 52).

Figure 11.3: The British as supportive ally ("Desert Dynamite," 1943, p. 47).

On their journey to examine the secret weapon, the two Russians teach a guerilla unit how to lure German tanks into an ambush for a deadly "Russian kiss" ("Blitzkrieg Boomerang!," 1943, p. 53). The guerrillas, in turn, equip Sotenko and Pavlikov as fur traders, which allows them to gain unobtrusive access to the Nazis' secret base. The duo soon discovers that the new weapon involves radio-controlled rockets. Using their engineering skills, they manage to reprogram a rocket so that it no longer targets Stalingrad. Instead, at the story's climax, readers see that the Russians have cleverly aimed the German rocket at its own base—which then disappears in a tremendous explosion.

The ingenuity and bravery of the two Soviet soldiers in this story line is palpable, particularly given the virulent U.S. propaganda that had condemned the USSR just a few years earlier. Indeed, except for the differences in their uniforms, one could almost mistake the pair for *American* heroes. For his part, the peasant's son is so impressed with them that he exclaims, "I wish I were a soldier like you!" The pair's reply is telling, as it comments not only on the valor of the Soviet people but on the spirit of the entire Allied cast—victims, heroes, and allies—"We all do what we can, little brother! All our men, women and our children!" ("Blitzkrieg Boomerang!," 1943, p. 55).

In this way, both victims and allies in *War Victory Adventures'* metaphoric construction of the war emerged as praiseworthy for their fierce resistance to the Axis powers. By continuously valorizing these supporting character roles, the series was in effect justifying the virtue of the Allied cause as well as emphasizing the likelihood of an Allied victory. After all, if the courage and effort of Axis victims and American allies were added to the righteous might of the transformed United States, how could the forces of good fail to vanquish the forces of evil in this, the greatest war of all time? In the view of Family Comics, at least, a just end to that war must have seemed inevitable.

Conclusion

Any reader of comic books in the World War II era could tell that the booklets' essential format aimed at telling stories. It is thus no surprise to suggest that *War Victory Adventures* relied on narratives. In fact, there is a sense in which these two comic books—and the thousands of others that appeared on the home front—worked at a fairly literal level of narrativity: here is a character I like, here is one I do not like, here is some action leading to closure, here is the satisfactory end, and so on. Although such an interpretation fails to go beyond the most obvious surface meanings, it is a legitimate way to explain the appeal of a given comic book and the attraction a reader might have to it.

Yet the foregoing analysis has established, I hope, that two additional levels of meaning are present in *War Victory Adventures* and, most likely, in many additional comic books from the home-front years. The first of these levels lies in the same realm in which presidents can envision the Cold War as a poker game between well-matched players (as Harry Truman did) or imagine the first Persian Gulf War as a strategic game of baseball (as George H. W. Bush did) (Larson, 1985; Kuusisto, 1998). This is the realm of metaphoric cognition, a pseudo-reality in which individual characters are but markers that signify the characteristics of a larger group or culture, as when a brave soldier at war comes to represent in the reader's mind the best qualities of that soldier's nation.

In *War Victory Adventures*, every character interacts on the literal level of meaning. Yet when considered in the aggregate, these characters can be seen as symbolically transferring their qualities to the country they represent. This transference is metaphoric, because it uses the traditional character roles from what Lakoff (2001, p. 27) calls the "just war fairy tale" (i.e., hero, villain, victim, helper) as source material to portray specific nations in a new way. One of humanity's most basic cognitive metaphors is states as persons, and the underlying logic of that metaphor is at play here (Lakoff, 1991). It is, then, a fairly simple rhetorical process to, say, identify the United States as a heroic figure, as all that is required is for a propaganda message to transfer ideas from the domain of heroes (brave, stalwart, fights the villain, etc.) to the specific domain of the nation. Both issues in the series embraced this metaphoric process enthusiastically.

There is, however, a third level of meaning in the two comic books, one that is a logical extension of the metaphoric level. As I have suggested, the source domains in the metaphoric realm all stem from traditional war stories, so it makes sense to consider what happens when those roles are established in a reader's mind. The answer, of course, is that the reader can imagine the underlying relationships spinning into narrative action. Just as when a group of playing children knows exactly how each individual should behave when it is decided who will play the cop and who will play the robber, so too does the reader of a tale that identifies heroes, villains, victims, and allies know what to anticipate next. This is the level of narrative cognition, and it is what would have allowed readers of *War Victory Adventures* to imagine with some degree of confidence the successful outcome of the war. After all, comic book heroes (at least those from the Golden Age) nearly always gave readers "a dose of reassurance that good would triumph over evil" (Streb, 1998, p. 12). If Family Comics was right in its apportionment of the war's metaphoric roles, then, the subsequent narrative outcome would likely seem to be a foregone conclusion to many readers.

In the end, *War Victory Adventures* thus combined metaphoric and narrative appeals to adapt the classic trope of good-vanquishing-evil into the specific circumstances of World War II. In doing so, the series presented the war as a dialectical struggle between good and evil. Home-front readers, to be sure, would have had little trouble deciding which side to root for in this colorful struggle. After all, they were themselves Americans. In the world of the comic book series, this single characteristic made them heroic by default—and perhaps even made them ready to become active participants in the war effort. Even if such readers were too young to enlist in the armed forces, they could still contribute by purchasing war stamps, gathering scrap metal, or even helping out at home. As "The Death Mask Mystery" protagonist Inspector Jordan advised a colleague—and, by extension, the comic book's readers—"this is no time to be taking bows! We have to keep punching!" (1943, p. 39). For those young comic book fans who found *War Victory Adventures*' metaphoric and narrative logic compelling, this advice must have seemed wise, indeed.

Notes

1. Of the National/DC superheroes, Batman was the least involved in the war, though Streb (1998) describes a 1943 issue in which both Batman and Robin use the Batplane to help prevent an Axis invasion (pp. 10–11).

2. In the World War II era, perhaps only moving pictures offered a similar synthesis of appeals.

3. It is worth noting that the series featured very little ethnic variation among its U.S. characters; every American character except one appeared to be from a Caucasian background (the exception was a black kitchen worker who appeared in just one panel) (Epp, 1943a, p. 8). Curiously, with the possible exception of Chickie Ricks, a 17-year old U.S. marine, all of the primary characters in the continued series are adults. This is in stark contrast to issue one, which Family Comics coproduced with the Treasury Department as a means of selling war stamps to children on the home front (U.S. Treasury, 1942). Despite the sudden absence of child characters, the advertisements in issues #2 and #3 make it clear that the series continued to see youngsters as a primary audience.

4. The only exception in the series was the adventures of Captain Red Cross, a typeset story line featured inside issue #3 ("The Story Behind," 1943). The issue's cover also offers a scene from this superhero's story, but it refers to him as "Captain Cross" (*War Victory Adventures*, 1943b, cover).

5. The difference between the two enemies here—with dehumanized Japanese and brutish, though still human, Germans—is consistent with a great deal of home-front propaganda from the time (Kimble, 2005, pp. 209–210).

6. In this sense, the fates of the series' villains are little different than those of the criminals traditionally faced by the likes of Batman and Superman.

7. Lakoff (2001, p. 23) notes that on occasion, the victim and the hero roles fall to the same nation, which gives the narrative a self-defense trajectory.

8. The story does not reveal Pavlikov's first name.

References

Arnold, M. (Ed.). (2006). *The best of the* Harveyville Fun Times! Saratoga, CA: Fun Ideas Productions.

Attack of the lone avenger! (1943). In *War victory adventures* (pp. 33–36). (Vol. 1, no. 2). St. Louis, MO: Family Comics.

Barkin, S. M. (1984). Fighting the cartoon war: Information strategies in World War II. *Journal of American Culture, 1-2*(7), 113–117.

Blitzkrieg boomerang! (1943). In *War victory adventures* (pp. 49–55). (Vol. 1, no. 2). St. Louis, MO: Family Comics.

Cazeneuve, A. (1943a). Masquerade for prey. In *War victory adventures* (pp. 21–26). (Vol. 1, no. 2). St. Louis, MO: Family Comics.

Cazeneuve, A. (1943b). Terror rides the waves. In *War victory adventures* (pp. 9–16). (Vol. 1, no. 3). St. Louis, MO: Family Comics.

Chafe, W. H. (2003). *The unfinished journey: America since World War II* (5th ed.). New York, NY: Oxford University Press.

The death mask mystery. (1943). In *War victory adventures* (pp. 32–39). (Vol. 1, no. 3). St. Louis, MO: Family Comics.

Desert dynamite. (1943). In *War victory adventures* (pp. 46–49). (Vol. 1, no. 3). St. Louis, MO: Family Comics.

Diemert, B. (2005). Uncontainable metaphor: George F. Kennan's "X" article and Cold War discourse. *Canadian Review of American Studies, 35*, 21–55.

Doherty, T. (1993). *Projections of war: Hollywood, American culture, and World War II*. New York, NY: Columbia University Press.

Dulles, A. F. (1942, December 28). A righteous faith. *Life*, 48–51.

Epp, M. (1943a). Chickie Ricks, pilot-fleet arm, U.S.M.C. In *War victory adventures* (pp. 1–8). (Vol. 1, no. 3). St. Louis, MO: Family Comics.

Epp, M. (1943b). Presenting Chickie Ricks, pilot-fleet arm, U.S.M.C. In *War victory adventures* (pp. 2–9). (Vol. 1, no. 2). St. Louis, MO: Family Comics.

Grohe, G. (1976). *He's watching you* [poster]. In A. Rhodes, *Propaganda: The art of persuasion, World War II* (p. 174). New York, NY: Chelsea House. (Original work published 1942).

Jackson, K. M., & Arnold, M. D. (2007). Baby-boom children and Harvey Comics after the code: A neighborhood of little girls and boys. *ImageTexT: Interdisciplinary Comics Studies*, 3. Retrieved from http://www.english.ufl.edu/imagetext/ archives/v3_3/jackson/

Jarvis, C. S. (2004). *The male body at war: American masculinity during World War II*. DeKalb, IL: Northern Illinois University Press.

Kimble, J. J. (2005). Whither propaganda? Agonism and "the engineering of consent." *Quarterly Journal of Speech*, 91, 210–218.

Kimble, J. J., & Goodnow, T. (2009). "You boys and girls can be the Minute Men of today": Narrative possibility and normative appeal in the U.S. Treasury's 1942 *War victory comics*. In P. M. Haridakis, B. S. Hugenberg, & S. T. Wearden (Eds.), *War and the media: Essays on news reporting, propaganda and popular culture* (pp. 112–125). Jefferson, NC: McFarland.

Koehler, K., & Ancona, V. (1980). *This is the enemy* [poster]. In *Paper bullets* (p. 1). New York, NY: Chelsea House. (Original work published 1942).

Kuusisto, R. (1998). Framing the wars in the Gulf and in Bosnia: The rhetorical definitions of the Western power leaders in action. *Journal of Peace Research*, 35, 603–620.

Lakoff, G. (1991). Metaphor and war: The metaphor system used to justify war in the Gulf. *Peace Research*, 23, 25–32.

Lakoff, G. (2001). *Metaphorical thought in foreign policy: Why strategic framing matters*. Berkeley, CA: Frameworks Institute.

Lakoff, G., & Johnson, M. (1980). *Metaphors we live by*. Chicago, IL: University of Chicago Press.

Larson, D. W. (1985). *Origins of containment: A psychological explanation*. Princeton, NJ: Princeton University Press.

Legrady, G. (2000). Modular structure and image/text sequences: Comics and interactive media. In A. Magnussen & H. Christiansen (Eds.), *Comics & culture: Analytical and theo-retical approaches to comics* (pp. 79–90). Copenhagen, Denmark: Museum Tusculanum Press.

McCloud, S. (1994). *Understanding comics: The invisible art*. New York, NY: HarperCollins.

Murray, C. (2011). *Champions of the oppressed? Superhero comics, popular culture, and propaganda in America during World War II*. Cresskill, NJ: Hampton.

Peril on the Pampas. (1943). In *War victory adventures* (pp. 23–30). (Vol. 1, no. 3). St. Louis, MO: Family Comics.

Pohl, F. K. (1993). *Ben Shahn*. New York, NY: Chameleon Books.

Rendezvous with revenge. (1943). In *War victory adventures* (pp. 10–20). (Vol. 1, no. 2). St. Louis, MO: Family Comics.

Scott, C. (2007). Written in red, white, and blue: A comparison of comic book propaganda from World War II and September 11. *The Journal of Popular Culture*, 40, 325–343.

The story behind the cover: Introducing Capt. Red Cross. (1943). In *War victory adventures* (pp. 40–43). (Vol. 1, no. 3). St. Louis, MO: Family Comics.

Streb, E. J. (1998, August). Truth, justice, and the American way: Propaganda and comic books in the Second World War. Paper presented at the meeting of the Comic Arts Conference, San Diego, CA.

Uncle Cal combats Axis U-boats! (1943). In *War victory adventures* (pp. 42–47). (Vol. 1, no. 2). St. Louis, MO: Family Comics.

U.S. Treasury Department. (1942, Summer). *War victory comics.* (Box 8, Folder 1). Odegard Papers, Franklin D. Roosevelt Presidential Library, Hyde Park, NY.

War victory adventures. (1943a, August). (Vol. 1, no. 2). St. Louis, MO: Family Comics.

War victory adventures. (1943b, Winter). (Vol. 1, no. 3). St. Louis, MO: Family Comics.

Waugh, C. (1947). *The comics.* New York, NY: Macmillan.

Weaver, D. (1943). Grimm, ghost spotter. In *War victory adventures* (pp. 17–22). (Vol. 1, no. 3). St. Louis, MO: Family Comics.

★★ 12 ★★

Beyond the Storylines

Even More Ways That Comic Books Helped Boys and Girls Help Win the War

David E. Wilt

In addition to winning the hearts and minds of the population, WWII propaganda in the United States—comic books very much included—also encouraged direct action on the home front. Participation in actual war work was one way of contributing, but even the most youthful citizens were urged to do their bit by taking part in appropriate home-front activities. Such activities had the potential to help the actual prosecution of the war. Yet they also fostered a feeling of direct participation in the conflict, giving individuals a personal stake in its outcome. Such a total-war effort, materially and psychologically, was in fact the ultimate goal of many U.S. propagandists.

Earlier chapters in this book have primarily examined the visual and verbal aspects of the narratives found in the comic books of the WWII era. This final chapter, in contrast, *excludes* the comic book stories themselves in order to focus on a variety of additional means by which comic books on the home front conveyed propaganda messages.[1] As I will demonstrate, eight discrete, formal components of comic books often played important roles in relaying such messages, including: cover content; supplemental cover content; editorials and letters; house ads; last-frame or incidental art messages; bottom-of-page messages; text-only stories; and public service announcements.

Two of these methods were wholly or partially narrative in nature—covers and text-only stories—while the other aspects were largely non-narrative, non-diegetic, and typically consisting of simple, declarative, war-oriented statements (such as "Buy Bonds" or "Save Scrap"). These elements appeared in many wartime comic books, working both singly and in combination to deliver myriad propaganda messages. A content analysis of comic books must of necessity examine all of these aspects to obtain a full picture of the extent of wartime references in the form. Thus, in what follows, I first examine the thematic emphasis of comic book propaganda during the war. The bulk of the chapter then explores how content regarding the home front emerged within the eight components mentioned above and provides examples as a way of demonstrating how even the smallest or least obvious elements inherent to the comic book medium could provide support for wartime propaganda campaigns.

Propaganda Themes in Wartime Comic Books

The U.S. government did not mandate inclusion of war-related content in the mass media. Instead, government agencies—most notably, the Treasury Department and the Office of War Information—advised, requested, suggested, and appealed for such content. Government officials ensured that useful material, from raw data to finished propaganda, was available to the media, which utilized it as each gatekeeper saw fit. There was no immediate quid pro quo; ad space for propaganda messages was donated, not sold (in fact, many of the propaganda campaigns themselves were created by advertising agencies at no charge). Indeed, from the comic book industry's perspective, there was no specific business reason for its booklets to feature war-oriented material at all. This notion was especially true regarding non-narrative elements that would be unlikely to inspire newsstand sales of comics.[2] Despite these factors, however, comic books promoted home-front activities repeatedly, and in a variety of ways. Thus, vigorous promotion of home-front activities appears to have been a deliberate, patriotic effort on the part of comic book publishers.

By far the two most prominently mentioned home-front activities in comic books were the collection of scrap material and the purchase of war stamps and bonds. Since the majority of comic book readers were generally assumed to be children, these two activities—which were well suited to juvenile participation—were naturally highlighted. Other home-front activities mentioned (if not promoted as strongly) were those that lent themselves readily to basic messages, visual or textual, and were also accessible to young people (for example, planting Victory Gardens). More adult-oriented topics, such as encouraging enlistment in the armed forces or employment in war-related jobs, promoting adherence to rationing, soliciting blood donations, and the like were less relevant to youthful readers and appeared in comic books much less frequently.[3]

Relatively few home-front messages or material (as opposed to the plentiful anti-Fascist messages) are seen in pre-1942 comic books. Although there are a number of references to national defense, numerous stories about enemy agents at work in the United States, and even a few references to defense bonds (the precursor to war bonds), major home-front topics such as scrap drives and rationing rarely appeared before the Pearl Harbor attack. However, in issues with cover dates from the late spring and early summer of 1942, comic books began a rapid conversion to a domestic war footing.[4]

The level of war-relevant material varied by publisher—some never devoted much space to war topics—but for most comic books, 1942 and 1943 were the peak period of war-relevant content.[5] In 1944 and 1945, topical references decreased significantly, although there were periodic upsurges, probably inspired by government suggestions. For example, the Fifth, Sixth, and Seventh War Loan campaigns and paper salvage efforts were all promoted in this later stage of the war. Occasional war-related content continued to appear in comic books dated in early 1946, some of it slightly altered with added text such as "now we can reveal the daring feat" ("The Target and the Targeteers," 1946, p. 11) to create the appearance of a retrospective feature. For the most part, however, stories about home-front topics quickly ceased after the war was over.

Home Front Content by Form

As noted above, propaganda messages from the war period were delivered in various forms in comic books, and different magazines used varying combinations of the methods. While virtually every publisher included at least some war-oriented content in its comic magazines, the amount and methodology were not always consistent (sometimes not even within a publisher's own line). Some comic books utilized most or all of the means described below (even if not always in the same issue), while others restricted their war-related material to the occasional patriotic cover image or topical joke.

Comic Book Covers

Comic book covers were in some ways analogous to wartime propaganda posters, since they generally delivered a message via a single large illustration and limited text. Although one can argue that some comic book covers do tell a story, they do not generally contain complex narratives (such as might be found in an interior comic story or text story). The primary purpose of a comic book cover is to sell the magazine by attracting attention on the newsstand, and only secondarily to list or preview the interior contents or to convey a propaganda message. Still, these differing goals were not mutually exclusive during the war.

While many covers of wartime comic books dealt with the war, the majority of them were action-oriented, depicting protagonists in battle with Axis enemies, rather than dealing with home-front matters. The content of covers varied by publisher, genre, title, and date. Table 12.1 analyzes a selected sample of titles from a variety of publishers.[6] It is important to keep in mind that I determined war relevance on the basis of the content of the primary cover art and text, and not on any added graphic elements or text (such as small flag symbols or text banners across the top of the masthead).

As one can see from these selected findings, covers specifically about home-front activities were relatively rare. Those that did exist were generally symbolic in nature rather than constituting attempts to portray actual home-front activities, although a few examples of the latter did appear. For instance, the cover of *Comic Cavalcade* #6 (1944) depicts Green Lantern, the Flash, and Wonder Woman participating in a scrap-paper salvage drive; Superman, Batman, and Robin do the same on the cover of *World's Finest* #13 (1944), and they plant a Victory Garden on the cover of *World's Finest* #11 (1943). The humorous cover of *Police Comics* #13 (1942) depicts the superhero Plastic Man fleeing from a group of children engaged in rubber salvage collection, while *Champ Comics* #24 (1943) features a simple, declarative word balloon ("Hey, pals! Collect junk for victory!") accompanying artwork of children towing a wagon labeled "Junk," with a dazed Hitler, Mussolini, and Hirohito sitting on the salvaged material (cover).

However, the majority of home front–themed covers took the form of overt appeals for readers to buy bonds. An interesting example occurred in July 1944, when Fawcett took the unusual step of producing nearly identical covers on eight of its major titles. Each featured the comic's star character holding an oversized $1 War Savings Stamp, and the text "Buy one of these War Stamps today!" (*Captain Marvel Adventures*, 1944, cover).[7] This message was both simple and direct, since it was delivered by a familiar authority figure and addressed to the reader personally.

The emphasis on war *stamps* in this and virtually all other instances of wartime comic book propaganda demonstrated the industry's awareness of the largely juvenile readership of comic books. As Lawrence R. Samuel points out, the stamps "were targeted to entry-level investors, that is, the under-class and children. . . . Besides being an ideal program to sell the war to children . . .

	Table 12.1. War-Oriented Comic Book Covers		
Publisher	**War-oriented/Home-front**	**Non-war**	**Ambiguous**
DC Comics (157 issues)	37 (24%) 12 (8%)	116 (74%)	4 (3%)
Fawcett (89 issues)	24 (27%) 6 (7%)	60 (67%)	5 (6%)
Timely (83 issues)	60 (72%) 0 (0%)	18 (22%)	5 (6%)
Ace (16 issues)	2 (13%) 0 (0%)	13 (81%)	1 (6%)
Quality (33 issues)	0 (0%) 0 (0%)	33 (100%)	0 (0%)
MLJ (61 issues)	33 (54%) 0 (0%)	27 (44%)	1 (2%)
Standard (95 issues)	65 (68%) 1 (1%)	22 (23%)	8 (8%)
Novelty Press (93 issues)	20 (22%) 11 (12%)	67 (72%)	6 (6%)
Total (627 issues)	**241 (38%) 30 (5%)**	**356 (57%)**	**30 (5%)**

Note: Home-front references are included in the War-oriented total. The percentage assigned to home front is the percentage of overall comic book covers that have home-front subjects, not the percentage of War-oriented covers with home-front content. Home-front content was defined as the depiction of, or major reference to, activities such as scrap collection, bond sales, the Red Cross, rationing, Victory Gardens, war production, etc. Depictions of enemy espionage and sabotage, even if they are shown taking place in the United States, were not categorized as home-front topics. The titles for each publisher were as follows: DC Comics (Action, Batman, Detective, Superman, World's Finest dated 1942–1945); Fawcett (Captain Marvel Adventures, Whiz, dated 1942–1945); Timely (Captain America, Marvel Mystery, dated 1942–1945); Ace (Super-Mystery, dated 1942–45); Quality (Smash, dated 1942–1945); MLJ (Pep, Zip, dated 1942–1945); Standard (America's Best, Exciting, Startling, Thrilling, dated 1942–1945); and Novelty Press (Blue Bolt, Target, 4Most, dated 1942–1945).

savings stamps represented the idea that the defense program was for Everyman" (1997, p. 18).

The focus on small-denomination stamps was not universal, however. Other publishers participated in the same summer 1944 Treasury effort but raised the ante: at least four comic covers used a photo facsimile of a $100 bond rather than a $1 stamp. On the July 1944 issue of *Looney Tunes & Merrie Melodies*, for instance, Bugs Bunny and Porky Pig are shown holding a $100 War Savings Bond. Bugs tells Porky, "Okay, Doc! One for me and one for you!!" above the printed text "Buy one of these bonds today!" (cover). *Walt Disney's Comics & Stories* 46 (1944) similarly depicted Donald Duck—costumed as Uncle Sam—with a $100 bond and the same printed text, while *Popular Comics* #101 featured various newspaper comic strip characters (including Smilin' Jack and Smokey Stover) holding a $100 bond and saying in unison, "Buy one of these bonds today!" (1944, cover). Novelty Press's *Target* 5/4, cover dated September–October 1944, also used the image of a $100 bond and the same printed text, this time on a bull's-eye background, with images of a plane, tank, and PT boat in the corners (1944b).[8]

Somewhat more allegorical were covers such as *Action Comics* 86, in which Superman buries a uniformed Japanese character (perhaps representing

Hirohito, or Tojo) in war bonds, saying, "And it isn't Superman who's doing this—it's the American people!" (1945, cover). An anthropomorphized war bond socks Hitler, Mussolini, and Hirohito on the cover of *Four Favorites* 11 (1943), while in the background, the various superheroes who appear in the comic sing "Der Fuehrer's Face." As with the *Action* cover, this image suggests that it will not be superheroes who defeat the Axis, but the American people, through their purchase of war bonds.

A more elaborate appeal emerged on the cover of the October 1942 issue of *Target*, which showed characters from "The Cadet" comic driving a steam-roller—with rollers covered in replicas of the ubiquitous Minute Man poster ("For Victory—Buy War Bonds and Stamps")—over a discomfited Hitler and Hirohito (1942b). The editorial in that issue discussed the meaning behind the cover:

> Actually, as you well know, Kit Carter and his cadet pal, Dan Merry, aren't really out there in the front lines steam rolling the Japs and Nazis much as they would like to be, but they're accomplishing the same thing by loaning to their Uncle Sam every dime and dollar they can raise. You too can and should help build Uncle Sam's steam roller to flatten the Axis by buying your share of War Bonds and Stamps. ("Ye Editors' Page," 1942a, inside cover)

This sort of deconstruction of a propaganda message was rare and actually appeared as part of a longer explanation of how a comic book cover was created. Still, it did provide an additional opportunity to encourage readers to participate in the war effort in collaboration with another method, the editorial (as discussed below).

On the whole, however, such home-front activities as purchasing war bonds and stamps were not ideally suited for wartime comic book covers, which typically stressed flamboyant action and patriotic allegories. Indeed, only five percent of the sampled covers (see Table 12.1) were directly home-front-oriented. Novelty Press, which had a policy of downplaying costumed superheroes and fantastic content, had the highest percentage of home front–themed covers (12%), followed by DC Comics (8%). Some publishers—even those with significant war-relevant cover content, such as Timely—did not feature home-front topics on their covers at all. Of course, this observation does not mean that most comic book covers were bereft of home front propaganda, as the following section illustrates.

Supplemental Cover Content

In addition to the main cover illustration, wartime comic book covers generally featured numerous additional graphic and textual elements. These supplementary cover features took various forms. A comic book's title, its price, the publisher's logo, and text or art that plugged subsidiary characters and stories could all function in propagandistic ways. In a few instances, even plain-text messages, such as "Back the 5th War Loan," were inserted on covers, usually above the title logo (e.g., *Batman Comics*, 1944, cover). During the major war-loan campaigns, larger boxes containing blocks of plain text promoting bond sales were occasionally added to covers instead.[9]

Some publishers overlaid small, war-relevant graphics or symbols on the cover art of their comics, regardless of whether or not the main illustration itself was war-oriented. The small-size cover graphics varied in design and usage by publisher but were generally not very eye-catching. The most notable, perhaps, were adopted by Standard Comics (also known as Nedor and Better). The vast majority of this publisher's comic books from fall 1942 until the end of 1945 featured a red, white, and blue pennant that read "Buy War Bonds and Stamps for Victory" on the cover (see Figure 12.1). Although variants of this method were used by many publishers, no other company continued this practice for so long or so consistently.[10]

However, other publishers did periodically add war-relevant material to their covers. In July 1942 some Standard and Fawcett comic covers had U.S.-flag-themed graphics bearing the motto "United We Stand"; in September, at least eight DC issues had a similar flag graphic, with text reading "Keep It Flying!" Moreover, in conjunction with Red Cross drives, small Red Cross graphics appeared on numerous covers in the spring of 1944 and again in 1945.[11]

Other publishers favored the Treasury Department's official war bond insignia, which was a representation of Daniel Chester French's *Minute Man* (a sculpture that stands in Concord, Massachusetts). Through the middle of 1942, the words superimposed on this image were "For Defense, Buy United States Savings Bonds and Stamps," while afterward they became "For Victory, Buy United States War Bonds and Stamps." On these covers, the Minute Man insignia is occasionally an integral part of the cover art, while at other times it looks as if it has been literally pasted on top of an otherwise non-topical cover.

Other repeated graphics included "Let's Go USA, Keep 'Em Flying!," featuring three blue airplanes in a white circle. Originally designed as a recruiting logo for the prewar aviation cadet program, this appeal was later used as a generically patriotic graphic, especially on comics from the All-American line. Elsewhere, on various issues dated July and August 1942, DC Comics experimented with

Figure 12.1: Standard Comics frequently used this pennant on its wartime covers (America's Best Comics, 1942, detail from cover).

a square cover graphic featuring Superman and two servicemen with the text "Superman Says Buy Defense Bonds, Help National Defense." This was a short-lived propaganda effort, since DC subsequently dropped any regular use of such cover graphics (*Adventure*, 1942, cover). Fawcett created a similar graphic featuring a saluting Captain Marvel and the standard text associated with the Minute Man but placed the result on the contents page of their publications rather than on the covers (e.g., *Captain Marvel Adventures*, 1943, p. 3). Meanwhile, a handful of 1942–1943 Fiction House comics carried a plain-text message that read, "Buy U.S. War Savings Stamps" in an extremely small white box on their covers (*Fight*, 1942, cover).

These small cover graphic images probably attracted little attention, so their propaganda value might not have been particularly significant. Indeed, some companies never used them at all. However, one should not discount the cumulative effect of these repeated propaganda messages, in concert with others in the same comic book, in other comics, and in the mass media in general.

Editorial Commentary/Letters Pages

Not all comic books published during the Golden Age had regular editorial/letters pages, but there were exceptions. For example, Novelty Press was one of the few publishers that consistently interacted with its readers, not only by soliciting and then printing letters but also by responding to them and by printing regular editorials, often on war-oriented themes.

Standard Publications' *Thrilling Comics* included the feature "Chats with the Editor," which contained a mix of editorial commentary and reader letters, although there was less interaction between the two sides than on the Novelty Press pages.[12] Even before Pearl Harbor, *Thrilling* editorials often addressed world events and were patriotic in nature. For instance, "All Out for Home Defense" told readers in 1941 that "all over this great and wonderful land, home defense brigades are on the march. . . . Every citizen can help! You too, boys and girls of America, must take your place in the ranks!" ("Chats with the Editor," p. 63). After the United States entered the war, this sort of theme continued, as when one 1942 editorial characterized readers as "Young Heroes of America" and stated:

> During this time of war and sacrifice, boys and girls, you have the sacred opportunity of showing your patriotism and loyalty. Make the most of it! You are the soldiers of the Home Front. . . . Many of you young heroes and heroines are collecting salvage materials, buying war savings stamps, building Navy aircraft models, extending hospitality to members of our armed services, tending victory gardens, and knitting socks and sweaters for the boys. More power to you! ("Chats with the Editor," p. 58)

Other titles that ran letters pages at times during the war years—mostly without specific editorial comment—included *Wings* (Fiction House), *Captain America* (Timely), *Superman* (DC), *King Comics* and *Ace Comics* (David McKay), and *Top-Notch Laugh* (MLJ).[13] Publishers often used such pages as both promotional ploys (prizes were awarded to readers whose letters were printed, thus encouraging participation) and as a means by which the editors could obtain feedback about popular and unpopular features of their comics.[14]

However, although the letters features presented an opportunity to promote home-front activities by the readers, the contents of reader letters mostly focused on favorite characters and stories, with sporadic suggestions for improvement. Occasionally, some topical comments appeared, as in the featured letter in *Top-Notch Laughs* #39. Here, U.S. Army Air Force private James E. Hancock wrote that "we are all . . . trying to defeat the Hitlers and Tojos and all others who don't like our way of life. . . . I also want you to tell all to buy War Bonds and stamps to help win through" ("Readers Page," 1943, p. 16). However, such letters were not common, and war-oriented editorial comments were also rare, with the exception of Novelty Press, which contained both numerous examples of letters from readers about their home-front activities and editorials encouraging such actions. In general, then, only Novelty Press magazines and Standard's *Thrilling* utilized editorial or letters-page communications regularly and to full effect for propaganda purposes.

House Ads

House ads were most often full- or half-page promotions for a particular company's other titles, upcoming issues, contests, and so on. During the conflict, war-oriented house ads often made overt appeals to readers to participate in specific home-front activities (see Figure 12.2). These non-narrative messages rarely attempted to convince or explain the issues to readers. Instead, they simply reiterated the importance and urgency of buying bonds, collecting scrap, or another home-front campaign; some were generic patriotic messages. Not all publishers regularly included house ads in their publications, using the space for other features or paid advertisements.[15]

Captain Marvel Adventures #25 contained two notable house ads. The first promoted *Whiz* comics but added wartime content: "Cats chase *little* rats! But Capt. Marvel and the other *Whiz* heroes handle *Axis* rats!" In the accompanying illustration, Capt. Marvel grasps a disheveled, subversive-looking fellow and asks: "*Now* what do you think Hitler's chances are?" (the response is "*Terrible!*") (*Captain Marvel Adventures*, 1943, p. 18). The second ad shows Capt. Marvel kicking three Nazi soldiers, and his alter ego, Billy Batson, shaking the hand of a GI, with the text: "Capt. Marvel says—Kick the Axis where it hurts, Buy bonds *steadily*, not in spurts! Keep buying War Bonds and Stamps! You've done your bit—now do your best!" (*Captain Marvel Adventures*, 1943, p. 45).

Daredevil Comics #14 (from December 1942) also contained two house ads, one for Comic House publications ("Stick to Comic House magazines, they're what you want!") ("It Can't Be Done!" p. 42), and a two-page centerspread depicting figures from American history (George Washington, John Paul Jones, General Pershing, Admiral Dewey, General MacArthur, and Abraham Lincoln) under the banner "We have never lost a war!.... And we must not lose this one!" The text urges readers to buy war bonds: "Let nothing stand in the way! *Buy all you can!! Defense Stamps come first!! Forward to Victory!!*" ("We Have Never Lost a War!" 1942, pp. 22–23). The unusual feature of this house ad, in addition to its large size and priority placement in the magazine, is the absence of star character Daredevil himself from the artwork. The anonymous tone, however, is somewhat offset by the cumulative gravitas of the famous Americans represented on the ad, who lend their historic authority to the appeal.

As these examples indicate, house ads used a personal, specific tone for their message. The readers of the magazine were targeted directly, and the messages contained somewhat more detail than comic book covers or other non-narrative methods, such as bottom-of-page messages or added cover graphics.

Figure 12.2: This house ad from Prize Comics features home-front activities
for both boys and girls ("What You Can Do," 1942, inside cover).

House ads were also very prominent and thus were likely to attract more reader attention, although since they were not intended to entertain, but rather to promote other comics (and in wartime, home-front activities), they might have been skipped or given short shrift by readers.

Last-Frame/Incidental Art Messages

The final frame of many wartime comic book stories was often devoted to messages about the importance of bond buying and other home-front activities, in addition to the usual teasers about the exciting story in the next issue (see Figure 12.3). This method of inserting home-front messages into comics was extremely popular among some publishers, notably Standard and Novelty Press. From the fall of 1942 through late 1945, virtually every story in Standard's *America's Best Comics, Exciting Comics, Startling Comics, Thrilling Comics*, and *Fighting Yank* concluded with a war-relevant message. Novelty Press regularly included last-frame messages in one or two stories per issue (in the spring of 1943, the majority of its stories contained them). Other publishers used this method of including additional home-front content, but not as consistently as Standard or Novelty Press.

Last-frame messages were sometimes presented as declarative statements by the protagonists of the stories—either as dialogue among characters or as an appeal made directly to the comic reader by the hero. At the end of the "American Eagle" story in *Exciting* #25, for instance, Bud (aka Eaglet) asks Tom (the American Eagle), "Swell action, Tom! What else is on the bill for today?" Tom, looking directly at the reader, replies: "Best of all—we're going down to buy some U.S. War Bonds and stamps!" ("The American Eagle," 1943, p. 23).

However, in other cases the home-front message appeared as a text box unrelated to the just-concluded comic book story, or as a combination of the two. For example, a "Dick Cole" story in *Blue Bolt* comics concludes with Dick and a friend each earning a $500 reward for the capture of two crooks. The final frame text caption references this plot point, then adds an additional, unrelated home-front message: "What did the boys do with the reward money? They bought war bonds, without a minute's hesitation! When you collect waste paper, don't pass up the small scraps such as envelopes, wrappings, ads, etc. They all add up!" ("Dick Cole," 1944, p. 10).

Such final-frame messages, because they were directly connected to comic stories, might have been consumed more readily—indeed, perhaps almost unconsciously—than house ads (which could be skipped), and messages delivered in other non-narrative methods. In each case, the story concludes and, without missing a beat, the reader is instantly urged (in many cases directly) to participate in the war effort by purchasing war bonds and by saving scrap material.

Figure 12.3: Last-frame messages, such as this one from Exciting Comics, inserted propaganda messages directly into the final point of the story line ("Crime Crushers," 1943, p. 49).

In addition to the final-frame messages, which were overt propaganda inserted at the end of stories, incidental war-relevant art and text messages also appeared in comic stories in the background or as throwaway gags. Unlike motion pictures or photographs, which could sometimes accidentally capture wartime references (for example, ration stickers on auto windshields or bonds posters on walls in the background), everything in a comic book story had to be deliberately written and drawn. Consequently, there were relatively few incidental topical images in wartime comics. Artists tended not to draw anything that was not relevant to the story, and only slightly more dialogue references appear (that is, wisecracks or comments about war-related matters in nonwar stories). The background messages that did exist were unobtrusive and probably had little propaganda impact on their own. The apparently random "Buy Bonds in This Bank!" sign in the background of an otherwise non-war-relevant, funny-animal comic strip, for example, seems likely to have gained little attention ("Billy the Kid and Oscar," 1943, p. 47).

Bottom-of-Page Messages

Some publishers used the white space at the bottom (or, occasionally, the top) of comic book pages to convey propaganda messages on a variety of topics. These one or two lines of text were printed outside the comic story itself but were highly visible to readers (see Figure 12.4).

The earliest example of this type of message found thus far is in *Boy Comics* #5, dated August 1942. However, the messages in this issue were mostly plugs

Figure 12.4: Even the blank space in the gutter at the bottom of the page was occasionally useful to comic book propagandists (Johnson, 1945, p. 38).

for publisher Comic House's characters and other titles, with only an occasional home-front message (such as "Help win the war—Buy Defense Stamps Now!" on p. 25). This message format began to appear regularly in mid-1944 in Standard comics and slightly later in Novelty Press titles, and was occasionally adopted by other publishers.

The Standard bottom-of-page messages ranged from the relatively generic, such as "Be an American—Buy War Stamps and Bonds!" to specifically youth-oriented appeals, such as "Too young to enlist—Buy War Stamps and Bonds!" (*The Fighting Yank*, 1944, pp. 1, 9) One of the messages also references the fiscal benefits of buying bonds: "The more you buy the more you'll have—Buy more War Stamps!" (*The Fighting Yank*, 1944, p. 13).

Novelty Press's bottom-of-page messages were heavily promoted as an added feature called "Q's & A's," with a question on one page and the answer on the following page (printed upside down). These were mostly factual trivia questions (or questions about something appearing in the comic story on that particular page) and presented as fun and educational matter. But interspersed with the questions and answers were topical messages, often in rhyme, such as "Saving paper, every scrap, will wipe the Axis from the map" and "Don't ever doubt it, the stamps you buy, will sweep the Axis from the sky" (*Blue Bolt*, 1944, pp. 22, 41).

Although they were both prominent and visible, however, such bottom-of-page messages lacked the detail, complexity, and authority of other message channels. Still, their presence in some comic books must have contributed to the overall, total-war ambiance of such wartime publications.

Text Stories

Comic books were required to contain several pages of text stories in order to retain second-class mailing privileges. Whether or not these stories were widely read is debatable—in one issue of *Target*, a reader suggested they be discarded, but the editors cited postal regulation requirements, concluding that text stories "must remain" ("Ye Editors' Page," 1942b, inside cover). These textual stories, usually rather generic fiction, often contained war-relevant material.[16]

A number of wartime text stories dealt with children who performed patriotic deeds, as in "Boy Volunteer," in which "Arthur Lee uses his Boy Scout knowledge to foil the Nazis!" (Jackson, 1943, p. 58), and "Aide to Uncle Sam," where "A Blind Newsboy Helps a Federal Agent Imperilled by Nazi Spies!" (Endicott, 1943, p. 37). Text stories about the heroic adventures of juvenile foreign nationals fighting to eject Axis invaders from their homeland also appeared in wartime comic books. Prominent examples included "Clarion Call," about a Chinese boy fighting the Japanese enemy (Sturdy, 1942, p. 27), and "Ragged Spy," which detailed the adventures of a young Russian battling the Nazis (1944, p. 37). These tales indirectly encouraged American youth—who were not living in occupied nations and thus could not confront the enemy directly—to be as patriotic as possible on the home front.

To reinforce this activist message, there were also numerous text stories about young people participating in home-front activities, as in "Junior Warden— Young Alfred Denton Does His Bit during a Blackout" (Hale, 1942, p. 35) and "Junior Red Cross Man—A Young Lad Does His Bit for Uncle Sam!" (Strong, 1942, p. 27). The text story in *Fighting Yank* #1 told the tale of one Eddie Forbes, who "was anxious to collect and sell as much scrap material as he could so that he would be able to buy defense savings stamps with the proceeds." When a crook tries to steal his father's tires (a scarce commodity during the war), Eddie knocks the thief out with an accumulated ball of scrap tinfoil (Donald, 1942, p. 38). The virtues of participating in scrap drives were also extolled in a text story in *Target* 4/12. Here a boy receives a letter from his brother in the Marines, which motivates him to throw himself wholeheartedly into a paper salvage drive; for his patriotic efforts, he is awarded his brother's Silver Star at a school assembly ("Paper Hero," 1944 pp. 34–35).

A more cautionary parable appeared in *Funny Animals* 2, which told the tale of a young boy eagerly anticipating many Christmas gifts. However, despite his parents' urging, he refuses to donate any of his many old toys to charity, and he has a dream in which toys are added to the list of rationed items. Not only does he not qualify for a toy ration, his father indicates that they are now too poor to afford any new toys, and that all of his existing toys have been taken away. Upon awaking, the story's protagonist vows to donate some of his toys to the cause. Furthermore, he realizes that he wants war stamps and bonds for Christmas, since purchasing them "will help Uncle Sam to fight for us and besides I'd save money and after the war I'll have something saved up to buy what toys and things I want" ("A Christmas Story by Uncle Don," 1943, p. 28).

Even comics aimed at very young readers—the so-called funny animal genre—utilized the text story format as a means of disseminating home-front propaganda. In *Ha Ha* #2, Flipsy Fox dreams of a "Ratzi" invasion and, when he awakes, decides to spend the million dollars he has won on war bonds (Jerome, 1943, p. 37). In the following issue, little Lou Rabbit sells war bonds to his animal neighbors: "Even old Miser Monk gave generously, because he knew that this was a chance for both patriotism and profit—at one and the same time!" (Markham, 1943, p. 40). Another funny-animal object lesson appeared in *Real Funnies* #2, as "George Gander Helps the War Effort" (Stanley, 1943, p. 33).

In general, this type of text story differed from stories with adult protagonists, whether war-oriented or not. By focusing on the home-front activities of young people, the stories provided a positive example for readers to emulate. Thus, they had more in common with comic stories featuring youthful protagonists such as the Little Wise Guys (Comic House), the Newsboy Legion (DC), or the Liberty Lads (Harvey) than they did with superhero or other war-action genre stories.

Yet text stories, while a kind of fictional narrative, still fall into a formal middle ground between comic stories and the non-narrative type of messages, thanks to their abbreviated nature and the often didactic style of writing used in their approach. Furthermore, the question of whether the majority of comic book readers actually took the time to read a page or two of rather densely packed type with a spot illustration or two (or none) makes the efficacy of these messages a bit dubious.

Outside Content

While most of the forms of propaganda discussed in this chapter were generated by the comic book artists or their editors and publishers, there is one final formal category that presented content created by outside providers— most often, by the U.S. government. Indeed, space was typically provided at no cost by publishers for government-sponsored messages, including open letters from Treasury Secretary Morgenthau and General "Hap" Arnold regarding home-front activities. Some of these messages were targeted specifically at youthful comic book readers, while others were general-interest propaganda. For example, the back cover of the government-sponsored *War Victory Comics* featured a message from President Franklin D. Roosevelt: "The United States does not consider it a sacrifice to do all one can, to give one's best to our nation, when the nation is fighting for its existence and its future life" (*War Victory Comics*, 1942, back cover).

In the summer and fall of 1942, more than a dozen comics from different companies published a full-page open letter from Treasury secretary Henry Morgenthau Jr. to the "Boys and Girls of America," in which he asked "every one of you forty million boys and girls" to buy at least one ten-cent Savings Stamp per week. "You would be lending your Uncle Sam two hundred million dollars every year," he added. Readers were informed that space for the ad had been donated by the publishers (Morgenthau, 1942, back cover; see Figure 12.5).

The Morgenthau letter was followed in late 1944 by another message to "the Boys and Girls of America!"—this time from General Arnold, Commanding General of the U.S. Army Air Forces. "We of the armed forces urge every young man and woman of pre-military age who has been filling a summer war job to return to school this autumn," he wrote. "Such work is important, but your education has top priority" (1944, p. 36).

The next year, five high-ranking American military officers sent an open letter to the public in support of the Seventh (and as it developed, final) War Loan. The appeal was reprinted in various outlets, including in facsimile on the cover of *Big Shot* #57 and *Popular Comics* #10, and (in a text-only version) on the editors' page of *Target* 6/5.[17] The letter read, in part: "We, upon whom has been placed the responsibility of leading the American forces, appeal to you with all possible earnestness to invest in War Bonds to the fullest extent of your capacity" ("Target Hits and Misses," 1945, inside cover).

There were other examples of such outside content, including full-page bond advertisements (i.e., not house ads, but the same sort of ads seen in mainstream magazines), as well as messages promoting groups such as the Civilian Service Corps ("If They Win," 1943, inside cover) and the Red Cross, in addition to generic patriotic messages. But the Morgenthau and Arnold letters in particular are interesting because they were specifically aimed at young people, and also had the authoritative imprimatur of high-ranking government officials. The "Boys and Girls of America" were so important, these letters suggested, that a cabinet secretary and the commander of the U.S. Army Air Forces felt it was important to use comic book pages to ask for help personally.

Conclusions

The comic book medium is capable of delivering information in a variety of ways: the stories alone deliver a narrative via a combination of text and visuals;

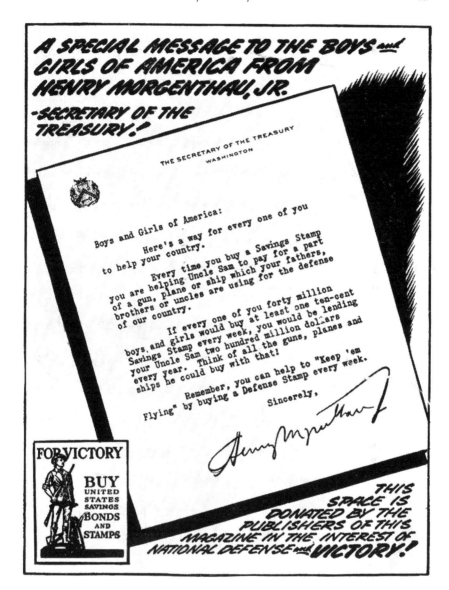

Figure 12.5: This open letter from Treasury secretary Morgenthau appeared in numerous comic books in 1942.

the cover, house ads, commercial advertisements, public service messages, editorials, text stories, and—as we have just seen—a number of additional methods relating to the format and typography of the printed comic magazine medium, are multifaceted and versatile. During World War II, all the tools of this information-dense medium were utilized for propaganda purposes.

As an example of the variety and number of messages contained in some wartime comic books, consider Standard's *Black Terror #7*, which was dated August 1944. Reflecting the reduction in page count that occurred during the war, this comic was 52 pages long (three of these pages were advertisements: the inside front and back covers, and the outside back cover). The cover art and all four comic stories inside—three Black Terror tales and one additional story featuring The Ghost—were war-oriented. Furthermore, the red-white-and-blue War Stamps pennant was present on the cover. The issue offered 44 textual, bottom-of-page messages (nine different messages, repeated several times each). Additionally, each of the four comic stories had a last-frame text message urging readers to support the war effort by purchasing bonds. Thus, in addition to the narrative content (the cover and the actual comic stories), the issue provided 49 more messages to readers concerning home-front actions they *should* take.[18] Although Standard's heavy use of the final-frame and bottom-of-page message format skews the total number of propaganda messages somewhat in this case (although some other methods are absent, such as house ads and an editorial/letters page), this issue does demonstrate how prevalent such non-narrative, war-relevant content was in comics of the era.

Of course, it would be impossible to prove the relative efficacy of the various methods of delivering propaganda in wartime comic books. One might speculate that personal appeals from popular and/or authority figures (e.g., the Morgenthau and Arnold letters, house ads, and other comic content in which stars such as Captain Marvel or Superman urged readers to buy bonds or save scrap) would have had a greater impact than anonymous text along the bottom of each page or the often-tiny and easily overlooked added cover graphics. Indeed, the latter seem to fall into the category of "nearly worthless" war references that the War Advertising Council called "A PLUG IN A SLUG" (Jones, 2009, p. 33). However, even such impersonal, repetitive, and brief messages could presumably produce a cumulative effect, especially when added to propaganda in mainstream magazines, motion pictures, posters, radio broadcasts, and so on. Taken together, all of this comic book propaganda, in its various shapes and forms, surely did its part to immerse Americans of all ages in the total war environment.

Notes

1. Outside advertising content is also excluded, with the exception of government-affiliated public service announcements.

2. One possible, if indirect, exception to this principle was the increased campaign to salvage waste paper in 1944: paper shortages restricted the number and size of comic books that could be printed, and while in the short run this might have had some beneficial effects on the bottom line (comics were reduced in size from between 64 and 68 pages to 52 pages, with no reduction in the cover price), in the long run publishers were unable to print sufficient copies of existing titles or add new comics to their line, despite wartime demand. A house ad promoting waste paper collection in "American Boys and Girls" 30 (1944) featured Uncle Sam warning readers: "If the paper shortage is not relieved by you, there will be no more comic magazines printed in the United States!" (p. 44).

3. In fact, there was even a major push in 1944 to encourage young people to *leave* temporary war jobs (including farm work) and return to school in the fall.

4. There was generally a 2–3-month lag time between the creation of a comic book's contents and its publication, and the cover date was usually at least a month later than the newsstand date—in other words, a comic hastily written and drawn in December 1941 would probably have been printed and distributed no earlier than March 1942 and might have carried an April cover date. Furthermore, publishers would have been reluctant to discard whatever backlog of unpublished material they had on hand, so full-blown war themes emerged in quantity only with issues dated summer 1942.

5. Comic book content overall generally followed the pattern of war relevance in other popular media: gradually increasing anti-Fascist messages in the period leading up to the attack on Pearl Harbor, a flurry of heavily war-oriented content in 1942 and 1943, followed by a gradual diminution of topical material in 1944 and 1945. For a comparison, the percentage of Hollywood films with war-relevant content was 30% in 1941, 55% in 1942, 63% in 1943, 51% in 1944, and 38% in 1945 (Shull & Wilt, 1996, pp. 80, 290).

6. This is not intended to be a random sample, but rather a representative one. Comic titles that were wholly or largely war-oriented (e.g., *Wings*, *Fight*) and titles or genres that were likely to have little or no war content (e.g., *Jungle*, *Funny Animals*) were omitted.

7. The Fawcett titles that used this motif were: *Captain Marvel Adventures* #37, *Master Comics* #52, *Whiz Comics* #56, *Captain Marvel Jr.* #21, *Captain Midnight* #22, *Don Winslow* #17, and *Wow* #27.

8. Nearly a year later, *Target* 6, #5 (July–August 1945) also used the image of a $100 bond—drawn rather than a photostat this time—as a centerpiece of its cover. The rationale behind an exhortation to purchase a $100 bond—which required a significant cash outlay that was unlikely to be within the immediate grasp of a young comic book reader—is unknown.

9. See, for example, the cover of *Whiz Comics* 66 (July 1945).

10. Standard comics dated June 1942 used the familiar "Minute Man" bond image, but the company subsequently decided to go with the tricolor pennant design, which was exclusive to their brand. Also published by Standard's Ned Pines, the Thrilling line of pulp magazines—*Thrilling Detective*, *Thrilling Wonder Stories*, *Startling Stories*, etc.—followed the same practice, with the covers of most issues from the fall of 1942 through the end of 1945 carrying the tri-color bonds pennant.

11. "Fight Infantile Paralysis" was another such graphic that appeared during the war years, although it was not directly war-oriented.

12. This feature ran in *Thrilling* from the first issue (in which letters from readers were solicited, with cash prizes for the best) until 1943. The majority of the page was taken up with editorial comments and a membership coupon for "The Thrilling Club," leaving a little space for brief excerpts from reader letters.

13. The longest-lived of these was probably "Wings' Air Mail" in *Wings*, which ran from mid-1942 throughout the war years and beyond.

14. *Blue Ribbon Comics* 3 (January 1940) contained a full-page house ad soliciting letters from readers commenting on the comic's features, promising $5 for the best feedback ("Boys and Girls Win a Prize for Your Letter," p. 64). However, no letters page appeared in subsequent issues.

15. Advertising was usually restricted to the inside front cover, inside back cover, and back cover of wartime comics; if a publisher could not sell this ad space in a particular issue, a house ad might be placed in one of these slots.

16. Some text stories were about characters who also appeared in comic stories in the same publication: for example, *Target* 2, #10 and 2, #11 (December 1941 and January 1942a) contain "Speck Turns Sleuth," a two-part story in which the protagonists of "Speck, Spot and Sis" are tricked into distributing foreign propaganda leaflets by an Axis agent. Text stories in Harvey titles sometimes told the "Story behind the Cover," as in *The Green Hornet* (1944, March) (pp. 42–43).

17. However, the bond-oriented cover of this comic did have text reading "Back Up Our Generals and Admirals." The cover of *Blue Bolt* 6/2 (August 1945) also had the "Back Up Our Generals and Admirals" text, along with portraits of seven military men, including Generals MacArthur and Eisenhower, and the generals/admirals open letter was printed on the editorial page of this issue as well.

18. The two one-page text stories in this issue were not available for review; it is conceivable that either or both of these were also war-oriented.

References

Action comics. (1945, July). (No. 86). New York, NY: Detective Comics.

Adventure comics. (1942, July). (No. 76). New York, NY: Detective Comics.

America's best comics. (1942, September). (Vol. 1, no. 2). New York, NY: Better Publications.

American Boys and Girls. (1944, February). In *Blue Beetle* (p. 44). (No. 30). Holyoke, MA: Holyoke.

The American eagle. (1943, February). In *Exciting* (pp. 15–23). (Vol. 9, no. 1). New York, NY: Better Publications.

Arnold, H. H. (1944, December). An important message to the boys and girls of America! (1944). In *Blue Bolt* (p. 36). (Vol. 5, no. 3). Philadelphia, PA: Novelty Press.

Batman comics. (1944, August–September). (No. 24). New York, NY: Detective Comics.

Billy the kid and Oscar. (1943, September). In *Funny Animals* (pp. 43–52). (Vol. 2, no. 10). Buffalo, NY: Fawcett.

Black Terror. (1944, August). (No. 7) New York, NY: Nedor.

Blue Bolt. (1944, December). (Vol. 5, no. 3). Philadelphia, PA: Novelty.

Blue Bolt. (1945, August). (Vol. 6, no. 2). Philadelphia, PA: Novelty.

Boy comics. (1942, August). (Vol. 1, no. 5). New York, NY: Comic House.

Boys and Girls Win a Prize for Your Letter. (1940, January). In *Blue Ribbon Comics* (p. 64). (Vol. 1, no. 3). St. Louis, MO: M.L.J. Magazines.

Captain Marvel adventures. (1943, July). (Vol. 5, no. 25). Louisville, KY: Fawcett.

Captain Marvel adventures. (1944, July). (Vol. 7, no. 37). Louisville, KY: Fawcett.

Champ comics. (1943, December). (Vol. 1, no. 24). St. Louis, MO: Family Comics.

Chats with the editor. (1941, June). In *Thrilling* (p. 63). (No. 17). New York, NY: Better Publications.

Chats with the editor. (1942, October). In *Thrilling* (p. 58). (Vol. 10, no. 2 [whole no. 30]). New York, NY: Better Publications.

A Christmas story by Uncle Don. (1943, January). In *Funny animals comics* (pp. 26–29). (Vol. 1, no. 2). Buffalo, NY: Fawcett.

Comic cavalcade. (1944, Spring). (No. 6). New York, NY: Gainlee.

Crime crushers. (1943, December). In *Exciting comics* (pp. 36–49). (Vol. 10, no. 3). New York: Better Publications.

Daredevil comics. (1942, December). (Vol. 1, no. 14). New York, NY: Magazine House.

Dick Cole. (1944, December). In *Blue Bolt* (pp. 1–10). (Vol. 5, no. 3). Philadelphia, PA: Novelty.

Donald, A. (1942, September). Home defense. In *The Fighting Yank* (p. 38). (Vol. 1, no. 1). New York, NY: Nedor.

Endicott, J. S. (1943, July). Aide to Uncle Sam. In *Thrilling* (p. 37). (Vol. 12, no. 3 [whole no. 36]). New York, NY: Better Publications.

Fight comics. (1942, August). (No. 20). New York, NY: Fight Stories.

The fighting Yank. (1944, August). (No. 9). New York, NY: Nedor.

Four favorites. (1943, August). (Vol. 1, no. 11). Springfield, MA: Ace Magazines.

Hale, H. (1942, January). Junior warden. In *Exciting* (p. 35). (Vol. 6, no. 1). New York, NY: Better Publications.

If they win . . . only our dead are free. (1943, June). In *The fighting Yank* (inside cover). (Vol. 2, no. 1). New York, NY: Nedor.

It can't be done! (1942, December). In *Daredevil Comics* (p. 42). (Vol. 1, no. 14). New York, NY: Magazine House.

Jackson, J. (1943, March). Boy volunteer. In *Startling Comics* (p. 58). (Vol. 7, no. 2). New York, NY: Better Publications.

Jerome, T. (1943, November). Flipsy Fox wins the sweepstakes. In *Ha Ha* (p. 37). (Vol. 1, no. 2). New York, NY: Creston.

Johnson, W. (1945, Spring). The cadet. In *4Most comics* (pp. 38–47). (Vol. 4, no. 2). Philadelphia, PA: Novelty Press.

Jones, J. B. (2009). *All-out for victory! Magazine advertising and the World War II home front.* Waltham, MA: Brandeis University Press.

Looney tunes & Merrie melodies. (1944, July). (Vol. 1, no. 33). New York, NY: Dell.

Markham, R. (1943, December). Lou Rabbit, super bond salesman. In *Ha Ha* (p. 40). (Vol. 1, no. 3). New York, NY: Creston.

Morgenthau, H. Jr. (1942, August). A special message to the boys and girls of America. In *Target Comics* (back cover). (Vol. 3, no. 6). Philadelphia, PA: Novelty.

Paper hero. (1944, April). In *Target* (pp. 34–35). (Vol. 4, no. 12). Philadelphia, PA: Novelty.

Police comics. (1942, November). (No. 13). Buffalo, NY: Comic Magazines.

Popular comics. (1944, July). (Vol. 1, no. 1). New York, NY: Dell.

Ragged Spy. (1944, October). In *Captain Marvel adventures* (pp. 37–38). (Vol. 7, no. 40). Louisville, KY: Fawcett.

Readers page. (1943, September). In *Top-notch laugh* (p. 16). (Vol. 1, no. 39). St. Louis, MO: MLJ Magazines.

Samuel, L. R. (1997). *Pledging allegiance: American identity and the bond drive of World War II.* Washington, DC: Smithsonian Institution Press.

Shull, M. S., & Wilt, D. E. (1996). *Hollywood war films, 1937-1945.* Jefferson, NC: McFarland.

Stanley, C. (1943, March). George Gander helps the war effort. In *Real Funnies* (p. 33). (Vol. 1, no. 2). New York, NY: Nedor.

Story behind the cover. (1944, March). In *The Green Hornet* (pp. 42–43). (Vol. 1, no. 17). New York, NY: Family Comics.

Strong, C. S. (1942, July). Junior Red Cross man. In *Exciting* (p. 27). (Vol. 7, no. 2). New York, NY: Better Publications.

Sturdy, C. (1942, October). Clarion call. In *Exciting* (p. 27). (No. 22). New York, NY: Better Publications.

Target. (1941, December). (Vol. 2, no. 10). Philadelphia, PA: Novelty.

Target. (1942a, January). (Vol. 2, no. 11). Philadelphia, PA: Novelty.

Target. (1942b, October). (Vol. 3, no. 8). Philadelphia, PA: Novelty.

Target. (1944a, April). (Vol. 4, no. 12). Philadelphia, PA: Novelty.

Target. (1944b, September–October). (Vol. 5, no. 4). Philadelphia, PA: Novelty.

Target. (1945, July–August). (Vol. 6, no.5). Philadelphia, PA: Novelty.

The Target and the Targeteers. (1946, February). In *Target* (pp. 11–17). (Vol. 6, no. 10). Philadelphia, PA: Novelty.

Target hits and misses. (1945, July–August). In *Target* (inside cover). (Vol. 6, no. 5). Philadelphia, PA: Novelty.

Walt Disney's comics & stories. (1944, July). (Vol. 4, no. 10 [whole no. 46]). New York, NY: Dell.

War victory comics. (1942, Summer). (Vol. 1, no. 1). St. Louis, MO: Family Comics.

We have never lost a war! (1942, December). In *Daredevil Comics* (pp. 22–23). (Vol. 1, no. 14). New York, NY: Magazine House.

What you can do to win the war [advertisement]. (1942, July). In *Prize comics* (inside cover). (Vol. 2, no. 10). New York, NY: Feature.

Whiz Comics. (1945, July). (Vol. 11, no. 66). Louisville, KY: Fawcett.

World's finest. (1943, Autumn). (No. 11). New York, NY: Detective Comics.

World's finest. (1944, Spring). (No. 13). New York, NY: Detective Comics.

Ye editors' page. (1942, October). In *Target* (inside cover). (Vol. 3, no. 8). Philadelphia, PA: Novelty.

Ye editors' page. (1942, November). In *Target* (inside cover). (Vol. 3, no. 9). Philadelphia, PA: Novelty.

★★ AUTHOR BIOGRAPHIES ★★

Derek Buescher (PhD, University of Utah) is Professor of Communication Studies at the University of Puget Sound in Tacoma, Washington. In addition to serving as Director of Gender Studies and Director of Forensics, he teaches courses in cultural theory, argumentation, and media studies. His research focuses on questions of citizenship within contemporary media and politics with particular emphasis on the challenges of ideology and orthodoxy in times of a perpetual war. In addition to essays published in *Critical Studies in Media Communication, Women's Studies in Communication,* and the *Alta Conference proceedings,* Professor Buescher has written collaborative projects on the state of debate forms in intercollegiate competition and tenure and promotion. He is currently coauthoring an argumentation textbook for Chinese students.

Travis Cox is a doctoral candidate at Texas A&M University in the Department of Communication. His research examines the intersection of visual rhetoric, gender, and popular culture.

Trischa Goodnow (PhD, University of Pittsburgh) is Professor of Speech Communication at Oregon State University. She recently published The Daily Show *and Rhetoric: Arguments, Issues and Strategies* with Lexington Press. Her next volume, *A Rhetoric of Film: Social Values and Social Change*, is an anthology to be published by Cognella Press. She has published essays in *Visual Communication Quarterly* and *The Handbook of Visual Communication* and coauthored an essay in *War and Propaganda.*

Jon Judy is an instructor of communications at Stark State College in North Canton, Ohio, and is a PhD student in education at Kent State University. He has taught mass media and film courses at Kent State, Cuyahoga Community

College, and Stark State and has presented papers at the Comics Arts, the American Culture/Popular Culture Association, and the National Writing Association conferences.

John R. Katsion is Assistant Professor of Communication Studies at Northwest Missouri State University in Maryville, Missouri. He has a PhD from Regent University in Communication Studies, and an MA from Minnesota State University (Mankato) in Speech Communication. His areas of research interest are the rhetorical ideas of Kenneth Burke, visual and musical rhetoric, and performance studies. He has presented on panels of the Religious Communication Association and the Visual Rhetoric Division in the above-mentioned areas. He has been teaching for over nineteen years at the university level in the areas of communication and performance studies.

James J. Kimble (PhD, University of Maryland) is Associate Professor of Communication & the Arts at Seton Hall University. He researches domestic propaganda, war rhetoric, and visual imagery. He is the author of *Mobilizing the Home Front: War Bonds and Domestic Propaganda* and of *Prairie Forge: The Extraordinary Story of the Nebraska Scrap Metal Drive of World War II*, as well as the writer and coproducer of the feature documentary *Scrappers: How the Heartland Won World War II*. His other research has appeared in edited books as well as academic journals, including *Women & Language*, *Rhetoric & Public Affairs*, *Southern Communication Journal*, *Communication Quarterly*, *Great Plains Quarterly*, *Women's Studies in Communication*, and *The Quarterly Journal of Speech*.

Christina M. Knopf earned her PhD in Cultural Sociology and Political Communication at the University at Albany in 2005. She has served the Speech Communication program at SUNY Potsdam since 2006 as Assistant Professor and is also affiliate faculty to the Women's & Gender Studies and African Studies programs. Dr. Knopf regularly presents her research at the National Communication Association and Eastern Communication Association conferences, in addition to presenting at the Rhetoric Society of America, the American Sociological Association, and the American Political Science Association, among other venues. Her earlier work was primarily concerned with the intersection of politics and religion, while recent work focuses on civil-military relations and military communication. She has published chapters in two edited anthologies (*What Democrats Talk about When they Talk about God*, D. Weiss, ed., and *The Rhetoric of American Exceptionalism*, J. Edwards & D. Weiss, eds.).

Steven E. Martin holds a PhD in Rhetoric and Public Address from The Pennsylvania State University. He is currently a professor of communication at Ripon College, in Ripon, Wisconsin. He has published several articles about the labor movement's use of comic books in the WWII era, including "Establishing Counter-Hegemony through Narratives: The Comic Books of the Congress of Industrial Organizations," in *Who Says? Working-Class Rhetoric, Class Consciousness and Community*, William DeGenaro, ed., University of Pittsburgh Press (2007).

Brad Palmer in an instructor of communication at Stark State College in North Canton, Ohio. He has taught persuasion, argumentation and communication theory for Walsh University, the University of Akron, and Stark State.

Elliott Sawyer is an independent scholar residing in Utah. He completed his master's degree at the University of Utah; his thesis is "Postfeminism in Female Team Superhero Comic Books."

Deborah Clark Vance, PhD, is Associate Professor and Chair of the Department of Communication & Cinema at McDaniel College in Westminster, Maryland. She has worked in both print and broadcast media. Her undergraduate work was in media studies at Northwestern University and her graduate study was in Intercultural Communication in the Department of Communication and Culture at Howard University. She teaches classes in media and culture, including a course on propaganda, with a research interest in exploring how individuals come to create their identities and how these constructs enhance or impede communication.

David E. Wilt is Professorial Lecturer in Film Studies at The George Washington University, and Systems Librarian with the University of Maryland Libraries. He received his PhD in Radio-Television-Film from the University of Maryland. Dr. Wilt is the coauthor of *Hollywood War Films* and *Doing Their Bit: Wartime American Animated Films*, the author of *The Mexican Filmography* and *Hard-Boiled in Hollywood*, and a contributor to a number of other books and publications.

Zou Yizheng is a lecturer at the Centre for China's Overseas Interests at Shenzhen University. He received his PhD in history at Hong Kong Lingnan University in 2014. Previously, he studied at Beijing University and taught in Linyi University in mainland China. His main research interests are Sino-U.S. relations, Sino-British relations, Hong Kong studies, and Chinese Overseas

Investment. Nine of his research articles have been accepted for publication in peer-reviewed journals, including *Critical Arts: South-North Cultural and Media Studies*, *The International Journal of the History of Sport*, *Biographical Literature* (in Traditional Chinese), and edited books.

★★ INDEX ★★

Page numbers in *italics* indicate illustrations.

Printed in Great Britain
by Amazon